MAX WEBER CLASSIC MONOGRAPHS

Selected and with new introductions by Bryan S. Turner

T0326183

MAX WEBER CLASSIC
MONOGRAPHS

MAX WEBER CLASSIC MONOGRAPHS

Volume III: The Sociology of Max Weber

J. Freund

With an introduction by Bryan S. Turner

Routledge
Taylor & Francis Group

LONDON AND NEW YORK

First published in 1966 in French as *Sociologie de Max Weber*
by Presses Universitaires de France

First English edition published in 1968
by Pantheon Books

Reprinted in 1998
by Routledge
2 Park Square, Milton Park, Abingdon, Oxfordshire OX14 4RN

Simultaneously published in the USA and Canada
by Routledge
711 Third Avenue, New York, NY 10017

First issued in paperback 2014

Routledge is an imprint of the Taylor and Francis Group, an informa company

Transferred to Digital Printing 2006

7-volume set
Volume III ISBN 13: 978-0-415-17454-1 (hbk)

Volume III ISBN 13: 978-0-415-75729-4 (pbk)

© 1966 J Freund; Introduction © 1998 Bryan S. Turner

Introduction typeset in Times by Routledge

British Library Cataloguing in Publication Data
A catalogue record for this book is available from the British Library

Library of Congress Cataloging in Publication Data
A catalogue record for this book has been requested

Publisher's note: These reprints are taken from original copies of each
book In many cases the condition of these originals is not perfect.
The paper, often acidic and having suffered over time, and the copy
from such things as inconsistent printing pressure resulting in faint
text, show-thorugh from one side of a leaf to the other, the filling in of
some characters, and the break-up of type. The publisher has gone to
great lengths to ensure the quality of these reprints, but wishes to
point out that certain characteristics of the original copies will, of
necessity, be apparent in reprints thereof.

INTRODUCTION

Bryan S. Turner

This study of the general sociology of Max Weber is Volume III of the Routledge and Thoemmes Press *Max Weber Classic Monographs* series. It was originally published in French in 1966 and continues to be regarded as the most valuable comprehensive overview of the sociology of Weber. This reprint of Julien Freund's study of Weber's social theory, which provides the student with a systematic and coherent statement of the sociological perspective, is an important contribution to modern scholarship. Generally speaking, apart from the work of Raymond Aron (1935; 1964; 1967), Weber's sociology has been strangely neglected in French academic life, especially in the social sciences. To take one obvious example, Michel Foucault, who was one of the leading French social theorists of the second half of this century, has made a profound contribution to the analysis of power/knowledge, discipline, systems of belief and the history of the self. Both Weber and Foucault converge on the study of the self in relation to religion, law and moral systems, and yet Foucault's response to Weber's work was late, limited and casual (Foucault, 1997: 224). Similar observations could be made about Pierre Bourdieu's very restricted use of Weber in his empirical studies of distinction, habitus and lifestyle (Bourdieu, 1990). Generally speaking, the French academy has been ignorant of or indifferent to Weber's sociology. While Freund is clearly sympathetic towards Weber's project, he intends, in his own words, to avoid the hagiographic approach of Paul Honigsheim and the negatively critical perspective of Leo Strauss. In this context, Freund's study has a unique status in contemporary Weberian exegesis.

The first important feature of Freund's approach is to see the critical interconnections between Weber's writings on the methodology of the social sciences and the empirical sociology of institutions (economics, religion, politics and law). Freund puts Weber's methodology and interpretative sociology at the front of his exegesis, and thus as the framework in which Weber's sociology can be understood. The epistemological problems of sociology are thus seen to be constitutive of the approach of sociology to values. It is interesting to compare this approach with Rheinhard Bendix's *Max Weber: An intellectual portrait* in which the methodological works are not considered at all, at least not as separate components of Weber's development as a sociologist (Roth and Schluchter, 1979: 16). For Freund, the problems of the social sciences in relation to the natural sciences are fundamental both to Weber's empirical studies and to his general values.

The second important feature of Freund's interpretation is to recognise the theme of rationalisation as the principal theme of Weber's sociology as a whole. Thus, while it has been commonplace to deny that there is a linking theme or key in Weberian sociology, Freund unambiguously places the discussion of rationalisation in the foreground. He distinguishes the rationalisation thesis from philosophical or normative accounts of reason and rationality. Freund claims that for Weber rationalisation was the historical product of western secularisation, scientific specialisation and technical differentiation. Weber often associated rationalisation with intellectualisation, that application of scientific principles to everyday life. This process of rationalisation was manifest in all spheres of society – religion, law, art, politics and economics. What Freund calls Weber's 'special sociologies' (economics, religion, politics, law and art) are thus the sites where the rationalisation process is to be discussed. Finally, Freund notes that Weber regarded rationalisation as (controversially) a process that has been particular to western civilisation.

These two issues – the integration of the methodological and value debate with the empirical sociology and the centrality of the theme of rationalisation – are the organisational principles of Freund's study of the sociology of Max Weber. The creative tension in this interpretation is that rationalisation and the coherence and meaningfulness of value commitments in Weber often appear to be contradictory and mutually destructive. As rationalisation increases, the enchantment (or meaningfulness) of the everyday world declines. In presenting Freund's study, I shall briefly outline these components in turn: philosophy of the social sciences, the theme of rationalisation in various institutional orders of society, the dispute over values and the tragic vision of life.

Weber shared with many late nineteenth-century philosophers and social scientists a critique of positivism as a solution to the issues raised by historicism and relativism (Antoni, 1959). In particular, Weber was influenced by what has been subsequently called the 'perspectivism' of Nietszche, which says that every approach to natural and social reality is from a particular perspective. Marxism, liberalism and utilitarianism are perspectives which identify certain key features of social reality. We cannot guarantee (in advance) whether one perspective is better than another; they are simply different. There is no way of avoiding this dilemma and we have to build it into the foundations of any social science. Weber did not however accept many of the nineteenth-century solutions of historicism.

There were basically two schools of thought: the so-called southwest German school of neo-Kantianism, which included Wilhelm Windelband and Heinrich Rickert, while the second school represented the position of Wilhelm Dilthey (Antoni, 1959). Windelband and Rickert stressed the difference between natural and human sciences, and between generalising and individualising approaches. Dilthey emphasised the centrality of the idea of interpretation, the lived experience of everyday reality (*Erlebnis*) as the bedrock of social data, and the role of irrational factors in history. Weber's methodology represents both an attempt to mediate between these two 'schools' and between the natural and the social sciences. It is also important to keep in mind the fact that Weber was trained both as a lawyer and as an economist, and his version of social science methodology was heavily influenced by issues in legal and economic theory. This training also influenced Weber's choice of subject matter.

Weber's methodology is treated with great clarity in Freund's exposition. The essence of the issue is twofold. On the one hand, sociology (and the humanities generally) is concerned with meaningful social action and not with behaviour, because actions are purposeful and meaningful. Social agents are also self-reflective about their actions and thus social reality has a very different constitution from the natural world. On the other hand, the social scientist is also part of that social reality and the values of the researcher are an important component of the process of research. In order to bridge the natural and the social science approaches, Weber developed a variety of methodological components: methodological individualism, ideal types, probability and causal analysis, sociological and historical treatment of variables, value analysis and the fact–value distinction. It is important to remember that in his own research and debates on research Weber employed a great variety of methods. In short, Weber was not rigidly or slavishly committed to a single methodological or technical approach or procedure. In order to understand Weber's methods, it is important to read his empirical sociology in some detail.

We can interpret Weber's empirical sociology as a series of studies of the processes of rationalisation; these processes are driven initially by the particular character of the economic ethics of the world religions. Rationalisation is the historical working out of fundamental cultural (religious) orientations to the social world. Rationalisation was particularly powerful in the case of Protestant Christianity, because its ethic of world mastery and asceticism produced a strong commitment to this-worldly transformation. Freund's treatment of the 'special sociologies' can be read in this light, namely as the manifestation of cultural complexities in the special domains of economics, law and politics. In order to present this analysis of civilisational history, Weber has to select from a wide variety of values a specific focus on the economic ethics of world religions. His historical and comparative sociology requires value analysis and value relevance. It requires both the interpretative understanding of the meaning of actions for individuals (methodological individualism) and a cultural analysis of the values formations of Christianity, Hinduism, Confucianism and so forth.

In response to the issues relating to values and research, there is a complex and frequently misunderstood account in Weber's philosophy of the social sciences of the role of values, value relevance, value neutrality and value analysis. Alan Dawe (1971) has pointed out that many critics of Weber have mistakenly assumed that values are a 'problem' in social research and that they have to be suppressed or expunged. On the contrary, for Weber values give us an insight into social action and, when carefully analysed, they give meaning and importance to social research. Values are relevant not superfluous to good sociological investigation. The fact–value distinction simply warns us against naively treating claims about values as if they were simply statements of reality. Furthermore, the notion of value neutrality does not mean that research can do without values; it was a professional criticism against professors in German universities who unfairly employed the authority of their chair to influence student values. It was not the duty of the professor to lay down the law *ex cathedra*, but to open the minds of students to the rational examination of values from a standpoint of neutrality.

Given his methodological principles, Weber concluded that social data or findings are always partial (because they are inevitably from a perspective) and provisional (because they are open to further explication). We live within a social world of competing and incompatible values within which we can never hope to achieve complete certainty or satisfaction. All of our conclusions are modified by the phrase 'for the time being'. Weber in fact employed religious terminology to describe this world by saying that we inhabit a world of polytheistic values. It is the duty of a scientist (a vocation) to try to make sense of this world and to behave responsibly within it. Of course, many of Weber's critics found his relativism and perspectivism somewhat shocking. His attempt to be scientifically responsible about values often appeared to younger scholars as indifference or as cynicism rather than value neutrality (Horkheimer, 1971: 51).

Weber's view of values and science was in fact a tragic view of reality. He believed that there is a contradiction between knowing and believing. In his final lectures, he often employed the analogy of the Garden of Eden where Adam, having eaten of the Tree of Knowledge, was no longer innocent and therefore was forced to labour and to toil. Similarly the rationalisation process means that social reality can no longer be apprehended innocently and naively. Social reality loses its sacred aura and its meaningful canopy. Rationalisation, of which sociology itself is a necessary part, makes the social world more intelligible and hence more predictable and controllable. Rationalisation makes the social world more intelligible, but also less meaningful. As social reality becomes more routinised, it is less sacred and less charged with significance. Hence, there was a tragic paradox between the growth of sociology as a science and the disenchantment of the world.

References

Antoni, C. (1959) *From History to Sociology: The transition in German historical thinking*. Detroit: Wayne State University Press.

Aron, R. (1935) *La Sociologie Allemande Contemporaine*. Paris: F. Alcan.

—— (1964) 'Weber und die Machtpolitik', *Zeitschrift für Politik*, Vol. II, pp. 100–13.

—— (1967) *Les Etapes de la Pensée Sociologique*. Paris: Gallimard.

Bendix, R. (1960) *Max Weber: An intellectual portrait*. Berkeley: University of California Press.

Bourdieu, P. (1990) *The Logic of Practice*. Cambridge: Polity Press.

Dawe, A. (1971) 'The relevance of values' in A. Sahay (ed.) *Max Weber and Modern Sociology*. London: Routledge & Kegan Paul, pp. 37–66.

Foucault, M. (1997) *The Essential Works: Ethics, subjectivity and truth*. London: Allen Lane, vol. 1.

Horkheimer, M. (1971) 'Value-freedom and objectivity' in O. Stammer (ed.) *Max Weber and Sociology Today*. Oxford: Basil Blackwell, pp. 51–3.

Roth, G. and Schluchter, W. (eds) (1979) *Max Weber's Vision of History: Ethics and methods*. Berkeley: University of California Press.

The
SOCIOLOGY
of
MAX WEBER

Julien Freund

Translated from the French by
Mary Ilford

PANTHEON BOOKS
A Division of Random House, New York

Foreword

An attempt is made in this brief study to give a clear exposition of Weber's sociological ideas, much as von Schelting has expounded his epistemological thinking and R. Aron his views on history. There is no intention of offering a personal interpretation or discussing those put forward by various authors, whether they adopted what might be termed a hagiographic approach, as did Honigsheim and Loewenstein, or tended to take issue with Weber, as did L. Strauss and L. Fleischmann.

I dedicate this work to the memory of one that was at my side when I first dipped into Weber's writings—André Lévy, the friend of my student years, my comrade-in-arms in a holding action, my confederate in the Resistance, my fellow-prisoner, shot by a firing squad at Songes, near Bordeaux, on July 29, 1944.

Contents

The Sociology of Max Weber

I

Weber's Vision of the World

———••◦∞◦••———

1. Reality and system

Nothing in Weber's thinking itself requires that we
begin a study of his sociology with a statement of his
general or philosophical concepts, but that seems the
easiest way of penetrating into his complex work and
giving it a semblance of unity—something, incidentally, which Weber himself deliberately refrained from
doing. His thinking is, in fact, characterized on the one
hand by a methodological, scientific and philosophical
dispersion which disdains a focal point, and on the
other by interest in all the antagonisms which can possibly exist and which in principle cannot be subsumed
under a single system. Perhaps, therefore, to attempt to
give a semblance of harmony to this intentional scat-

tering is to be unfaithful to Weber's thought? We would answer that question in the negative, for a number of reasons.

To begin with, this dispersion of Weber's is the very opposite of incoherence, of confusion of subject matter, and even of eclecticism. He was passionately concerned with rigorously defining the concepts he used and distinguishing between different orders of problems and different levels of any one problem. We have only to look at his methodological work to see how ruthlessly he hunted out errors of logic, ambiguities, slipshod reasoning and lack of precision. He was so little of an eclecticist that he never wearied of denouncing the practice of compromise at the level of ideas as one of the scientist's most dangerous pitfalls. Not only, in his view, is a moderate solution, a middle-of-the-road line, no more justifiable scientifically than an extreme position; it is generally also a tangle of ambiguities. Objectivity can be attained only by aiming at the greatest possible single-mindedness and precision, even at the cost of challenging deep-rooted prejudice and entrenched opinion by an extreme judgment, provided that the judgment itself is perspicacious and well-founded.

To put it another way, the scattering of Weber's efforts was the natural consequence of his concern with rigorous, indeed, meticulous analysis, used as a tool to separate what is logically incompatible and to establish such relationships as may be discerned at a given stage of research. He was not blindly opposed to systematization as such, but believed that, because research is by definition an unending process, scientific data are constantly liable to more or less radical correction and no definitive system can possibly be devised. In the interests of his work, a scientist may attempt at a given moment to systematize the sum total of knowledge acquired in a science or in some one sector of it, provided that he makes it clear that he is only hypothesizing, with due regard to the possibility of other interpretations and systematizations on the basis of other assumptions and of the future development of his discipline. For the present, and so long as scientific knowledge is not complete—an eventuality no man can foresee—every system is necessarily no more than a point of vantage, and other, equally justified viewpoints can be opposed to it.

It follows that any synthesis of human evolution, or of science as a whole, or even of one particular branch of it, such as sociology, is futile; indeed, should it claim universal and final validity, it would be antiscientific. The most that can be said for it is that it might usefully anticipate later developments or serve as guidance for research. In short, the scientist is free to unify a few relationships provisionally; he cannot, as a scientist, unify all knowledge in a self-contained system.

Secondly, Weber's thinking implies certain correspondences, whether conscious or unacknowledged, between seemingly antinomical subjects. His commentators are right in stressing the fact that he radically dissociates knowledge and action, science and politics; but it would be a mistake to regard this as an unfortunate or "maddening" contradiction, not so much because such an attitude is foreign to Weber's temperament as because it is at odds with the spirit of his *Weltanschauung*. On the contrary, there is a genuine unity in the conduct he requires of the scientist on the one hand and of the man of action on the other. The strict separation he seeks to establish between value and fact, or between will and knowledge, is aimed not only at clearly defining the logical essence of the two types of activity, their respective spheres and consequently the kind of problems each is capable of solving with the means peculiar to it, but also at enabling them to collaborate more successfully, because their very separateness will have eliminated confusions that would only have hampered them both.

Only through the delimitation of scientific work is action given its full meaning, with the corollary that it can freely make value judgments, something that is outside the scope of scientific objectivity. Science gives the man of action a better understanding of what he wants and what he can do; it cannot tell him what he ought to want. The fact that science is incompetent to choose final objectives does not mean that those objectives are futile or useless, but simply that they belong to the sphere of beliefs and convictions, which are as essential to man as is positive knowledge.

Despite their antinomy, there is correlation between scientific rigorousness and freedom of choice, in that both must serve their goals single-mindedly if the twin dangers of error and sterile exaltation are to be avoided. There is yet another, and deeper, affinity between them. In a sense, Weber's conception of science is governed by his idea of politics, namely, that the multiplicity and antagonism of values and objectives find their parallel in the multiplicity and antagonism of the points of view from which a phenomenon may be scientifically explained. Despite its rigorous concepts and precise demonstrations, science is not free of rivalry among hypotheses and competition among theories, each based on a number of ascertained and ascertainable facts, sometimes perhaps too carefully chosen to suit the needs of the cause, to the exclusion of other, equally well-established facts. In other words, Weber's theory of science is a reflection of his theory of action, save that the first attempts to overcome the contradictions which are the lifeblood of the second. This is the crux of the problem which, following Rickert, Weber calls "value-orientation." We shall return to it later, for this is not the place for a detailed discussion of the various correspondences in Weber's thinking. We shall discover them one by one in the course of this critical commentary, particularly in connection with the methodological relationship between the "ideal type" and the categories of objective possibility and adequate causality.

Lastly, although Weber always refrained from relating his investigations and explanations to any single focal point or principle, he nonetheless starts from the basic assumption that empirical reality is extensively and intensively infinite. This means, first of all, that reality surpasses our power of understanding, so that we can never come to the end of our exploration of events and of their variations in space and time or act on them all; next, that it is impossible to describe even the smallest segment of reality completely or to take into account all the data, all the elements and all the possible consequences at the moment of taking action. Knowledge and action are never quite completed, for all knowledge leads to further knowledge and every action to other actions. Neither any one science nor all sciences taken together can give us perfect knowledge, because the mind is not capable of reproducing or copying reality, but only of reconstructing it with the aid of concepts. And there is an infinite distance between the real and the conceptual. Thus we can never know more than fragments of the whole, for the whole is a singularity which defies the sum total of all conceivable singularities. It defies even the knowledge we have acquired, for that knowledge, no matter how solid in appearance, is laid open to question the minute a scientist discovers a new and hitherto unthought-of point of vantage.

Whatever method we use, we can only impose an order of relationships on reality, not exhaust it. To arrive at such an order, we might apply the generalizing method, which aims at establishing general laws by reducing qualitative differences to precisely measurable quantities. This procedure despoils reality of its wealth of singular characteristics by constructing concepts which are increasingly impoverished in content as they gain in general validity. Another method, which might be termed the individualizing method, stresses the distinctive and qualitative aspects of phenomena. Nevertheless, inasmuch as it seeks to achieve knowledge, it cannot do without concepts either, although they may be richer in content than in the preceding case. But concepts of whatever kind are incapable of completely reproducing reality. Consequently, if we add up the results achieved by both methods, the sum will inevitably fall short of the fullness of reality, since in any case those methods can yield only some aspects of the empirical world. For this reason, Weber was firmly opposed to all systems—whether classificatory, dialectical or other—which, after constructing as close a network of concepts as they are able, claim that they can deduce reality from it. Such philosophies, which he calls "emanationist," are suspect in every respect.

2. *Scientific sociology and reformist sociology*

These views of Weber's are basic to our understanding of the sense in which his sociology represents a veritable turning point in the history of that discipline; henceforth, sociology was to become a positive and empirical science in practice. Despite all protestations of faithfulness to the scientific spirit and speculations on the possibility of applying to the study of society the usual procedures of the scientific method (observation, experimentation, induction leading to the establishment of laws, quantification and comparison), the various sociologies of the nineteenth century were far more doctrinal than genuinely scientific. Thus Comte, Marx and Spencer, for example, all preferred romantic synthesis to modest, precise and cautious analysis. These thinkers took it for granted that science and the philosophy of history are intimately related, one being a necessary extension of the other.

We leave aside the question whether their idea of science was correct or not. What matters in this context is that they all started from a conception of society, culture and civilization as one whole; the objective spirit of Hegel, the dialectical materialism of Marx and the humanitarian approach of Comte have this in common. In other words, they all presupposed an a priori unity between past and future history, making it readily possible to discern what they deemed to be the unique and global course of the future. In their scheme, historical development occurs in stages, in the sense that each stage constitutes a logical premise for the next, so that the individual is reduced to submitting passively to the immanent and progressive rationality of evolution until it reaches its final flowering. They saw no need to analyze too closely the actual structures of particular societies or various human groups, since only the facts which confirmed the doctrine postulated at the outset were held to be of importance.

It is clear, therefore, that the nineteenth-century sociologies merely used science for their own ends and that their primary objective was to change existing society. They were, in fact, closer to reform than to science. Their analysis of what existed served merely as a pretext for bringing about what ought to be and for furthering social transformation.

And what of Durkheim? In 1895, when Durkheim published his *Rules of Sociological Method*,[1] Weber was a professor at the university of Freiburg-im-Breisgau, and far more concerned with economics and social policy than with sociology. With that book, Durkheim undoubtedly laid the groundwork for sociology as a positive and autonomous science, independent of metaphysical hypotheses and eschatological predictions.

Durkheim's work has given rise to much sterile polemics and unfair criticism; we would, on the contrary, stress his merits: he was the theoretician of scientific sociology, even though in practice he failed to abide by his own distinction between a judgment of reality and a value judgment. The crux of the contradictions in Durkheim's conception is to be found at this level, and nowhere else. He mistakenly interpreted "collective consciousness" as an ascertainable fact, whereas it is no more than a hypothesis which, if treated as such, can be useful in research. Equally open to criticism is his definition of a social fact as an object, inasmuch as Durkheim regarded collective manifestations as constituting a separate category, a specific group of phenomena distinguished by definite characteristics from those studied by the other natural sciences. The error, in this case, lies in classifying the sciences on the basis of a division of reality into several series of *sui generis* phenomena (physical, biological, psychic, social, etc.), each with its separate existence and incapable of explanation in terms of each other. Such compartmentalization is alien to the scientific spirit, for one and the same phenomenon can be studied by history as well as by sociology, psychology, biology or physics. While each science constitutes an autonomous discipline with its own postulates, empirical reality, on the contrary, cannot be divided into independent segments to be apportioned to the various sciences much as politics divides the world into independent states.

These faults, which are to be attributed to the weakness of Durkheim's theory of knowledge, did not, however, affect his intention to make of sociology a positive science. Durkheim's profound error was to reintroduce surreptitiously into his work those very value judgments which he rightly condemned in theory; he thus helped to perpetuate a confusion which he had been the first to denounce, going so far as to say that unless it was eliminated, sociology could not aspire to the rank of a positive and empirical discipline. This is not the place to list all the unverifiable evaluations in Durkheim's work. Let us merely note, for example, that he regarded society as "good," without putting forward any more valid scientific proof than do those who deem it to be bad. He believed not only that society is endowed with moral authority, but also that it is the bearer of reform because it is the vehicle of rationality, and he thought, moreover, that rationality can have only beneficial effects.

He thus believed in moral progress through social progress, and he even felt that his sociological studies could be used as a basis for a new social system, the correctness of which could be scientifically proved. Similarly, he hoped that sociology would be capable of producing more durable social structures than those which had collapsed with the fall of the Empire in 1870. What is more, he believed that he could reduce not only morality and politics, but also the theory of knowledge and the spirit of religion to simple sociological factors. These are but a few evaluations among many.

All these statements and positions are, of course, value judgments outside the competence of any science, yet Durkheim put the authority of sociology behind them. Consequently, despite his theoretical intentions, he frequently marred scientific inquiry by introducing ideals proper to a certain kind of scientism, and virtually undermined his own project of establishing a positive science.

While Durkheim's intentions have justifiably been compared with Weber's, despite the countless other differences between them, it remains that Weber was the first in practice to place sociology on a strictly scientific basis. Indeed, what strikes us in Weber's work is the total absence of preconceived doctrines or a priori syntheses. He was a pure analyst, whose sole concern was to gain a sound knowledge of historical data and to interpret them within verifiable limits. He was, of course, helped by his encyclopedic scholarship, which no other sociologist has since equaled. Readers of his work are both astounded and gratified at his equally profound knowledge of the history, economics and law of all countries, the subtleties of the various religions of China, India, Europe and Africa, and the formation of the scientific spirit and the evolution of the arts. True, his immense documentation sometimes makes it difficult to follow his reasoning; but the useful comparisons which it enabled him to make preserved him from rash and premature generalization. Not that Weber systematically resisted synthesis; he attached a definite value to it as an intellectual procedure in formulating the circumscribed significance of a given phenomenon, but he had an aversion for those vast constructions which, while pretending to make rational forecasts, become involved in predictions bordering on prophecy.

Weber was too familiar with the surprises, disguises and reversals of history to allow his rigorous analysis to be influenced by any enthusiasm or regret he might have felt concerning the coming of socialism or the future of capitalism. Sociology must be faithful only to the scientific postulates which make it what it is, and not to convictions which are alien to it, be they moral, religious, political or esthetic; in particular, its business is to discuss genuinely sociological problems in a scientific manner, and not to confirm or refute a philosophical doctrine. It should not be Marxist or naturalistic, spiritualistic or materialistic; its sole duty is to be a true science. Errors and inadequacies undoubtedly occur in Weber's work, but they are the errors of a scientist. They are due, for example, to lacunae in information or to weaknesses in critical interpretation stemming from failure to make the necessary comparisons; but they are always verifiable.

Obviously, such a conception of the sociologist's work is not inspiring. Weber was the first to recognize that, paradoxically, the scientist's passion has its depressing side:

> And whoever lacks the capacity to put on blinders, so to speak, and to come up to the idea that the fate of his soul depends upon whether or not he makes the correct conjecture at this passage of this manuscript may as well stay away from science. He will never have what one might call the "personal experience" of science. Without this strange intoxication, ridiculed by every outsider; without this passion . . . according to whether or not you succeed in making this conjecture; without this, you have no calling for science and you should do something else.[2]

If there is any progress recognized by science, it is the progress of knowledge, for what is known today will be outstripped tomorrow.

The work of any sociologist who claims to be a scientist is basically critical; it consists in analysis and verifiable interpretation. This critical approach, however, is also constructive, not in the sense that it permits the elaboration of a philosophical doctrine, but in the sense that it contributes to the formation of the science of sociology which, like other disciplines, cannot progress save on the basis of solid documentation, verified relationships and clear and precise concepts. The fact that the results of sociological study can be put to practical use in furthering political, economic or technical ends has no bearing on their validity in logic; they are scientifically valid because they are true, or approximately accurate, and not because they can also serve purposes alien to science. Sociology is not any more concerned than is physics with foreseeing the ultimate destination of world evolution. It is concerned, however, with the problem of meaningfulness, inasmuch as human activities, institutions and associations are teleological in character, being established, or developing, with a goal in mind.

Sociology would clearly be failing in its duty if it ignored such questions. Yet there is only one way of dealing with them scientifically: to concentrate on the specific and particular meaning of a given activity or institution, as circumscribed by its purpose and the means at its disposal, and to recognize that the same institution, for example, may vary in time and that therefore its meaning too may vary, so that within a single generation it may come to mean the opposite of what it had before, or be held in esteem by one group and ridiculed by another. This brings us face to face with Weber's concept of value-orientation, which will be discussed at some length later. Here we shall merely define it briefly.

Political and economic activities, for example,

have for man a general meaning which is determined by their purposes. Independently of this rationally determinable meaning, a socialist and a capitalist will attach yet another significance to them. Similarly, a modern state means something different from a Greek city. Meanings of this kind cannot be scientifically categorized except through value-orientation, itself a variable. Thus, when we study the Greek city historically or sociologically, we can determine the meaning it had for men of that era only in the light of the basic values towards which they were oriented. But we historians and sociologists of the twentieth century may find a different significance in that institution by relating it to our own values, or by studying the meaning attached to it by political writers of the sixteenth century and relating it to their values.

What is important, in making our judgment on the meaning of the Greek city, is that we should always clearly explain which order of values we are using as our frame of reference, or we may create a confusion prejudicial to scientific work, perhaps by attributing our scale of values to the Greeks or vice-versa, or by hopelessly mixing up several different value orders. These various types of value-orientation are all equally legitimate, but we must be careful to distinguish between them, lest our work lose all scientific worth. In fact, all fallacious, specious and sophistic reasoning stems from this kind of confusion. When the historian and the sociologist study any particular phenomenon, be it the state, bureaucracy, law, a social class or a political party, they will not do truly scientific work unless they confine themselves to ascertaining the meaning of that phenomenon and indicate their value-orientation. Naturally, no one can stop them from looking for a more general meaning, in line with what they take to be the direction of world evolution on the basis of a defined system of values, but at this point they stop being scientists and become philosophers or prophets.

3. *Rationalization*

Weber adhered to this method as strictly as he could in his sociological work and in dealing with his students. He was neither phrase-making nor merely expressing a conviction, but stating a rule which he personally observed, when he declared that a professor, when teaching, must avoid taking any position based on value-judgments, but must confine himself solely to the problems within his province, whereas he is free to assume the role of demagogue or prophet on the street and in the press—in short, wherever there is a possibility of free discussion and public criticism. The soberness of Weber's own teaching was equaled only by the passion with which he defended his personal views in public. In other words, he too had his vision of the world, the essence of which will be found in his famous addresses, "Science as a Vocation" and "Politics as a Vocation."[3] He shows little affinity with the authors of the major syntheses of the nineteenth century, except perhaps Fichte, but on the other hand he is very close to such writers as Baudelaire, Schopenhauer, Nietzsche, Dostoievsky and Burckhardt. The predominant concept in that personal vision is, we believe, what he called "rationalization."

Weber's rationalization is not to be confused with the notion of the rationality of history, which professedly directs human evolution on a course of universal progress culminating in a sort of feast of reason, in the sense of a flowering of true justice, genuine virtue, equality, peace, etc. It is, rather, the product of the scientific specialization and technical differentiation peculiar to Western culture, and Weber sometimes associated it with the notion of intellectualization. It might be defined as the organization of life through a division and coordination of activities on the basis of an exact study of men's relations with each other, with their tools and their environment, for the purpose of achieving greater efficiency and productivity. Hence it is a purely practical development brought about by man's technological genius.

Weber also described rationalization as a striving for perfection, in other words, as an ingenious refinement of the conduct of life and the attainment of increasing mastery over the external world. As we shall see later, he analyzed its evolution in all major branches of human activity—religion, law, art, science, politics and economics—while being careful not to go beyond the limits of what is objectively ascertainable in any analysis intended to be scientifically valid. Only in the two addresses to which we have referred and in his essay on ethical neutrality[4] did he venture to strike a personal note in explaining his conception of rationalization and delineating its philosophical and metaphysical implications as he saw them.

While Weber treats rationalization as a phenomenon peculiar basically to Western civilization, he clearly does not view it as some metaphysical force propelling world evolution in a determined direction toward a theoretically foreseeable ultimate goal. On the contrary, it is the by-product of the activity of a certain type of men, who may or may not transmit it to the rest of humanity. More precisely, it relates to the meaning which those men attach to their activities, and not to the ineluctable goal of world evolution announced by the "emanationist" philosophies of history. The civilizations of the Incas and the Aztecs, for example, did not contain in embryo the immense potentialities of Western civilization. Weber therefore regarded technical proficiency as one of the fundamental characteristics of that civilization, without, however, reducing all Western culture to that one factor.

Although he was one of the sociologists who laid most stress on the importance of technology, he rejected Marx's technological "deviation."[5] He took the view that to establish the close connection that Marx did between economic system and technical development (hand-mill and feudalism, steam-mill and capitalism) was to be guilty of "emanationism." As Weber saw it, what technology teaches us is respect for the creative genius of individuals who, thanks to often highly ingenious inventions, succeed in transforming the living conditions of an entire community. Far from regarding each epoch as the inevitable consequence of the one preceding it, a sociologist should be capable of seeing those features which make it unique, even as they give every civilization its originality: each one is a masterpiece. In other words, the fact that we can establish cause-and-effect relationships between epochs should not make us ignore, on the one hand, their singularity and, on the other, the creative part played by the individuals who, through their personal contribution, have helped to give each of them its own distinctive character.

Increasing rationalization is far from representing progress in the usual sense of the word, or even from being reasonable. Although it is based on scientific techniques, it cannot be said to constitute an advance in knowledge in the sense of a better understanding of our way of living. For instance, what does a computer operator know of the theorems and scientific laws which went into the building of the device? Or we might consider even simpler examples, which are Weber's own. The man who takes a streetcar or an elevator has little notion of the principle on which those machines work, nor are the motorman and the elevator operator much more enlightened. What exactly do we know of the properties of currency, since financial experts themselves are not in agreement on the subject? The consumer buys any number of products in the grocery without knowing what substances they are made of. By contrast, "primitive" man in the bush knows infinitely more about the conditions under which he lives, the tools he uses and the food he consumes.

The increasing intellectualization and rationalization do *not*, therefore, indicate an increased and general knowledge of the conditions under which one lives. It means something else, namely, the knowledge or belief that if one but wished one *could* learn it at any time. Hence, it means that there are no mysterious incalculable forces that come into play, but rather that one can, in principle, master all things by calculation.[6]

It would be an even more grievous error to believe that rationalization brings reason in its train, in the sense not only of enlightenment but also of individual or collective moral progress. The fact is that it affects external social organization and not man's private intellectual life. There is at least as much reason in tradition as there is in technical progress, even when it comes to foreseeing the future. Under a traditional system, one generation knows fairly accurately how the next generation will behave; consequently, while it may lack scientific knowledge, it has the consolation of certainty. In this connection, Weber might have cited Pascal, who found it entirely reasonable that the eldest son of the queen should succeed the king, because that arrangement obviated vainglorious rivalries and claims of superior ability or virtue. He might also have asked whether increasing rationalization had made men more peace-loving, more moral, more conscientious or more tolerant. Is a criminal who rationally organizes his enterprise any less guilty than a murderer in a traditional society? Inversely, is Socrates a philosopher of lesser stature than, say, Husserl or Sartre? Weber, however, chose instead to cite Tolstoy, thus going directly to the heart of the problem and giving his investigation far greater depth.

The proponents of rationalization regard it as eudemonistic. The truth is that, beneath its apparently boundless surface optimism, it may well be profoundly pessimistic, and concerned only with giving some coherent shape to despair. Is it in truth the key to happiness? Abraham died, laden with life's blessings, having enjoyed all that life had to offer. There was nothing more he could expect on this earth. Rationalized man knows that his life is provisional and uncertain; he suffers because happiness is a thing of tomorrow, or of the day after, and because he is caught up in a movement which never stops amazing him and luring him on by fresh promises. Rationalization is thus Utopian in character; it leads man to believe that happiness is for his children, his grandchildren, and so on. Why should not today's man enjoy it himself? Through what injustice? Hence the attraction of improved external conditions, always equally remote but constantly more desirable, makes him miserable in the present. Happiness continuously postponed prevents him from being content with what he has. As for death, he sees it merely as an obstacle preventing him from enjoying happiness; it is an absurdity. And when death becomes meaningless, life does too. Thus increasing rationalization and intellectualization transform the dialectics of the inner and the outer world into that of a real void and an imaginary plenitude. All meaning crumbles and only irrational appearances are left.

That progress exists is undeniable, but it is not present everywhere. Hence the problem is to locate and define it, for rationalization is not in itself necessarily a sign of progress. Weber demonstrated this in connection with music in his brief study "The Rational and Social Foundations of Music."[7] Let us take painting as an example: the paintings of the primitives, who were not acquainted with perspective, are no less beautiful than those of the artists of the Renaissance and later periods. A work of art is "finished"; it can be neither surpassed nor improved upon, nor can it grow old. Or, if we consider government, we find that, under modern systems, the citizens are "consulted" on political issues, but that they have no greater voice in decisions than they ever had, to say nothing of the fact that decision-making continues to be an area of conflict and power. In the economic sphere, owing to industrial technical development, primary needs are more easily satisfied, but other needs, hitherto regarded as secondary, have become pressing. Thanks to psychology, psychophysiology and psychoanalysis, we have a better understanding of certain phenomena, such as sensations and the motivation of feelings and passions; but love has not become more perfect or jealousy less heinous. It is generally believed that, because of the transformation they have brought about, the Mormons are better adapted to conditions in the Salt Lake area than were the Indians who inhabited it before them; but such a judgment is entirely subjective, for technical progress is apt to cause us to regret life in the open, the charm of solitude and the restfulness of silence.

Progress has a meaning in the realms of science and technology—wherever the accumulation of knowledge makes further discoveries possible, as, for example, where greater technical ability allowed architects to resolve the problem of vaulting empty space and gave birth to the Gothic style. Yet it can hardly be said that Gothic represents an advance over Romanesque. In short, whatever is quantitative is capable of progress; the purely qualitative is not.

Nevertheless, increasing rationalization and intellectualization have had one decisive consequence, on which Weber laid great stress: they have disenchanted the world. With the progress of science and technology, man has stopped believing in magic powers, in spirits and demons; he has lost his sense of prophecy and, above all, his sense of the sacred. Reality has become dreary, flat and utilitarian, leaving a great void in the souls of men which they seek to fill by furious activity and through various devices and substitutes. A prey to precarious relativism, to uncertainty and tedious scepticism, they attempt to furnish their souls with the bric-a-brac of religiosity, estheticism, moralism or scientism —in brief, with a sort of pluralist philosophy which extends an indiscriminate welcome to the most heterogeneous maxims from every part of the world. Mysticism becomes mystification, community becomes communitarianism, and life is reduced to a series of unrelated experiences. Academicians and intellectuals are begged for a message, although by the very nature of things they are entrenched each in his own specialty. Flattered at having this role thrust upon them, they pass off a fraudulent hodge-podge of pious platitudes as prophetic utterance. Rationalization and intellectualization have stripped the world of charm, and men endeavor to make up for it through emphasis and militancy.

Faced with this situation, Weber saw only two possible solutions: either to go back to the tranquillity of the old churches, or to face the future with courage, which generally means fortitude in dealing with humble everyday tasks. Essentially, Weber's stand is that of the individualist undecided between two types of activity: the Promethean and the Epimethean.

4. *Antagonism of values*

Despite the superficial progress they have brought about in all fields of human activity, rationalization and intellectualization have made no inroads on the empire of the irrational. On the contrary, as rationalization increases, the irrational grows in intensity. This is a key idea of Weber's, and, although he never stated it in so many words, it dominates his entire philosophy. What does rationalization apply to? Thanks to the forecasts which science and technology are able to make by calculating probabilities, man succeeds in rationalizing external relationships; but nothing else. As Weber explains at the end of his "Essay on Some Categories of Interpretative Sociology," these are basically relationships among the artificial products which man himself has fashioned, which he is capable of mastering and controlling, and in which he can place his reliance simply because he can assess their scope and effects. It is at this level that rational goal-oriented conduct is most meaningful; it is easiest to understand because it is based on a technical evaluation of the relationship between the end and the most adequate means. The fact that it is the most readily understandable kind of conduct does not, however, mean that it is the most frequent, although Weber would have liked it so. Nevertheless, his deep belief, which he expressed more than once in his studies "The Objectivity of Knowledge" and "Politics as a Vocation," was that life and the world are fundamentally irrational.

What did Weber mean by irrationality? He categorically rejected the idea that human freedom is either based on the irrational or introduces it into the world.

> The error in the assumption that any freedom of the will—however it is understood—is identical with the "irrationality" of action, or that the latter is conditioned by the former, is quite obvious. The characteristic of "incalculability," equally great, but not greater than that of "blind forces of nature," is the privilege of the insane. On the other hand, we associate the highest measure of an empirical "feeling of freedom" with those actions which we are conscious of performing rationally—i.e., in the absence of physical and psychic "coercion," emotional "affects" and "accidental" disturbances of the clarity of judgment, in which we pursue a clearly perceived end by "means" which are the most adequate in accordance with the extent of our knowledge.[8]

Thus irrationality has its source, first of all, in our affective life, inasmuch as we remain subject to the same passions and the same needs, and secondly, in our relationship to power, regardless of whether we bow to authority or rebel against it. It also finds its expression in chance and in unforeseeable circumstances; this applies both to natural phenomena and to individual and collective behavior. Weber vehemently opposed what he called the "ridiculous prejudice of the naturalist dilettantes" who believe that collective or mass phenomena are more rational and more objective than individual reactions. Finally, he laid particular stress—and this is the most original aspect of his conception—on what he termed the "ethical irrationality" of the world, which is characterized by axiological irrationality on the one hand, and by the paradox of the consequences on the other.

In our world, numerous values and ultimate goals confront each other, and their very pluralism sustains irrationality. Despite opinions to the contrary, truth, goodness and beauty are separate and irreconcilable. Not only can a thing be holy without being beautiful, good or true; it can be good without being either true or beautiful and precisely because of those elements in it which are neither true nor beautiful; it can be true without being holy, good or beautiful and to the extent that it is none of these.

This idea of the antagonism of values stems directly from Weber's intuitive notion of the infinite diversity of reality. The disenchantment of the world brought about by rationalization is powerless before that eternal struggle which the Greeks, still under the spell of gods and demons, expressed in their polytheism. That multiplicity is the truth of the human experience. In fact, even as the Greeks sacrificed in turn to Aphrodite, Apollo, and the gods of the city, we attempt to serve peace, justice, love, truth, and equality; were we to select any one of these values, even temporarily, we might offend and vex the rest.

Here lies the reason for Weber's deep-rooted animosity to those unitarian philosophers of history who hope at last to reconcile all values and goals at a final stage of evolution. In reality, this ultimate unification very often depends on the exclusion of certain values, such as politics and religion, so that it does not remove the causes of antagonism. It is of course possible, in some circumstances, to achieve a compromise among all the goals in question, but such agreement is tentative at best and subject to sudden collapse, despite the requirements of expediency and the counsels of wisdom. To put it plainly, the antagonism of values is irreconcilable.

Furthermore, it is to be found at all levels of human activity. An effort to harmonize such basic points of vantage as economics, politics, morality, art, religion and science is doomed to failure, for no harmony necessarily exists between power, need, interest, purity and knowledge. The reason for this lies not only in differences of temperament and taste, but in the choice itself, which is essentially a matter of conflict. Every choice implies rejection. Moreover, a conflict may arise within any one activity; for instance, within a religion, not only as between Catholicism and Protestantism, but within Protestantism or within Catholicism. Similarly, how are we to decide whether one culture is superior to another: the French to the German, for instance? There, too, different gods and values are locked in combat, no doubt for all eternity. Or again, it is surely commendable to live according to the precepts of morality; yet the moment a man attempts to overcome evil, he will be faced with, for example, the opposition between the evangelical precept of non-resistance and the desire to combat evil by violent means. He may choose between these two attitudes, but no ethical theory on earth is capable of determining which is preferable or superior to the other; and, worse still, all such theories are likely to conflict.

In short, a particular end, such as justice or equality, conceals an antagonism beneath its very ambiguity. The man who chooses justice will come to the crossroads where commutative and distributive justice part company, while the man who wants equality will be faced with the dilemma whether those of greater merit should be given more or whether, on the contrary, more should be required of them.

The second aspect of ethical irrationality is the paradox of the consequences. For a clearer understanding of what this implies we shall briefly recall the famous distinction between the ethics of conviction and the ethics of responsibility. The adherent of the first is a man of principle and uncompromising singleness of purpose, inspired solely by a sense of obligation to do what he deems his duty, without regard for the consequences. A case in point is the doctrinaire pacifist who clamors for peace at any price, without taking into account the circumstances, the balance of forces or the problems involved. Another example is the man who demands that everything relating to a sensational case be brought to light, regardless of the passions that the revelation may provoke or of its disastrous consequences for others. This is the unconditional morality of all or nothing; consequently, when such a man meets with resolute opposition, he often does an about-face and embraces millenarianism, either attributing his powerlessness to human stupidity or advocating extreme violence on the pretext of putting an end to all violence.

The proponent of the ethics of responsibility, on the contrary, bears in mind what is possible, and looks for the most suitable means of achieving the desired end, being aware not only of the final purpose and of his responsibility toward others, but also of the possible consequences. The two forms of ethics are thus clearly differing typical constructs, but in practice it is perfectly possible to act with both conviction and a sense of responsibility in working for a cause. Indeed, Weber saw in such a union the hallmark of the "genuine" man.

Nevertheless, at the typical construct level at which the opposition between the two kinds of ethics is clear, it will be observed that only the conduct of the partisan of the ethics of responsibility is rationally goal-oriented, since his evaluations take into account not only the irrationality of the world and the available means, but also the foreseeable consequences. The conduct of the partisan of the ethics of conviction, on the other hand, is irrational, or rational only in terms of value-orientation, since it is unconcerned with means and consequences. At best, such a person takes refuge in a cosmo-ethical "rationalist" ideal, because he cannot bear the irrationality of the world as it is. Purity of conviction does not necessarily ensure the possibility of attaining a "good" end by using similarly "good" means; some of the means may be dishonest, or at least dangerous, and some of the consequences undesirable.

In any event, no system of ethics is in a position to say at what moment and to what extent a good end justifies dangerous means or consequences. This is the stumbling-block encountered by every kind of Simon-pure ethics of conviction and, more particularly, by every ethical system based on a religious doctrine, for, as Weber explains at length at the close of his address "Politics as a Vocation," man's experience of the world's irrationality has been the driving force of all religions. The man motivated by political conviction must know that no one active in public affairs can avoid either violence or compromise with the powers of darkness, and that he can achieve the purpose in which he believes only by surrounding himself with a human apparatus, a following, so that he must needs expose himself to the irrationality of violence.

Consequences are of two kinds—foreseeable and unforeseeable. The latter especially, through their very paradoxicality, reveal the irrationality of the world. One of the fundamental and least questionable facts of history and human experience is that the result of an activity, especially political activity, seldom corresponds to the hopes and original intentions of the agents. The most unsettling aspect of action when measured by the yardstick of conviction is the antinomy between intention and result. This is true of so circumscribed an operation as a strike and so spectacular an upheaval as a revolution. That good can lead only to good, and evil to evil, is not a tenable proposition. The real situation is infinitely more complex. The purest and noblest intentions may give rise to the most disastrous consequences. If good produced only good results, action would be a simple matter, and all moral problems and conflicts of duty or conscience would be resolved by pure logic. There would be commendable actions on the one hand and blameworthy actions on the other, and we would need only to choose the first, without a qualm or a doubt. Such a Manichean attitude is, of course, in line with the intellectualist rationality of the ethics of conviction, but it is contradicted by the realities of life.

The paradox of the consequences is further complicated by the uncontrollable and undefined repercussions of various acts on each other, which make it impossible to foresee how and when an action, once initiated, will end. Weber remarks that engaging in any activity, particularly in political activity, is not the same thing as getting into a carriage (or a taxi) which can be stopped at will. The consequences, and the consequences of these consequences, will not cease at the wish or command of the person who has initiated the action.

5. Weber's personality

Now that these various ideas of Weber's have become part of the common domain of philosophy, it is difficult to conceive the violent and bitter opposition he encountered in his lifetime. Naturally, he had students and some enthusiastic followers who laid claim to enjoying his confidence (some of whom, unfortunately, have made a career of Weberianism in the United States), but he had no true disciples. His thinking remains controversial, even as he wished. In a letter of April 18, 1906, addressed to Gottl-Ottlilienfeld, he asked the latter to attack his (Weber's) ideas as violently as he pleased should he find them open to challenge. Weber was and remains a source of inspiration; he never wanted to be a master. There is no Weberian school, as there is a Marxist, a Comtian and even a Durkheimian school.

Indeed, on a number of occasions Weber found himself completely isolated, abandoned by those who had called themselves his best friends. This isolation was no doubt due to his political attitude and, more particularly, to his hostility to the rash undertakings of

Kaiser Wilhelm II. But he was similarly isolated even on the purely scientific terrain of the discussion of the concept of ethical neutrality, for instance at certain memorable meetings of the Association for Social Policy. Some of his positions on public affairs aroused the fury of nationalist students, who went so far as to invade his class-room to prevent him from lecturing. A perusal of the pious biography written by his wife, Marianne Weber, affords but the merest inkling of the outbursts, revolts and scandals he provoked. Those who knew him say that he was like a volcano in constant eruption, at the same time retaining an inward calm which added to the confusion of those who argued with him. He was always able to preserve his detachment, despite his never dormant curiosity, which led him to be as concerned with some abstruse detail about ancient China as with the most vital events of his own day. He was first and foremost a scholar. Once or twice he yielded to the temptations of a political career, but met with failure. He was too interested in politics in human terms to make a vocation of it.

One is tempted to ask what he might have accomplished had he resolutely embraced that career. The question may not be altogether idle, but it is beside the point; from what we know of Weber's character, he did not see a personal future for himself in politics. Even as in his academic career he always refused to play the role of a master surrounded by disciples—he much preferred open discussion—so he also shrank from putting himself in a position where he would have to recruit a human apparatus, a following. Yet that, as he recognized himself, is the first requisite for effective political action.

In all things and all circumstances, he was essentially independent, and this explains in part some of his apparently contradictory statements and attitudes. The same impulse prompted him to advocate both the shooting of the first Polish official to set foot in Danzig and the execution of Count von Arco, the assassin of Kurt Eisner, who had headed the revolutionary government of Bavaria. Again, although he detested Ludendorff, Weber was prepared to defend him against unjust attack. He actively opposed the exclusion of anarchists, socialists and Jews from university faculties, and had only contempt for the revolutionary movement that sprang up following the defeat of 1918. And while he came out in support of pacifist students, he advocated "chauvinism" should the peace be merely unilaterally imposed by the Allies.

On the scientific level, it may well be asked why Weber, who was understood to be an atheist, should have concerned himself so much with the sociology of religion. This subject takes up three thick volumes of his collected works, not to mention a projected fourth volume on Islam and the chapters on religion in his *Wirtschaft und Gesellschaft* (Theory of Social and Economic Organization). All in all, this is the major part of his sociological work. We have no desire to embark on a discussion of Weber's religious sentiments; but we must stress again his intellectual independence, allied with his scrupulous scholarship, which resolutely excluded any reflection of the subjective opinions of the man from the work of the sociologist. The fact is that all social, economic and political structures have always been, and still are, impregnated with men's religious convictions. Hence to neglect this capital aspect of the study of society would be to mutilate sociology; what is more, to combat religion in the name of science would be contrary to the scientific spirit of objectivity. And since religion is one of the antennae of human sensibility, its disregard must result in a misunderstanding of the phenomenon of culture. Weber would no doubt have subscribed to Miguel de Unamuno's fine epigram: only God is an atheist.

2

Weber's Methodology

———————·•◆◆•·———————

1. The naturalistic method and the historical method

Weber's epistemological ideas must be viewed against the background of the methodological quarrel which divided German academicians toward the end of the nineteenth century. One after another, economists (Schmoller, Menger), psychologists (Wundt), historians (Lamprecht, E. Meyer, von Belov), philologists (Vossler), philosophers (Dilthey, Windelband, Rickert), and other, less known, writers joined in the debate. The bone of contention was the status of the human sciences (also called the historical sciences, the social sciences, the intellectual sciences, the cultural sciences, etc.): should they, as the positivists claimed, be assimilated with the natural sciences or, on the contrary, be regarded as wholly autonomous?

Inevitably, the debate was soon sidetracked into a discussion of the classification of the sciences, and at this stage those who held that the human sciences must be autonomous became divided among themselves. Some, Dilthey among them, believed that such a classification should be based on difference of subject, a distinction being drawn between the kingdom of nature and that of the human mind or history; they felt that reality could be subdivided into independent sectors, each the realm of a separate category of sciences. Others, including Windelband and Rickert, rejected such fragmentation, claiming that reality is indivisible and always identical with itself, and they proposed division on the basis of logic. Different sciences, they argued, study reality from different angles, and the guiding principle of classification should therefore be the difference in the methods used: a scientist seeks either to discover general relationships and laws, or to study the particular aspects of a given phenomenon. According to this view, then, there are two principal methods: one which might be termed the generalizing and the other the individualizing method. This would imply the existence of two fundamental categories of sciences, which Windelband called nomothetic and idiographic and Rickert called natural and cultural sciences. For example, although psychology is mainly concerned with mental phenomena, it proceeds in a naturalistic fashion and therefore falls under the heading of the natural rather than of the cultural sciences.

While Weber accepted the distinction between

generalizing and individualizing methods, he rejected Windelband's and Rickert's conclusions, notably their classification of the sciences on the basis of differences of method. According to Weber, there is no reason to classify psychology among the natural rather than among the cultural sciences. He saw no valid ground for reserving one of the two methods for one category of sciences, the other for the other. On the contrary, he maintained that every science uses each method in turn, depending on the circumstances. According to the needs and aims of research, both sociology and psychology have recourse to either the generalizing or the individualizing method; similarly, both biology and astronomy on some occasions seek to establish laws and on others study the unique characteristics of a single phenomenon.

Consequently, while the distinction between the general and the particular and between the different procedures they call for is logically valid, it is wrong to say that in practice the natural sciences use exclusively the naturalistic or generalizing procedure and the cultural sciences the historical or individualizing procedure. The first also concern themselves with particulars (for example, the special properties of a planet or a tissue), while the second may well attempt to establish general laws.

Neither method is preferable or superior to the other. True to the spirit of Kantian epistemology, Weber denies that knowledge can ever be a reproduction or a faithful copy of reality, in either extent or understanding. Reality is infinite and inexhaustible. Consequently, the fundamental problem of the theory of knowledge is that of the relationship between law and history, between concept and actuality. Whichever method is used, that method must make a selection from the infinite variety of empirical reality. Thus, because of its objective, the generalizing method divests reality of all its random and unique aspects by reducing qualitative differences to precisely measurable quantities which can serve as a basis for a general and legitimate postulate. The individualizing method, on the other hand, neglects generic elements and concentrates its entire attention on the qualitative and particular features of phenomena. In this sense, both depart from reality to serve the needs of conceptualization, without which scientific knowledge is impossible. Consequently, there is no ground for claiming that, when held up against reality, either of these methods is more valid, more appropriate or more complete than the other.

These insights give authenticity to Weber's theory of method. Inasmuch as method is a technique for acquiring knowledge, it is subject to the law that applies to all techniques, namely, efficiency. No one can say a priori that some one procedure per se is better than another; everything depends on the scientist's perspicacity, the aim of his research and his skill in applying the particular procedure, so that its validity can be determined only retrospectively, in the light of the results obtained. Not only is there no universal method, but the usefulness of a procedure varies according to the project; it may be effective in one case and fail in an analogous one. The very question whether a method may legitimately be used in a particular science sets up a spurious problem. Weber felt strongly that this was not a point to be treated dogmatically: a method must advance knowledge rather than be faithful to an imaginary ideal of cognition; if science means unlimited research, there cannot possibly be a perfect or ideal method or even a definitive procedure.

Weber repeatedly refuted, in particular, August Comte's conception of a hierarchical classification of the sciences, with one science dependent on the other, so that the social sciences could arise only on the basis of the already existing natural sciences. This dogmatism caused Comte to deny psychology the status of an autonomous science; he called it a branch of biology, and believed that there could be only one science of society, whereas the natural sciences are many. According to Weber, there can be as many sciences as there are different avenues of approach to a problem, and we have no right to assume that we have exhausted all possible avenues of approach.

For the same reason, he regarded as sterile the attempts of philosophers to give the human sciences a common foundation; for example, by reducing them to psychology. Since every science has its own premises, it is autonomous, and none can serve as a model for the others. To try to make of psychology the foundation of sociology, on the pretext that the latter in its research encounters psychic phenomena, is thus no more than an intellectual pastime. Does not sociology also come to grips with geographical, medical, economic and political phenomena? Why not base it then on geography, medicine, economics or politics? The status of sociology as an independent science, in Weber's view, thus depends solely on the specific problems it seeks to resolve.

2. Quantification and actual experience

In the light of these considerations, Weber severely criticized two conflicting concepts which were accepted in his day (and in our own) as governing scientific investigation in history as well as in psychology and sociology, namely, quantification and actual experience.

It is a mistake, Weber argued, to believe that valid scientific cognition is possible only in quantitative terms. In point of fact, quantification and measurement are methodological procedures and no more; as such, they cannot be the end goal of science, for science means truth for all who want truth. Weber accordingly attacked, on the one hand, the prestige enjoyed by mathematics in the traditional theory of science and, on the other, the simplistic attitude of certain scientists and sociologists who think that they have accomplished scientific work merely because they have translated various observations into numbers and equations. The fact that mathematics happens to be chronologically the first to have achieved scientific exactness does not endow it with logical superiority. In fact, the mathematical procedure, like any other, entails a selection from among the various aspects of infinite reality; it is therefore valid only within the scope of its own postulates and has no jurisdiction over anything beyond. It is consequently neither a universal nor an exemplary method. While it would be ridiculous to question the exactness of mathematical propositions and their usefulness in practical application, that is no reason for setting mathematics above the other disciplines. Every scientist is entitled to decide for himself which concepts are of use to him and how rigorous they need to be for the purposes of his research. Weber denied that rigorous conceptualization can be attained only through the use of figures; it may also result from criticism, logical rationalization, exact observation or intuitiveness.

Many theories of science, modeled on the mathematical pattern, actually contradict our experience of extensive and intensive infinity, because they start from the assumption that reality can be deduced from concepts. Scientistic imperialism presupposes that, as scientists go on discovering increasingly general laws, it should one day be possible to construct so rich and complete a system of concepts that all reality could be deduced from it. But those who hold this view forget that a concept is by nature selective, and that the sum total of concepts—in other words, of selections—can never equal the sum total of reality. The infinite is not an accumulation of finite things, to say nothing of the fact that generalization cannot recapture the particular, having ignored it in the course of its operations. The various philosophical systems of the nineteenth century expected miracles.

Nevertheless, since all procedures which are effective in the sense that they advance science are good, Weber saw no objection to using quantification in sociology if it produces results. As an economist, he had himself made use of figures; for example, in a long essay entitled *Zur Psychophysik der industriellen Arbeit*. And in his essay on psychophysical law and the theory of marginal utility he ridiculed those who opposed that method out of dogmatic prejudice. To say, however, as do some American sociologists, that Weber has been the main proponent of the mathematization of sociology is to go too far, and anyone truly familiar with Weber's ideas is aware that he also poked fun at those who, like Solvay, for example, attempted systematically to reduce all social life and social phenomena to a mathematical formula.

What can figures add to phenomena whose meaning is self-evident? They are likely only to introduce confusion into perfectly clear problems and give a scientific appearance to work which does not deserve that name. By making social usefulness a numerical variable in an equation, we cannot turn this variable into a precise concept; it will continue to be based on a series of subjective and indeterminate value judgments. To what order of judgments do the categories of productivity or social energy belong? To that of science or of evaluation? Many sociological studies which rely on quantification add nothing to our knowledge and are therefore absolutely useless. What matters is to distinguish clearly between a numerical measurement which can help us to grasp a problem, and the fashionable pseudo-scientific approach where a difficulty is thought to have been resolved simply because it has been dressed up with figures, equations or graphs.

Other theoreticians of science, proceeding in the opposite direction, hold that sociology and its related disciplines can be founded on intuition, by which they mean either empathy (*Einfühlung*) or the reliving of an experience (*Nacherleben*)—in other words, direct knowledge of others through a sort of self-projection into their experience.

Weber's objection to this was that intuition pertains to the realm of feeling and is therefore not a means of scientific cognition, for not only does the latter require the elaboration and construction of concepts, but those concepts must also be precisely defined. Their place can never be taken by experience, which is diffuse, personal, incommunicable and unverifiable. It is an esthetic, and not a scientific, approach to reality. Moreover, most people have a mistaken notion of intuition; intuition can never encompass the infinite diversity of reality, for it too is selective. We can therefore never relive through empathy more than a few aspects of our own or another's experience; instead of reproducing or repeating an earlier state of being, our intuitive cognition of it simply constitutes another original experience.

Leaving aside the role of intuition (which Weber did not underestimate), an actual experience as such never represents scientific knowledge. It can be transmuted into such knowledge, but only provided it is subjected to the usual processes of conceptual transformation, verification and other methods of establishing proof, it being understood that a proposition may be scientific without necessarily being subsumed under any law. In any event, a piece of knowledge is scientific only if it has been made valid for all, and not if it is merely pleasing to some.

The same preconceived notion lies at the root of the theory of quantification as of the theory of actual experience, namely, that physical evolution is more rational than psychic or human evolution. Only the conclusions drawn in the two cases differ. In the first case, the irrational factor is regarded as negligible and it is felt that all elements of human activity should as far as possible be reduced to those of nature; in the second, it is sought to preserve whatever is irrational and to build up around it a science with its own principles and methods, even should they be in contradiction with those of the natural sciences.

Weber's objection was that both positions are essentially unscientific. To begin with, science knows no boundaries and in principle can deal with all of reality; consequently, there is no reason to exclude the irrational from its field of investigation. Secondly, two mutually contradictory sciences are inconceivable. Any analysis claiming to be scientific must be subject to the rules of control, verification and proof which apply to all positive and empirical sciences. This is no mere pious hope on the epistemologist's part, for it must be recognized that physical change is just as rational or just as irrational as psychic change.

What is generally understood by irrationality? Unpredictability and chance. But is the number of pieces into which a free-falling rock will break on landing any more predictable than an act performed under the stress of passion? Are we better able to foretell the weather a month from today than a man's future conduct? Conversely, an action which uses the appropriate means in pursuit of a specified end is fully as rational as a general law of physics; consequently, it too is accessible to nomological knowledge. A military command and a criminal law rationally take into account a number of anticipated consequences, in the same way as an engineer constructing a bridge or a farmer using chemical fertilizers. Consequently, there is no difference in kind between the predictability of natural phenomena and that of the consequences of a human action.

It is true that the concept of irrationality also has

another meaning: it is identified with freedom of the will. This idea is based on the assumption that the difference between the natural and the cultural sciences rests on the opposition between inertia and freedom. In Weber's opinion, this thesis is as fallacious as the previous one. As we have seen in section 4 of the preceding chapter, the idea of human freedom is no more irrational than determinism, since we associate the highest measure of an empirical feeling of freedom with those actions which we are conscious of performing rationally.

Consequently, the difference between quantification and actual experience can hardly be said to lie in the opposition between determinism and freedom, since there can be as much irrationality and incalculability or, conversely, rationality, in the one as in the other. It would be a distortion of scientific work to apply it to the task of proving that one of these concepts is right and the other wrong, and it would be contrary to the very essence of science to seek to establish that either of them has sole competence in a given category of sciences. Such an undertaking lies outside the sphere of positive research. Determinism and freedom are no more than data, which should be accepted on the same basis as chance, insanity, life, etc. Hence they can be neither the starting point nor the aim of research.

In fact, necessity and freedom are both situated in an area which transcends empirical knowledge and escapes its jurisdiction; the scientist cannot, therefore, be guided by them in his work. He may take them into consideration as hypotheses, but he cannot pronounce on their metaphysical validity without abandoning the domain of science for that of unverifiable value judgments.

We cannot, of course, in this short work, describe Weber's methodological conception in every detail. We shall therefore confine ourselves to an analysis of those concepts which he himself regarded as most significant.

3. Causality, value-orientation and value-interpretation

Science deals only with what is. Its job, therefore, is to explain what is, and it generally does so by looking for the causes. Unfortunately, the causal relationship has given rise to endless misunderstanding and confusion. Thus, causality is sometimes equated with legality, in the sense that only a condition which can be subsumed under a law deserves to be called a cause. Wrong! says Weber. An accidental effect can be traced back to a cause fully as much as a phenomenon which is deemed to be necessary; basically, whatever occurs in the world had to occur in just that way and not in any other. In other words, every phenomenon, accidental or not, is what it had to be. Consequently, a unique phenomenon, too, is the result of causes, some of which may have represented unique circumstances. For example, in analyzing the causes of a war, we cannot exclude the particular decision taken by those who started it. More generally, whatever is itself produced in turn produces an action (*bewirkt und wirkend*). In brief, what is regarded as an effect from one point of view may in turn serve as a cause, just as an event identified as a cause may from another point of view be seen as an effect.

Causality may be understood in two ways: as the *ratio essendi* and as the *ratio cognoscendi*. We might begin by taking an example cited by Weber—Goethe's letters to Frau von Stein. Reading them may help us to perceive causally the real influence which his relations with Frau von Stein had on Goethe's development (causality in the sense of *ratio essendi*). The letters may also give us a better understanding of what was characteristic of Goethe's personality or of the German educational milieux of his time. In that case, they are no longer real links in the causal chain of Goethe's actual, historical development, but solely a means of understanding a type of man or a type of culture (*ratio cognoscendi*, or a heuristic means).

Or let us take a non-Weberian but more classic example: the causes of war. In analyzing the causes of World War I, we shall take account of the Sarajevo assassination, the Austrian ultimatum, etc.; these events have the value of causes in the sense of *ratio essendi*, being genuine links which really helped to precipitate the hostilities. If, on the other hand, we speak of the economic causes of war, we are dealing with the question on another level—the typical level, that of the *ratio cognoscendi* of war in general. It is to be regretted that both historians and sociologists are apt to confuse these two ways of interpreting causation, to the detriment of clarity and scientific explanation.

The truth of the matter is that the generalizing method does not use the causal relationship in the same way as the individualizing method. In its full and original sense, causality comprises two basic ideas: the idea of rational action, a sort of dynamic between two qualitatively different phenomena, on the one hand; and the idea of subsumption under a general rule, on the other. The generalizing method tends to eliminate the idea of action and consequently that of cause, and to retain only the idea of law in the sense of a mathematical equality between the phenomena under consideration. In the individualizing method, on the contrary, the idea of a rule tends to disappear and the accent is on the qualitative uniqueness of evolution in general or the qualitative specificity of one of its fragments.

There is no ground, however, for claiming that the former way of treating causality is more valid than the latter, or that causality is out of place in the historical sciences, or again that analysis of historical causation must needs be less rigorous or less scientific than any other analysis.

We must go deeper yet into the matter. The knowledge we gain through causality (in the realm of nature as well as in that of culture) is never more than a fragmentary and partial view of reality, based on a probability estimate. Since the diversity of reality is extensively and intensively infinite, causal regress has no end. If we wanted to exhaust the causal cognition of a phenomenon, we would have to take into account the sum total of evolution, for all of it has in some way contributed to producing the particular effect we are seeking to analyze: ". . . the appearance of the result is, for every causally working empirical science, determined not just from a certain moment, but 'from eternity.' "[1]

Each method confines itself to those aspects of development and of phenomena which it deems to be important in the light of its presuppositions, and neglects the rest. On every occasion, we content ourselves with what Weber terms an adequate reason, which is to say that we effect a selection from the infinite diversity confronting us. In principle, no aspect or element is negligible; if we treat some of them as such, that is because of the object of our curiosity and the purpose of our research. The result is that, despite the theoretical hypothesis *causa aequat effectum*, in which casuality is seen in terms of a mathematical equation, in practice causal research always establishes an inequality among the various phenomena in that it treats some as important and essential and others as secondary and negligible. The naturalistic method ignores chance, accident, and similar factors which cannot be subsumed under a law; such subsumption is thus its criterion of selection. What criterion is employed in the historical or individualizing method?

Weber calls it by a name he borrowed from Rickert: "value-orientation." At first glance, this concept seems to be ambiguous, since, if the historian or the sociologist is free to deal with values, which are known to be variable, surely he leaves the door wide open to subjective errors. In those circumstances, can the practitioners of the human sciences conceivably comply with the principle of objectivity? In order to clarify the meaning Weber assigns to this concept, let us first state what it is not, and only then define its nature and its role.

First of all, value-orientation has nothing in common with a value judgment or an evaluation, ethical or other, of the subject treated. That would, in fact, be in direct contradiction with that "ethical neutrality" which Weber, as we shall see later, fervently defended with reference to sociological and economic studies. An evaluation which praises or condemns, approves or disapproves, has no place in science, precisely because it is purely subjective. Conversely, value-orientation has nothing to do with any objective and universal system of values arranged in a univocal and definitive hierarchy. The edification of such systems is the domain of metaphysical philosophy; furthermore, unlike Rickert, Weber did not believe it possible to construct a system of this kind that would be generally acceptable. Whether we like it or not, values, in the sense of evaluation and a system of values, depend on our feelings and wishes; they relate to our faith in ultimate ends, which escape the jurisdiction of science. Consequently, they cannot serve as a basis for theoretical knowledge.

Value-orientation determines the questions we put to reality. If a historian were asked why, for example, he was interested in the French Revolution or in Fichte's philosophy, or a sociologist why he studied social relationships in a workers' settlement or the living conditions of university students, either would doubtless reply that the subjects were interesting ones, or again, that they were important. Weber was not content with such vague answers, and put yet another pertinent question: why is a particular question important, and in relation to what? The reply to both parts of this question involves reference to values. For development as such is not concerned with meaningfulness; it offers no criterion for our curiosity or interest, nor does it furnish the reasons why we regard some things as important and others as secondary. Once a scholar has chosen a topic for study, he assembles documents and data and makes his choice among them, deeming some essential and others insignificant.

On what basis does he make his selection, if not that of value-orientation? Value-orientation thus represents that arbitrary moment which precedes all study and all scientific work (perhaps, from a certain point of view, a useful comparison could here be made with what we take to be axiomatic). It is within the limits of this selection that the scientist or scholar applies the regular procedures of scientific investigation: accurate observation, criticism of texts, surveys and documents, determination of causal relationships, comparison, etc. It is at this level that he must eschew evaluative appreciation, in the sense of approving or disapproving, for purely personal reasons, of the segment of development, the action of a hero or the example of social behavior which he is studying; and at all times, he must be careful to afford the reader an opportunity to verify the correctness of his reasoning and the soundness of his statements.

The values to which the sociologist and the historian relate reality are naturally variable. Weber even speaks of "our" values, meaning, for example, that the sociologist who studies Puritanism at a given period is able to give us new insights into this doctrine and its role in history by confronting the values of the men of that time with our own. Consequently, a specialist in the human sciences can, by referring to the relevant values, give us a modified or entirely fresh view of a problem because he attaches importance to elements neglected by other scholars who were oriented toward other values. It will thus be seen that differences in value-orientation condition the various points of view from which reality can be examined. It is as absurd to believe that any sociologist could arrive at a final conclusion regarding the phenomenon he is studying as it is to think that the truth could be expressed in a single proposition or morality in a single action.

No sociologist is in a position to furnish us with a complete picture of social relationships under a capitalist system, but each one sheds some new light on the question because, starting from the values toward which he is oriented, he makes fresh comparisons, raises new problems, discovers hitherto unthought-of aspects. It is the combination of all possible viewpoints that gives us the clearest picture of a problem. No one scientist can exhaust what we know of reality; on the contrary, reality becomes increasingly intelligible in its complexity as more and more historians, sociologists, economists and students of politics examine it in the light of yet other values. For that very reason, a contemporary historian will find Thucydides' account of the Peloponnesian War fully as interesting as that of a more modern author, and a sociologist will not think Saint-Simon, Comte or Durkheim dated, but will profit by reading them.

We can now readily grasp the role and meaning of value-orientation. Given the extensive and intensive infinity of empirical reality which no science can wholly encompass, value-orientation is seen to be that principle of selection which is the precondition for at least partial knowledge. More precisely, value-orientation is the subjective factor which enables a scientist to acquire a limited objective knowledge, always provided that he is conscious of this inevitable limitation. In other words, the personality of the sociologist or the historian must necessarily influence his work. Science varies constantly as new problems are brought to light because reality is being viewed from fresh points of vantage. Far from limiting the field of study, value-orientation broadens its horizons. It also demonstrates that research is unending. A scientist and his school may think that they have said the last word on a given subject, but another scientist will reopen it because he has discovered another set of values to which it can be oriented. Science is the creation of all scientists.

> The cultural problems which move men form themselves ever anew and in different colors, and the boundaries of that area in the infinite stream of concrete events which acquires meaning and significance for us, i.e., which becomes an "historical individual," are constantly subject to change. The intellectual contexts from which it is viewed and scientifically analyzed shift. The points of departure of the cultural sciences remain changeable throughout the limitless future as long as a Chinese ossification of intellectual life does not render mankind incapable of setting new questions to the eternally inexhaustible flow of life. A systematic science of culture, even only in the sense of a definitive, objectively valid, systematic fixation of the problems which it should treat, would be senseless in itself.[2]

In order further to pin down the role of value-orientation, we might set out the following points: (*a*) it determines the selection of the subject of study, i.e., it enables us to detach a definite object from reality, which itself is diffuse; (*b*) once the topic has been chosen, it guides us in sifting the essential from the secondary, i.e., it defines the historical individuality or uniqueness of the problem in effecting a choice from an infinitude of details, elements and documents; (c) in this operation, it supplies the reason for establishing a relationship between various elements and the meanings we assign to them; (d) it also indicates what causal relationships are to be established and how far causal regression should go; (e) lastly, because it is not a value judgment and requires clear and articulated thinking for the verification of our propositions, it eliminates mere personal experience and vague emotionality.

In consequence, all human sciences necessarily proceed by means of interpretation. This is the method we use to understand the meaning of an activity or a phenomenon and the significance of various elements in their relationship to each other, as is suggested by the two German words, *deuten* (interpret) and *bedeuten* (signify). Since evolution itself is devoid of all meaning, and therefore humanly indifferent, interpretation based on value-orientation endows it with meaning by affording verifiable proof of both the motives and the purposes of an activity. This idea of verifiable proof (*Evidenz*) is of great importance; to quote Weber, "all interpretation, as does science generally, strives for clarity and verifiable proof."[3]

By using the method of demonstration which is peculiar to it, mathematics endeavors to make evident, and to prove, numerical and quantitative relations; the human sciences, and in particular sociology, use interpretation to make evident, and to prove, meanings.

Misunderstandings often arise because interpretation can proceed on several levels, and Weber was careful to distinguish between those levels. Three are basic. First, there is what he termed philological interpretation; it consists in grasping the literal meaning of a text, in criticizing documents and studies, etc. This is the preparatory work required in all the human sciences, the accompaniment of any study of sources. Next, there is what he called evaluative or ethical interpretation; it consists in assigning a value to the subject and making a favorable or unfavorable judgment on it. This type of interpretation ranges from purely emotional evaluations, by means of empathy, of the events and circumstances of our daily lives, to the higher and more refined sphere of esthetic appreciations and moral judgments. Lastly, there is what Weber termed rational interpretation, whose aim is to enable us to grasp, through causality, or through comprehension, the meaningful relationships between different phenomena or different elements of the same phenomenon.

To the extent that the first type of interpretation effects a selection among documents and sources, it bears some relation to value-orientation. The second type, which makes a direct value judgment of an object, is not a scientific method, although the scientist must sometimes take it into account in his work, for he cannot disregard the fact that one activity is generally deemed good and important, while another is censured. He must not, however, allow himself to be influenced by such evaluations, but must study, for example, the phenomenon of prostitution with the same strict objectivity as the phenomenon of a religious belief. Nevertheless, only rational interpretation is a determining factor in the formulation of a scientific proposition.

As noted above, this last type of interpretation is

the one which looks for meaning, whether the scientist is attempting to determine the significance which certain individuals—the Puritans, for example—attached to their acts because they related them to their religious values, or whether he uses modern values as a frame of reference to discover the historical or sociological meaning of a doctrine, an event, or the evolution of a situation. Consequently, we are here talking about analysis, the purpose of which is to determine the values toward which a given activity is oriented, and not to evaluate that activity as good or bad in the light of subjective ethical convictions.

In such interpretation, Weber emphasized, it is essential to employ the regular procedures of scientific cognition and to subject them to verification. That is why he also called such rational interpretation "causal" or "explanatory" interpretation. It is of particular importance in sociology, when the meaning of an activity is analyzed. Every activity involves a means-and-end relationship; in particular, we can understand with a high degree of verifiable proof an activity oriented toward a consciously realized end and carried on with full knowledge of the most appropriate means. In such a case, the means become the causes of the chosen end. It is essential for analysis to remain at the level of what is empirically given, since it must endeavor to grasp the meaningful relationship between the means used and the goal set, without passing judgment on the ethical value of either goal or means. For example, it is within the province of sociology to attempt a rational interpretation of the significance of certain police measures by explaining why they were taken and what were their consequences, but not to evaluate those measures positively or negatively, or to pass judgment for or against the police. Sociology cannot dispense with rational interpretation in that sense, for then it would be unable either to understand an activity or to explain it. This notion, of course, is linked to the concept of understanding; we shall come to it again later, in the chapter dealing with Weber's idea of "understanding" or "interpretative" sociology (*verstehende Soziologie*).

4. The *"ideal type"*

Every science worthy of the name defines its concepts precisely. The naturalistic method has the advantage of dealing with concepts—such as power, force, mass, energy—which are entirely unambiguous because they can be expressed in figures. The same concepts, when used by the human sciences, are exceedingly vague and constantly give rise to misunderstanding and confusion. When history or sociology deal with such notions as capitalism, socialism, Protestantism or productivity, they encounter still greater difficulties, because the content of those ideas varies from epoch to epoch and from school to school. What was understood by Calvinism in the seventeenth century is not what we mean by it today. True, the term carries some meaning for everyone, but a scientist cannot be satisfied with such imprecision.

If we concede that the content of a historical concept varies from one period to another, we must each time specify in what sense we are using it, lest we confuse our analysis and arrive at inconsistent results; for example, by drawing, for capitalism in general, conclusions which hold true only for a certain type of capitalism at a given time, or by attributing to Christianity as a whole a rule of conduct which applies solely to one of its historical forms. The historian and the sociologist think that they are scientifically describing reality, whereas the language they use is made up of terms which have not been evolved by reflection, which are full of ambiguities, and which can be understood only approximately and without certainty. How can an analysis be precise if the intellectual tools it employs are not?

In order to give the concepts utilized in the historical method the necessary rigor, Weber evolved his notion of the "ideal type."

> An ideal type is formed by the one-sided accentuation of one or more points of view and by the synthesis of a great many diffuse, discrete, more or less present and occasionally absent concrete individual phenomena, which are arranged according to those one-sidedly emphasized viewpoints into a unified analytical construct.[4]

The ideal type is thus the sum total of concepts which the specialist in the human sciences constructs purely for purposes of research. As we have seen in connection with value-orientation, Weber rejects the old view of science as capable of penetrating to the essence of things in order to unify them in a complete system which would be a faithful reflection of reality. In his opinion, no system is capable of reproducing all reality, because reality is infinite, nor can any concept wholly reproduce the utter diversity of particular phenomena. In short, there is no knowledge which is not hypothetical. The ideal type is but another instance of the selection which the historian and the sociologist must always make, since they necessarily approach reality from certain points of view which are determined by their value-orientation.

However, value-orientation merely gives direction to the work and helps to eliminate inessentials; it does not in itself ensure the necessary precision of concepts. That is the function of the ideal type. It offers a means of concept construction appropriate to the historical or individualizing method, which, as we have seen, sets itself the goal of studying reality and single phenomena in all their uniqueness.

Weber's question is this: how are we to formulate a precise concept of a unique piece of reality, seeing that we must eschew generalization in the sense of drawing analogies and noting resemblances with other segments of reality, for to do so would mean to subordinate phenomena to laws or generic concepts which would despoil them of what is distinctive, special and unique about them? Or, to put it more briefly, is it possible to formulate individualized concepts, since it is commonly thought that all concepts are general by their very nature? Capitalism is a particular manifestation of economic life, as Protestantism is of religion and romanticism of art; similarly, capitalism in ancient times had its own characteristics, different from those of modern capitalism, while Anglo-Saxon capitalism, for example, differs from capitalism as it exists in continental Europe.

To attempt to explain capitalism or Protestantism by subsuming them under the general concepts of economics or religion would mean to leave out those aspects which give them originality (although that procedure may also help us to understand them better, for the individualizing method does not exclude the generalizing method). Equally meager results are obtained if we attempt to define unique segments of reality by the addition of features common to all the forms of capitalism or Protestantism, or by establishing an average of the features peculiar to the various forms of those two phenomena. The same problem arises in connection with most historical and sociological notions, such as the Greek city-state, rural economy, the artisan system, or socialism.

For Weber, the solution to the problem lies in a special concept of type. The term can mean the sum total of common traits (average type), but it can also stand for a certain stylization, in which the characteristic, distinctive, or "typical" elements are stressed. Let us proceed by analogy. Avarice is a general concept, but the miser portrayed by Molière in *L'Avare* is a type. Harpagon is not an average miser; through a process of enlargement, exaggeration and amplification, Molière has endowed him with a characteristic individuality; he is, as it were, an ideal miser. He does not sum up the traits common to all misers; rather, he is a stylized character, the embodiment of all that is typical in that particular predilection. *Mutatis mutandis*, it is in such a manner that we must understand Weber's definition of the ideal type, in which he speaks of accentuation or one-sidedly emphasized viewpoints according to which the traits and characteristics of individual phenomena are arranged in a unified analytical construct.

Such a conceptual construct is "ideal" in that it is

never, or only very rarely, encountered in all its purity in real life. The ideal type of capitalism as an analytical construct, for example, unites those characteristics which give it its originality as an economic doctrine, although they may be found only as diffuse phenomena in reality and although any one of them may be absent in a concrete economic organization. The ideal type of capitalism also comprises its various trends and its final goals, even if they are nowhere fully attained. The incidence of any one element is thus less important than the characteristic and original quality which distinguishes this particular economic system from the rest.

Equally to be stressed is the idea of one-sidedness; it enables us to give the ideal type the required precision, since it is a precondition both of the enlargement of characteristic traits and of the formulation of a coherent and non-contradictory analytical construct. Rising above the practical applications of the capitalist doctrine, which are usually ambiguous, being the result of compromise, the ideal type offers a rational "blueprint" of that doctrine, i.e. its logical organization as distinct from the fluctuations of reality. It thus constitutes an ideal and consistent representation of a particular historical entity, obtained through the Utopian rationalization and one-sided accentuation of characteristic and original traits, for the purpose of giving a coherent and unambiguous meaning to elements in our day-to-day experience which would otherwise seem incoherent and chaotic.

In order to avoid any possible misunderstanding, Weber explained his concept of the ideal type in terms not only of what it is intended to be, but also of what it is not intended to be. To begin with, the ideal type does not attempt to grasp the reality of things classified in a hierarchy of species and genera, whether within a system of natural laws or within an assemblage of general components faithfully reflecting such a system. The ideal type is not to be identified with reality in the sense of expressing reality's "true" essence. On the contrary, precisely because it is unreal and takes us a step away from reality, it enables us to obtain a better intellectual and scientific grasp of reality, although necessarily a fragmented one. Moreover, since value-orientation is involved, our ideal typical construct of, say, an epoch or a doctrine, for the purpose of penetrating their meaning, will certainly differ from the concept formed of that epoch by those who lived in it, or from the meaning of the doctrine which its proponents attached to it. Depending on the nature of our research, we can construct the ideal type of liberalism on the basis of the values to which its proponents related social conditions, but we can also construct other ideal types by relating liberalism to our own values or to those of an opposing school of thought.

Secondly, when we call our construct an "ideal" type, that term has nothing in common with an ideal in the ethical sense, i.e. that which ought to be. The ideal type is not intended to be in any way exemplary, and must not be confused with an ethical model, or even with a practical rule of conduct. It seeks perfection of a logical, not a moral, order, and it excludes all value judgments. Although this kind of confusion is tempting and is of frequent occurrence, a scientist who constructs the ideal type of Christianity with a view to studying its cultural significance must not relate Christianity to his own subjective and personal idea of what it ought to be. It is, on the other hand, possible to construct an ideal type of what Christianity regards as its ideal form or its final goal.

It may well seem pedantic to transform most of the ideas which historians and sociologists take for granted into ideal types. Yet that is the only way to arrive at a precise definition of concepts and to avoid hollow rhetoric, fallacious reasoning, ambiguity and pernicious error.

Let us take free trade as an example. A number of modern economists have ridiculed this theory, claiming that it is anachronistic and outstripped by events and therefore of no conceivable usefulness in economic research. Weber agreed with their criticism of the liberal school which held that free trade obeyed natural laws and which elevated it to the rank of a philosophy or of an empirically valid rule expressing the essence of economics. In his view, however, the notion of free trade is useful as a Utopian rationalization of trade relations formulated by thinkers who sought to grasp the meaning of trade. It would therefore be wrong, he felt, to underestimate its heuristic value as an ideal type, for by discarding it we might well misunderstand the nature of trade.

The case of Marxism is no different. Marxist laws and constructs are extremely useful as ideal types, but it would be altogether mistaken to regard them as empirically valid or as reflecting economic reality.

Consequently, it is preposterous to criticize specialists in the human sciences for making new constructs; that is the price we pay for the progress of science, to say nothing of the fact that such work is essential because problems and viewpoints alter constantly as civilization itself evolves and changes. For this reason alone, a definitive synthesis of reality is out of the question. The scientist, therefore, must never lose sight of the limitations of the concepts with which he works. At the very moment when he believes that he has charted the future, humanity may suddenly change course. He can never understand more than a finite and ceaselessly changing part of the chaotic and prodigious flow of events in time. And it is this fact that defines the role and methodological significance of ideal types.

Weber did not regard ideal types as goals of cognition, as in themselves summing up or containing reality or constituting a complete scientific system. They are only instruments, heuristic means of establishing unambiguously the meaning of the subject under investigation. More precisely, they are purely experimental procedures which the scientist evolves deliberately and arbitrarily, according to the needs of the investigation, and which he abandons without a qualm if they do not meet his expectations. Thus their value is determined solely by their helpfulness and effectiveness in research. If they are not helpful or effective, or cease to be so, the sociologist is free to construct other, more serviceable ideal types. In themselves, ideal types are neither true nor false, but simply, like any other technical tool, useful or useless.

These considerations are bound up with Weber's concept of science. If science means unending research, then the concepts it uses must necessarily be constantly outstripped, since it is through such outstripping that knowledge advances. Hence the need for constantly evolving fresh ideal types, not only because "the eternally onward-flowing stream of culture perpetually brings new problems,"[5] but also because mankind perpetually probes, from different angles, even that reality with which it is familiar. This eternal youth of science compels the scientist to strive for precision.

Indeed, it is just *because* the content of historical concepts is necessarily subject to change that they must be formulated precisely and clearly on all occasions. In their application, their character as ideal analytical constructs should be carefully kept in mind, and the ideal type and historical reality should not be confused with each other. It should be understood that, since really definitive historical concepts are not in general to be thought of as an ultimate, and in view of the inevitable shift of the guiding value-ideas, the construction of sharp and unambiguous concepts relevant to the concrete *individual* viewpoint which directs our interest at any given time affords the possibility of clearly realizing the *limits* of their validity.[6]

If need be, the scientist may construct different ideal types of the same phenomenon; as many, in fact, as he may deem necessary for a clearer understanding of that phenomenon from all possible points of view. He may formulate an ideal type of Christianity or, taking Christianity as a generic concept, construct, depending on his line of research, ideal types of primitive Christianity, medieval Christianity, or the Jesuitical, Gallican, Catholic or Protestant forms of Christianity; and he is also entirely free, in choosing to accentuate one characteristic in preference to others (for example, charity in faith, the legal organization of churches, or

Christian social structures), to construct a number of ideal types of the evolution of Christianity in general or of some one of its historical forms. Thus, Weber did not reject the possibility of elaborating ideal types of an evolution. None of these constructs would resemble the others, nor be encountered in empirical reality, but each could rightly claim to represent the "idea" of Christianity in so far as it was a selection of characteristics to be found in reality and significant by reason of their singularity.

Consequently, precisely as there exists a great variety of different viewpoints representing different value-orientations, so the most diverse principles may be brought into play in selecting typical relationships which can be arranged in a unified analytical construct. The reason is readily apparent: since our knowledge of infinite reality is of necessity partial and fragmentary, it is also bound to be approximate. The multiplicity of ideal types simply serves the purpose of making this approximation as close, as circumstantial, and as clear as possible.

Thus the true role of the ideal type is to be an intelligibility factor on the two levels of research and exposition. Let us consider the first case. The construction of ideal types enables us to make judgments involving causal imputation, not because the ideal types themselves are meant to serve as hypotheses, but because they allow us to construct hypotheses, drawing on an imagination enriched by experience and disciplined by methodology. That is a point of basic importance. By using a rationally devised Utopian concept, we are able to determine what is unique about a course of events, a doctrine or a situation by showing, in each particular case, to what extent reality departs from the unified and unreal analytical construct. The ideal type thus serves as a kind of yardstick.

Let us suppose that we want to study the artisan system in the Middle Ages. We will construct an ideal type based on the distinctive and typical features of the organization of artisan groups. We will then compare it with empirical reality, and will thus be in a position to determine whether medieval society was strictly an artisan society or whether, on the contrary, elements of some other economic system (such as capitalism) were already apparent in it. We will then be in a position to proceed to causal imputation. Similarly, the construction of an ideal type of the urban economy in the Middle Ages will enable us to ascertain to what extent some particular city exemplified that economic system or obeyed the principles of an older regime or, on the contrary, presaged a new form of organization. Being unreal, the ideal type has the merit of offering us a conceptual device with which we can measure real development and clarify the most important elements of empirical reality.

At the exposition level, the ideal type lays no claim to reproducing reality; what it does is to afford precise and unambiguous means of expression. As a rule, those historians and sociologists who repudiate ideal-typical constructs on the pretext that they are useless or ponderous use them just the same, but unwittingly and illogically, with the result that they may on occasion pass off their value judgments as scientific conclusions or remain entirely in the sphere of the affective. What are such generic terms as Christianity, feudalism, manager, value, or, to introduce a more modern notion, industrial society, if not so many ideal types? There is no law to prevent the sociologist from proceeding by suggestion, but in so doing he should not imagine that he is acting scientifically.

Weber was fully aware of the shortcomings of his theory, which, moreover, he presented only in broad outline, without pursuing all its methodological implications. He has often been criticized for his failure to do so. The major part of the immense literature concerned with his work deals with his theory of knowledge, and in particular with the concept of the ideal type, often in an altogether negative manner. That in itself is an indirect recognition of the importance of the question he posed. He replied in advance to his future critics by inviting them to meditate on his propositions until they were in a position to offer something better.

Weber's theory may be regarded as the most lucid and coherent of the many endeavors made to give greater precision to the concepts used in the human sciences. True, it leads to a scattering of approaches and analyses at the expense of systematization. The question is whether a scientific system is more important that the possibility of obtaining scientifically valid results. For it is undeniable that the ideal-type method has the advantage of preserving, by means of precise concepts, the unity and originality of a historical phenomenon whenever we seek to study it in its singularity. Understood in this way, the ideal-type theory can provide the basis for a further study of the historical method, in contrast to the purely negative criticisms of it, which can never rise above negation.

5. *Objective possibility and adequate causation*

Finally, the ideal type is the cornerstone of the theory of objective possibility and adequate causation. Weber explained these two categories mainly in his essay on the methodology of history.[7] He did not restate the theory in connection with his sociological studies, but simply applied it to various important sociological concepts, such as goal-oriented action. We shall follow the same course and proceed from an analysis of historical methods to one of sociological methods.

The theory of objective possibility raises the problem of causal imputation in another form. To attempt to explain a historical event by subsuming it under a general law is to distort history, which is made up of a succession of singular events. The only appropriate method is that of individualization, which relates a particular event to particular causes or to a particular complex of causes, which Weber called a "constellation." Although all the components of such a constellation have a part in bringing about the event, they do not all have equal importance in the eyes of the historian. The historian makes a selection among them, and we are consequently faced with the problem: how is he to assess the importance of a cause?

In answering this question, Weber cites several conclusions drawn by Eduard Meyer, one of the foremost German historians of the present century. Meyer declares, for instance, that the victory of Marathon was of the greatest historical significance for the future of Greek culture, and that Bismarck's decision precipitated the Austro-Prussian war of 1866, but that, on the

other hand, the two shots fired in Berlin on the night of
March 1848, and which touched off the revolution
there, were not determining causes, since the atmosphere in the Prussian capital had been such that almost any incident might have led to disturbances.
These and similar judgments, which are to be found in
the works of all historians, attribute greater importance
to some causes than to others. The problem Weber
raised is this: by what logical operation does the historian assign unequal significance to the antecedents of
an event which he proposes to analyze?

If he is to give their proper importance to the bat-
tles of Marathon and Sadowa, and to the shots fired in
Berlin, the historian must at least implicitly ask himself: what would have happened had the Persians been
victorious, or had Bismarck not made that particular
decision, or again, had the two shots not been fired?
This is much like the question which the criminologist
or the judge asks himself when he seeks to determine in
what circumstances an individual may be said to be
responsible for his acts, with the difference that the
judge then proceeds to weigh guilt and possibly to impose a penalty. If we consider the matter, we shall see
that the historian mentally isolates some one cause (the
victory at Marathon, Bismarck's decision, the shots),
that he abstracts it from the constellation of antecedents, and that he then asks himself whether or not the
course of events would have been the same without it.
Meyer recognizes that, if the shots had not been fired,
the revolution would nevertheless have occurred, and
that this particular cause is therefore of minor importance; on the contrary, if the Persians had conquered at
Marathon or if Bismarck had not taken his decision,

Meyer believes that events would have followed a different course and that, consequently, these causes were determining factors.

To put it more precisely, in effecting such an abstraction the historian constructs a possible course of events in order to determine which were the actual or "adequate" causes. "In order to penetrate to the real causal relationships," says Weber, "we construct unreal ones."[8] In short, drawing on his knowledge and on the sources available to him, the historian imagines a possible development, one that might have taken place had the cause in question been removed, and in that way evaluates the significance and importance of that cause for the historical development known to have taken place.

What makes such a possibility objective? Let us take the battle of Marathon as an example. That battle decided between two possibilities. The first was a Greek victory, which took place and which therefore determined the actual course of history, bringing in its train Greek independence, the development of a free mind and spirit oriented toward the things of this world, and the flowering of a culture concerned with science, philosophy and the many other "humanist" values from which we still draw sustenance. The other possibility was a Persian victory. In the light of what we know of Persian policy in conquered lands, for example of the attitude of the Persians toward the Jews, it seems possible that the Persian king would have sought to utilize the local religion as an instrument of domination in Greece too. The chances are that he would have encouraged a theocratic-religious culture in Greece based on the mysteries and the oracles.

The possibility of such a development is objective because our suppositions rest on our knowledge of the general lines of Persian policy in conquered countries and of the presence of theocratic-religious elements in Greek life. Objectivity is ensured by our positive knowledge of conditions in Greece and by our nomological knowledge, based on empirical rules. Hence this is not an arbitrary assumption, a gratuitous hypothesis, but a rational supposition supported by a number of known facts.

Like the ideal type, objective possibility constructs an "imaginary picture," a Utopia, except that, instead of accentuating characteristic traits, it abstracts one or several elements of the actual situation in order to discover what might have happened. Objective possibility, representing as it does a reasoned judgment, is not tantamount to "not knowing," since it is a supposition based on what we know from experience. Nevertheless, it would be a mistake to conclude that a condition thus removed from a constellation of antecedents must necessarily be the only cause of the event under study; the significance we attach to it is simply that of one important condition among others, for history does not know single causes. Moreover, the theory of objective possibility does not for one moment affirm that, in the event of a Persian victory, a theocratic-religious culture must inevitably have developed, but only that it would have been a probable consequence of such a victory. It forms no judgment as to what must necessarily have happened in that case, since only what actually did happen —the Greek victory—is real.

Consequently, in imputing causal significance to a condition isolated in the light of objective possibility, we may say with R. Aron, who sums up Weber's position very well, "we have no need to describe in detail what would have happened; it is enough for us to know that things would have been different."[9]

We can now understand the nature of causality in the human sciences which use the historical method: it is probabilistic. The reason is not only that our knowledge is imperfect, owing in many cases to the paucity of data, but also that the antecedents are countless, so that we are obliged to construct an imaginary course of events in order to select the more important antecedents. Besides, no matter how complete our knowledge, the inevitable moment of selection, which is bound to be subjective, would suffice to introduce the element of probability. Despite the apodictic nature of their propositions, without the mathematicians there would never have been any mathematics; and history without historians to write it and in so doing to put new questions to the flow of events is equally unthinkable.

The degree of probability of an objectively possible construct is variable. Despite the climate of insurrection prevailing in Berlin in 1848, no historian can say with certainty that the revolution would have occurred anyway, without the two shots. This means that, although the objective possibility that the course of events would have been different had the two shots not been fired is slight, it cannot be said that the shots had no significance whatsoever. Conversely, although there is a very high degree of objective possibility that Greek civilization would have developed along theocratic-religious lines in the event of a Persian victory, it cannot be said that such a development would have been absolutely inevitable. The role of the category of objective possibility is thus not to form judgments as to the necessary sequence of events, but to weigh the significance of the various causes of an event. When the probability resulting from an objectively possible construct is very high, Weber suggests that we speak of adequate causation, and when it is low, of accidental causation. Thus a theocratic evolution in Greece would have been, not the necessary, but an adequate, consequence of a Persian victory. On the other hand, the shots in Berlin in 1848 fall under the heading of accidental causes, assuming that the atmosphere was conducive to insurrection. Weber's refusal to employ the term "necessary," and his substitution of the term "adequate," was motivated by the desire to do nothing to disguise the irrational character of evolution, which never has any meaning of its own, but only such meanings as we assign to it. He thus opposed the naturalistic and purely determinist conception of history, while maintaining the validity of causal explanation.

In a word, history itself is not rational, but the historian is able to rationalize it in some measure; in fact, to the extent that he succeeds in formulating probabilistic objective judgments in the form of an adequate relationship between cause and effect, he makes a scientific knowledge of history possible, despite the irregularities due to chance or accident and despite the intervention of the human will. No logical obstacle prevents the existence of a science which is concerned with the unique.

Although history deals with particular acts of will, or decisions, whereas sociology seeks to establish general rules, both use the same method in some respects, since both are concerned with human activity. Weber saw no difference in kind between individual action and social or collective action. The development of Hellenic culture, for example, while a separate and unique phenomenon, was not the work of a single man, but of a society. Consequently, a sociologist who wants to operate with strictly defined concepts is also obliged to construct ideal types (city, bureaucracy, domination, etc.) and to work with the categories of objective possibility and adequate causation.

We will discuss the relationship between history and sociology later on; but it may be useful at this point to indicate in what way the sociologist makes use of these two categories. Unlike the statesman or the business executive, who evaluates the different possibilities open to him before taking action, the sociologist, just as much as the historian, is faced with a completed action or a given behavior, and must a posteriori explain its causes and motives, seek to understand its purpose and analyze the means used to attain it. In order to discover whether the means employed empirically by a man or a group of men were suited to the end in view, our sociologist must construct the ideal type of rational goal-oriented action, by which we mean an imaginary picture of an objectively possible action, taking into account the planned goal and the available means, in order to determine whether the means actually used were adequate for the purpose.

In this way, he is able to measure the gap between the ideal-typical objectively possible action and the empirical action, and ascertain the part played by irrationality and chance or by the intrusion of accidental, emotional and other elements. For, as Weber stresses repeatedly, the teleological relationship between the means and the end, as for example the proposition that x is the appropriate or adequate means for attaining the end y, is simply an inversion of the causal relationship: y follows x. In other words, if a human action, whether individual or collective, implies a causal relationship, the categories of objective possibility and adequate causation are automatically applicable to it.

The sociologist pursues two purposes. He may content himself with simply describing the social action of individuals or groups as it actually and empirically occurred; but he may also seek to establish whether that empirical action led to results compatible with the agent's intentions, in terms of the given situation. A basic characteristic of social action is that it is significantly related to the behavior of others, in that the agent counts on the others to comply with an explicit agreement or with the accepted social norms, or else that he bears in mind the possibility of penalties if those norms are violated, or again that he hopes to put the others in a difficult position. Once a sociologist asks himself whether the agent was really able to count on a certain behavior on the part of the others and consequently whether the agent's suppositions were correct, he can obtain an answer only by constructing, on the basis of the given situation viewed objectively, an ideal action showing the adequate means of attaining the proposed end.

Hence it is only by comparing the agent's real action with an ideal construct that the sociologist can discover whether the agent was right in making the assumptions by which he was guided, what mistakes he made in the course of his undertaking, and what unforeseeable external elements intervened to make the action deviate from its original objective.

6. *Ethical neutrality*

Ethical neutrality is a subject on which Weber differed, sometimes violently, with most of the methodologists of his day. It is a sensitive issue, for it is not concerned solely with the principles governing the construction of theoretical concepts, but also with the practical attitude of the scientist in his everyday life, and it raises the still more touchy point of intellectual integrity.

Reduced to its simplest form, the problem is this: is it right for a scientist to take advantage of the prestige he has gained by purely scientific work to seek to impose his personal and partisan views on others? Great is the temptation for a mathematician, a biologist, a historian or a sociologist, especially if he has attained some eminence, to intervene in his capacity as a scientist in political or economic decision-making, on the ground that his experience in theoretical research is a guarantee of his competence in a sphere of beliefs and evaluations. This practice is so common that one forgets to ask whether it is not fraudulent. Certainly no one today would deny the need to distinguish between science and faith. However, the question goes beyond purely religious considerations; it also concerns the expression of ethical, political and other beliefs.

Weber's position tends to arouse particular ire because it is absolutely free from bigotry. He asserted, for example, that an anarchist who as a matter of principle denied the validity of law and convention could be a good teacher of law, precisely because his convictions could equip him to perceive problems in legal postulates which most jurists take for granted. On the same grounds, Weber opposed those of his colleagues who held that socialists and Marxists should not be allowed to teach in a university. What was unpardonable in his eyes was that a man should present his personal, subjective convictions as scientific truths by cleverly confusing, supposedly in good faith, empirically ascertainable and scientifically verifiable observations with attitudes and value judgments having no other justification than belief in questionable and arbitrarily selected final goals. To avoid all misunderstanding, Weber drew a distinction between two levels of scientific activity, namely, teaching and research.

He was not opposed in principle to evaluations being handed down from the professorial chair. In any case, he felt that this was not a matter for scientific discussion and therefore could not be definitely resolved, since it was itself dependent upon an evaluation, and in particular on the country's educational policy. Nevertheless, in an age when university specialization has triumphed along with freedom of opinion, it is hard to see, Weber argued, why a scientist should feel compelled to impart a *Weltanschauung* to his students in addition to the specialized material which he teaches. Professorial prophecy is not a specialty. Moreover, while at the outset such lumping together of precise analyses and personal value judgments may earn the professor an easy triumph, it ends by boring his audience.

For the sake of his personal dignity, if for nothing

else, the professor should concentrate on the teaching required of him, instead of playing the cultural reformer without the practical means of carrying out reforms, or parading the qualities of a statesman while lacking that basic requirement, a state to organize. To make a show, on the slightest excuse, of personal impressions, which moreover are often insipid, is in bad taste. A professor does not express his personality by giving everything a personal touch but rather by the quality of his work and of his courses. To use a lecture room as a public forum betrays a lack of understanding of the purpose of a university. The student must perforce remain silent, and it is therefore unkind and unfair to him to try to impose one's own convictions upon him, safe in the knowledge that no contradiction will be forthcoming. Common honesty demands that a professor who wants to disseminate his ideals should employ the means available to every citizen: public meetings where contradiction is permitted, membership in an organization or group engaged in propaganda, publication in the press, literary or political essays, conversations with the man in the street, etc.

Weber accompanied these reflections of an ethical nature by considerations pertaining to the sociology of pedagogy. Not only should the professor not seek to impose his personal values, said Weber, but he should also refrain from making pronouncements on matters which the authorities would like him to take up. For the authorities, he pointed out, are not alone in trying to influence universities; certain professors become the conscious or unconscious spokesmen of pressure groups and special interests. In any event, if a lecture hall is deemed to be a forum for the discussion of ideological and practical problems, the right of reply must be freely granted to dissenting views. The university is not the private preserve of any one doctrine. Absolute freedom to advocate practical goals must lead to the adulteration of purely professional work and to the discrediting of the very function of the professor.

It is important, however, to understand exactly what Weber meant by ethical neutrality in teaching; it has nothing to do with pusillanimity, with refusing to form or to express an opinion out of fear, hypocrisy, or concern for one's career. Here again, a man must take full responsibility for his acts and acquire sufficient poise to assert his independence as a teacher. Such independence, however, is possible only on condition that the professor is neither the tool nor the fanatical servant of influences external to the university, whatever they may be, whatever their significance and however generous their ethics.

In Weber's opinion, the professor should adhere to the following course: fulfill his task with simplicity, suppressing his personality in order solely to dispense instruction; in explaining the matters within his province, never ignore disagreeable facts, particularly those which might be embarrassing for his personal views; and distinguish between empirical observations and value judgments, between research and private conviction. Lucidity thus becomes the paramount virtue of a university lecture. When a teacher expounds a problem in economics, sociology or political science, it is not his business to look for the proper moral attitude or to make up a colorful nosegay of those cultural values which comfort him most; his business is to serve the discipline which he teaches. If, on occasion, he cannot refrain from making value judgments, let him at least have the courage and the honesty to make clear to his students what part of his lecture is based on pure logical reasoning or empirical explanation, and what part is composed of his personal evaluations and subjective beliefs. This naturally presupposes that he is able to grasp the difference between the sphere of science and that of conviction.

So long as the professor accepts this obligation, there is no objection to his making evaluations or expounding ex cathedra a philosophy founded on ethics or on culture generally. For all anyone knows, such a method may even lead to the discovery of unsuspected problems. In any event, no professor can tell another what his conduct should be, since, as we have seen, ethical neutrality in teaching is itself the outcome of evaluation.

The position is somewhat different in the case of research, however. By its very nature, science abhors value judgments. Its object is not to act on personal conviction, but to show that its propositions hold for all those who want to know the truth.

It has been and remains true that a systematically correct scientific proof in the social sciences, if it is to achieve its purpose, must be acknowledged as correct even by a Chinese—or—more precisely stated—it must constantly strive to attain this goal, which perhaps may not be completely attainable due to faulty data. Furthermore, the successful logical analysis of the content of an ideal and its ultimate axioms and the discovery of the consequences which arise from pursuing it, logically and practically, must also be valid for the Chinese. At the same time, our Chinese can lack a "sense" of our ethical imperative and he can and certainly often will deny the ideal itself and the concrete value-judgments derived from it. Neither of these two latter attitudes can affect the scientific value of the analysis in any way.[10]

This means that, at the level of research, the distinction between science and conviction is a logical necessity, and that it is a sin against the spirit of science to make it conform to subjective beliefs. Difficult as it may be to draw the line between empirical observation and practical evaluation, the scientist must do so to meet the demands of science.

Obviously, there is nothing to stop a sociologist from taking as his subject of research the opinions of different individuals on the same question, but he will cease doing scientific work the moment he himself expresses an opinion on those opinions. His task is to interpret, to analyze, to describe a situation, using all the resources of the scientific method, but not to contribute his own views or to call one opinion right and another wrong.

Thus we see that science may deal with evaluations, provided that it does not evaluate them. In short, a scientist should not be naturalistic, or spiritualistic, or even scientistic. If he encounters facts which he is unable to explain with the available tools of scientific research, he must neither deny them in the name of a subjective conception of science, nor ignore them, nor relegate them to the realm of superstition, but simply admit that he cannot explain them. Unlike axiology, science has no need of apologetics. By embarking on ethical justification or the commendation of cultural values, it adds nothing to its objective validity. On the contrary, it runs the risk of mistaking its own meaning, as well as the meaning of ethics.

Consequently, the scientist who wishes to remain within the fixed boundaries of science must renounce all philosophies, including those which lay claim to a scientific basis. All that the scientist can do for the man of action is to tell him, once the goal has been chosen, which are the most appropriate means of attaining it, and what are their possible consequences—in other words, what price he may have to pay for reaching the desired end. Science may also help the man of action to understand the importance of his project and to become more fully aware of the circumstances and conditions of his activities and perhaps alert him to the values with which he may come in conflict. It may in no case influence him in the making of a decision. That is a matter for choice and not for theoretical knowledge. In brief, science can tell us what we can do and in some cases what we want to do, never what we ought to do.

To sum up, while in the sphere of teaching ethical neutrality remains a problem to be solved by each professor in his own way, it is a logical necessity in scientific research. The duty of the physician is to find the drugs or the treatment that will cure his patient; it is not for him to appraise the value of life or to say whether or not life is worth living. That question involves other than merely medical and scientific considerations. The task of the art historian is to study works of art, their origins, and the evolution of artistic trends, and not to reply to the question: Should man create art? The sociologist's job is to analyze the structure of society, the nature of conventions, law, politics, and economics, and not to play at being a social reformer or lay down the law as to the best form of society. Weber remarks that certain scientists and a few professors who never grew up still cling to the naive and optimistic belief that they will one day discover the road to individual and social happiness. To know what such a hope is worth it should suffice to read the passage where Nietzsche sits in judgment over the last men to have discovered happiness. We can keep on asking science: What must we do? How should we live? Science will give us no reply, for science is theory. Each one of us must look within himself, and his greatness or his weakness will supply the answer.

3

Interpretative Sociology

---

1. The concept of interpretative sociology

Sociology is commonly defined as the science of
social facts. Difficulties begin, and differences of opinion and misunderstandings arise, as soon as we attempt
to define the term "social fact." Although a few attempts have been made to analyze its content (it is
collective by nature and implies external coercion), sociologists generally resort to enumeration, and say that
social facts are all the various structures of society,
institutions, customs, collective beliefs, etc., taken as a
whole. Seen from this angle, sociology becomes a basically formal science. Sociologists of this persuasion
study in turn crime, law, custom and their evolution in
different human communities at different periods, from
the primitive societies to those of our own day.

    Durkheim's position was more subtly differentiated. He divided sociology into two principal sections: social morphology, the purpose of which is to describe social structures as affected by geographical, ecological, demographic, economic and other factors; and social physiology, the object of which is to study the operation of these structures with a view to discovering the laws that govern their development. Nevertheless, one has the impression that Durkheim saw social facts as developing autonomously, as though in obedience to their own internal dynamics, without the participation of man. Only on occasion did he hint at an interaction or a reciprocal relationship, which he was careful not to explore.

The originality of Weber's contribution lies in the fact that he did not sever social structures and institutions from the multifarious activities of man, who both builds them up and endows them with significance. Central to his sociology, therefore, is the concept of social action (*soziales Handeln*); he was concerned not with appraising or evaluating social structures as good or bad, useful or ill-advised, but rather with achieving the most objective understanding possible of how men evaluate and appraise, use, create and destroy their various social relationships. He thus sought to understand actual man living in society. He did not deny the usefulness of purely static and descriptive studies of various social groups, such as Toennies' differentiation of the categories of society and community, but he supplemented them by a statistical analysis intended to show how men generally live in the midst of all these structures.

His vocabulary is in itself significant. What interested Weber was how man behaves in his community and society, how he forms and transforms these relationships. Accordingly, instead of the terms *Gesellschaft* (society) and *Gemeinschaft* (community), he used the terms *Vergesellschaftung* (associative relationship) and *Vergemeinschaftung* (communal relationship). He took the view that to study the development of an institution solely from the outside, without regard to what man makes of it, is to overlook one of the principal aspects of social life. The development of a social relationship can also be explained by the purposes which man assigns to it, the benefits he derives from it and the different meanings he attaches to it in the course of time. Hence the importance of what Weber called meaningful relatedness (*sinnhafte Bezogenheit*), through which we are able to understand, quite apart from objective development, the subjective meaning which a social relationship holds for man and by which he is guided in his social conduct.

Let us take the framing of a law as an example. Weber pointed out that, when the drafting of a new law or a new paragraph in the statutes of an association is under discussion, those persons at least who are particularly interested in the matter usually examine the purpose of the legislation very thoroughly. However, once the law has become familiar, its original meaning, on which its authors were more or less agreed, may be forgotten, or cannot be grasped because of some change in interpretation, so that only very few judges and lawyers are capable of truly perceiving the end for which these confused legal norms had once been agreed upon. The public, on the other hand, no longer has any knowledge of the reasons for and the empirical validity of these norms, and consequently of the possibilities to which they give rise; and this, Weber said, could have the most shocking consequences.[1]

It might even be said that no one is more aware of the validity of a law, the interpretation usually placed on it and the penalty it carries than the man who intends to break it.

Weber's purpose is now clear. He at no time rejected the general conception of sociology as a discipline concerned with establishing general relationships and gaining nomological knowledge. Furthermore, he himself worked along those lines when he constructed ideal types of an association, an institution, domination, law and bureaucracy, or when he established statistically, using the general rules of experimentation, the meaning men commonly attach to a social relationship to which they submit. However, as we have seen in the preceding chapter, he refused to restrict sociology to this aspect alone. Any science may apply either the generalizing or the individualizing method, depending on the needs of research. And if it is true that the scientific examination of a problem is never completed and that its scope should not be narrowed by prejudice or preconceived philosophical notions, there is no reason why sociology should, as a matter of principle, ignore individual phenomena.

Explanation by means of general laws and interpretation of a particular case are equally legitimate methods, and neither of them should be given preference. They are, in fact, mutually complementary, and we can dispense with neither in our attempt to master, as far as we are able, the infinite diversity of social reality in the process of change. On the contrary, sociology would only suffer if we forbade it to use certain research methods which can add to our knowledge. Consequently, when Weber used the term "interpretative" sociology, his intention was certainly not to assign a higher place to interpretation than to explanation or to condemn other sociological approaches, but merely to show that they are inadequate, sometimes deliberately so, and that they betray a narrowness of vision. His sociology is interpretative in the sense that it opens up new possibilities to traditional sociology.

If limitations are to be placed on sociology, they should be of an altogether different kind. Weber was aware of an imperialistic tendency on the part of his contemporaries—a desire to annex to sociology such related disciplines as human geography, demography, ethnology, ethnography, and the study of civilization in general. Such a claim, Weber felt, is untenable, for these are all autonomous sciences, each with its own research goals. The idea is as preposterous as would be the attempt to make of economics a branch of botany or geology because it is concerned with a country's vegetable and mineral resources or, conversely, to subordinate botany and geology for that reason to economics.

Not that sociology should take no notice of demographic, geographical or ethnological research. On the contrary, it should—and does—take into account birth and death rates and racial characteristics in just the same way as hereditary traits and the findings of psychoanalysis, climatology or jurisprudence. But it regards all these phenomena as problems to be resolved by the other sciences, and not solely by the sociological method. In other words, to sociology they are purely data, that is to say, conditions and circumstances surrounding social behavior, which must be taken into account as such in any explanation of meaningful human relationships. The same is true of man-made objects. A machine is of no interest to sociology in itself, but only to the extent that it may cause meaningful changes in human associations. Let us suppose that a scientist discovers that a certain phrenological feature indicates special aptitude for the exercise of authority. Such a discovery would in itself have no sociological import, which would arise only if such special people were able to influence social relationships and alter the meaningful relatedness of superiors to inferiors.

While respecting the autonomy of the different sciences, each of which explores a given segment of reality from a specific point of view, Weber stressed that all sciences must inevitably interact. That is readily understandable. Society is not a single essence; rather, it is made up of many networks of relationships, exchanges and conflicts permeating the different spheres of human activity: politics, economics, religion, law, the arts, etc. In that sense, we may speak of a sociology of politics, a sociology of economics or a sociology of religion. This does not mean that sociology would in any way supplant or replace political science or economics, since both these disciplines have their own tasks and problems; but when sociology sets itself the goal of understanding, from its own particular point of view, in what way, and to what extent, politics and economics exert a meaningful influence on the social behavior of men within certain associations by causing them to establish new or modify old relationships, it becomes political or economic sociology. In other words, the sociology of politics and the sociology of economics do not constitute autonomous disciplines, but are merely subdivisions of the sociologist's work in dealing with the different aspects of social reality.

Sociology has unity in that it examines the infinite diversity of reality from a specific point of view. Hence the following definition:

> The term "sociology" is open to many different interpretations. In the context used here it shall mean that science which aims at the interpretative understanding of social behavior in order to gain an explanation of its causes, its course, and its effects.[9]

Two of the terms used in this definition, "interpretative understanding" (*Verstehen*) and "social behavior," call for special comment.

2. *Interpretative understanding*

Weber's critics have frequently stressed the ambiguities of his concept of interpretative understanding. He did not, of course, invent this method (it was first advanced by the historian Droysen around 1850). Moreover, Weber's theory contains elements from various other sources (Dilthey, Rickert, Simmel, Gottl-Ottlilienfeld, Lipps, Jaspers, etc.). We will not enter here into details regarding the idea of interpretative understanding which properly belong to the history of philosophy, but will simply explain what Weber meant by it.

It is bound up both with his theory of interpretation (so much so that in some parts of his work the two concepts are confused) and with that of causality. In his view, the purely naturalistic method alone cannot possibly make human behavior intelligible to us, because it deals only with external relationships, while interpretative understanding, on the other hand, if it is to be valid, must overcome the ambiguities of the subjective approach and submit to the normal procedures of scientific research. All in all, Weber recognized the legitimacy of the interpretative method as worked out by his forerunners and contemporaries: it cannot be dispensed with if objects in the process of change are to be made intelligible.

Nevertheless, instead of examining the purely philosophical questions it poses, he concentrated on its scientific validity. There are, after all, different ways of understanding, some of which may be valuable for esthetic appreciation or for direct experience, but not compatible with the requirements of scientific exactitude. The question which Weber raised is this: To what extent is interpretative understanding, as a sociological method, capable of establishing truths which are valid for all who want the truth?

In contrast to a purely naturalistic explanation, interpretative understanding always aims at grasping the meaning of a behavior or a relationship. Although Weber occasionally used the term "meaningful structure" (*Sinngebilde*), he did not dwell on the philosophical problems it poses, such as this: does it exist in a sphere of its own, which is neither physical nor psychic? He was content to note that human behavior has a context of meaning which we must grasp if we are to understand the behavior itself. On the other hand, he analyzed the different ways of understanding the term "meaning." Dogmatic disciplines, such as logic, metaphysics and jurisprudence seek to determine the "just," "true," or "correct" meaning of a relationship. Thus, for example, a lawyer may seek to define the precise or just meaning of a paragraph in the statute book, and a logician to formulate correct and non-contradictory propositions.

The so-called empirical disciplines, such as history and sociology, are concerned with the purpose subjectively pursued by men, or groups of men, engaged in a particular course of action. These disciplines seek to understand the goal (whether logically correct or not) toward which these men in practice orient their action. Any study of the musical theory of the Pythagoreans is obliged to accept at the outset the calculation that 12 fifths = 7 octaves, which we know to be "wrong," just as a study of the practices of Roman surveyors or Florentine bankers must take account, without attempting to correct them, of the mistakes which, in the light of our knowledge of arithmetic and trigonometry, we know them to have made. In dealing with rules which convention accepted as valid and toward which human conduct was subjectively oriented, an empirical study must understand them in the same way as we understand the man who correctly uses the proposition $2 \times 2 = 4$, or the Pythagorean theorem, or who is guided by the "lessons of experience" in choosing the most appropriate means to the desired end.

Being an empirical discipline, sociology is concerned only with the interpretative understanding of subjectively meaningful conduct. But how are we to grasp its meaning? At this point Weber makes a further distinction between what he calls direct empirical understanding and explanatory understanding. Our understanding of the multiplication of two numbers, or of what we read on the printed page, or of anger as expressed by a natural movement, or again of the behavior of a woodcutter felling a tree or a hunter aiming his gun, is of the first type. The second type of understanding is indirect, because it relies on the motives of the acts to supply their meaning. It is in this manner that I understand the meaning which a man attaches to the calculations in which he engages in working out an accounting problem, or the action of the woodcutter who fells trees for a living, or that of the hunter who engages in his sport for his health.

Each of these two types of understanding may be either rational or irrational. The direct understanding of the meaning of an arithmetical operation or of the behavior of the woodcutter felling a tree is rational, as is the motivational understanding of the action of a person working to gain a livelihood. The direct understanding of a fit of anger, on the other hand, as well as the motivational understanding of a person who uses a gun for purposes of revenge or loses his temper out of jealousy, are irrational. Yet however different these forms of understanding may be, they are all based on certainty, quite apart from scientific research. To understand, one might say, is to grasp the certain meaning of an action.

Certainty, however, may vary in degree according to circumstances. The highest degree consists in the intellectual understanding of a rational activity; for example, of a mathematical operation. A merely adequate degree of certainty characterizes our understanding of the experiences of others which we are capable of sympathetically sharing; for example, of mistakes which we are inclined to make ourselves. The certainty of such understanding, achieved through empathy and imagination, diminishes as the activities in question are further removed from our own approaches. At the outermost limit, we accept them simply as data, of the same order as a psychophysical reaction or a heredity factor; the heroic feats of charity of a virtuoso of otherworldly love and the rationalistic fanaticism of a champion of human rights fall into this category. On the other hand, we are the more capable of sympathetically reliving and understanding such irrational reactions as fear, jealousy or desire for vengeance, the more susceptible we are ourselves to such emotions.

The certainty of understanding may thus be impaired, either because unintelligible external elements such as chance are involved, or by the psychological bewilderment we may experience on seeing, say, two persons reacting differently to the same situation. Motivational understanding may be similarly handicapped where the avowed reasons for an act are only pretexts concealing deep-lying conflict and opposing desires. In such cases, interpretation must rely on the findings of the sciences which deal with such problems—biology, psychology, psychoanalysis, etc. In short, interpretative sociology regards such unintelligible phenomena as simple data and takes account of them in the same way as it takes account of physical or climatological phenomena, or again of such factors as nutrition and senescence.

Although this may not be the position apparent

from some of his writings, it would seem that Weber did not regard interpretation as a purely psychological process. In his criticism of Simmel for taking that view, he pointed out that interpretation is properly a logical method whereby we may be enabled to grasp the significance of an activity or mode of behavior. Even if we are unable to understand, with rational certainty, either Buddhist contemplation or the mysticism of Christian monks, through our inability to relive such experiences empathically, the fact remains that they are meaningfully oriented to the world, and we must try to understand them by drawing on the work of scholars who have dealt with them.

Hence Weber warns against interpreting the meaning attached by the subject to his behavior as constituting the "internal aspect" of that behavior. That is an unfortunate locution, to say the least, for interpretative sociology is not in the least concerned with enumerating the psychic and physical manifestations and elements which accompany, or even result in, meaningful goal-oriented behavior. Moreover, if we remember that, according to Weber, the most complete interpretation is one involving the rationally or intellectually certain understanding of the meaning of, say, a mathematical operation, we cannot possibly class him among the psychologists. His theory has been found by some to be ambiguous because of his stress on reliving (*Nacherleben*) and empathy (*Einfühlung*), those terms being mainly used by methodologists of the psychological school. It will therefore be useful to explain the role which interpretation plays in the general anatomy of Weber's sociological method.

One thing is certain: grasping the subjective meaning of an activity is facilitated by interpretative understanding, and in particular by reliving through empathy. Nevertheless, Weber says that only an "adequate" level of understanding can be reached by such means, and declares: "To be able to put one's self in the place of the actor is important for clearness of understanding but not an absolute precondition for meaningful interpretation.[3] For example, it is not necessary to be Caesar in order to understand Caesar. In other words, interpretation is never more than a useful auxiliary method; it is not indispensable. It makes the sociologist's work easier; it helps him to grasp problems whose very existence he might otherwise not have suspected, but it is not the last word in methodology.

Weber's real problem is other than this, and it arises on two different levels: how to establish, on the basis of interpretative understanding, a rational and accurate ideal type of social behavior which would be compatible with the rational interpretation discussed above and would facilitate scientific work; and how to endow the interpretative method with the greatest possible objective validity. We shall deal with the latter question first and discuss the other in conjunction with Weber's concept of social behavior.

Rationally verifiable behavior comprises all those meaningful relationships which are susceptible of purely intellectual understanding. However, such rational verifiability is scientifically valid only if it can be established by the ordinary methods of scientific work. "To be sure, every interpretation strives to achieve utmost verifiability. But even the most verifiable interpretation cannot claim the character of being causally valid."[4]

If it is necessary to verify even a mathematical proposition which is demonstrably correct, there is obviously every need to verify proof obtained by empathy, for experiential knowledge, whether it results from personal experience or from reliving the experience of another, does not as such have the validity of scientific observation. Weber's objections to purely intuitive cognition which refuses to accept the discipline of rigorous conceptualization apply here as well. Thus, even while advocating motivational research as against the partisans of the naturalistic approach, he laid equal stress on the fact that only causal explanation can give interpretative research the dignity of a scientific proposition. In his view, an interpretative understanding is no more than an auxiliary means of grasping the meaning of an act, and must be confirmed by causal imputation or substantiated by statistical data. Then, and only then, can interpretative sociology establish general rules.

Weber's position on this point never varied. Consequently, his theory cannot possibly be assimilated to Dilthey's, who regarded explanation and interpretation as two independent methods. According to Weber, any relationship which is intelligible through interpretation should also be capable of causal explanation. It is not surprising, therefore, that he should have made frequent use of the expression "interpretative explanation" (*verstehende Erklärung*).

The combination of explanation and interpretative understanding gives added meaning to causal imputation, which now becomes meaningful causality (*sinnhafte Kausalität*); in other words, causal relationships (*Kausalzusammenhänge*) become meaningful relationships (*Sinnzusammenhänge*). This is one of the most original features of Weber's theory of causality. In establishing a cause-and-effect relationship, the naturalistic method, unlike the historical method, does not take the human element into account. If the explanation of an activity or social behavior is limited to causal relationships alone, the sociologist is not satisfied, precisely because a human activity is unintelligible to us unless we understand its meaningful orientation to objects, means and ends. Even functional sociology is not adequate from this point of view. Something more is needed, and that something is interpretative explanation; our knowledge is not complete until we have both explained an activity causally and grasped its subjective meaning.

At the same time, Weber's concept of the link between causality and interpretation differs altogether from that underlying those philosophies of history which, while making use of value-orientation, look for meaning in some more or less apocalyptic last end. In Weber's view, interpretation and causal explanation must be limited to a finite segment of infinite reality: that segment which in the given case happens to be the subject of positive research. Obviously in such a case interpretation can never achieve the value of an apodictic truth. As Weber remarks, the additional benefit gained through interpretative understanding as against simple causal observation is dearly bought, since the price we pay is the hypothetical and fragmentary character of the results. Yet there is a benefit: unlike the claims of the philosophies of history, the findings of interpretative sociology are verifiable, and this gives them at least some degree of objective validity.

3. Various types of social behavior

The second problem mentioned above relates to the possibility of grasping the meaning of social behavior with the highest degree of proof. What is behavior (*Handeln*) in general, and social behavior (*soziales Handeln*) in particular? Behavior, says Weber,

> will be called human "behavior" only in so far as the person or persons involved engage in some subjectively meaningful action. Such behavior may be mental or external; it may consist in action or omission to act. The term "social behavior" will be reserved for activities whose intent is related by the individuals involved to the conduct of others and is oriented accordingly.[5]

Weber explains further that social behavior may be oriented to the past, present or foreseeable future behavior of others (revenge for a past attack, defense against present attack, or preparation of defensive measures to prevent a future attack). The "others" may be one or several isolated individuals or an indefinite number of persons. Thus, the use of money is social behavior because the conduct of the individual who accepts it or pays it is oriented to the expectation that numerous but undetermined "others" will make meaningful use of it as a medium of exchange.

It follows that a behavior which is oriented solely to the possible reactions of inanimate objects cannot be termed social, any more than can the religious conduct of a person engaged in solitary prayer. Lastly, not every type of contact between human beings constitutes a social relationship. An accidental collision of two cyclists is not a social relationship, for example; but such a relationship arises if they try to avoid hitting each other, or if, after the collision, they exchange insults or peacefully discuss their mishap. Accordingly, the fundamental requirement for social behavior is its meaningful relatedness to the conduct of others.

Where such relatedness does not exist, the uniform conduct of a number of persons cannot be termed social; for example, the fact that people on the street all open their umbrellas at the same time to protect themselves against rain does not constitute social behavior. Even imitative and traditional acts are not social behavior if they are mere repetition of a gesture for its own sake and are not related to the behavior of another person. Obviously, in practice the line of demarcation between purely reactive imitation and imitation which is meaningfully oriented is often far from clear; generally speaking, a determination has to be made in each particular case. The same may be said of certain types of behavior which, while taking place in isolation, are nevertheless influenced by the group.

Without pursuing all the fine distinctions Weber draws, let us merely note that in interpretative sociology the difference between behavior which consists simply in the simultaneous or successive conduct of a number of persons and behavior which is meaningfully oriented to the conduct of others is absolutely basic. While the latter category of behavior alone is of interest to interpretative sociology, because it is the primary form of more complex types of behavior, such as those of groups, institutions, and associations, the former category could nevertheless be studied by causal sociology.

This remark of Weber's is further evidence of what
he meant by interpretative sociology: its purpose is
neither to replace nor to go beyond existing sociology,
but to supplement it by shedding light on hitherto neglected aspects. Let us add that, while meaningful relatedness of conduct to the conduct of others is essential, the agent himself need not be aware of it. In many
cases, the task of discovering this unrealized relatedness falls to the interpretative sociologist, and results
from his efforts to render a particular form of social
conduct intelligible. A difficulty arises at this point,
which has to be resolved by regular scientific research:
Is the meaning which the sociologist attributes to a
behavior the same as that which the agents themselves
consciously or unconsciously attach to it?

Since all interpretation strives to achieve the utmost certainty, the problem is to define social behavior
in the most rationally verifiable manner. To this end,
Weber distinguishes between rational goal-oriented
(*zweckrational*) conduct, rational value-oriented (*wert-
rational*) conduct, affectual (*affektuell*) conduct and
traditionalist (*traditional*) conduct.

Following Weber's own procedure in defining
these four types of behavior, we shall begin with the
type least susceptible of verification—traditionalist behavior. This lies on the borderline between what can be
explained by purely causal sociology on the one hand
and by interpretative sociology on the other, because it
is frequently simply an automatic reaction in unconscious obedience to custom, and therefore comprises
unintelligible elements. But it may also border on rational, value-oriented behavior, when the agent regards
tradition as a value worthy of respect. Of course,

strictly traditionalist behavior is not often met with in practice. It is not necessary, however, that it should be, since to Weber it is an ideal type, to be used to determine whether, and how closely, some specific conduct approaches traditionalist conduct in the purest sense, or departs from such conduct either in the direction of simultaneous activity capable only of causal explanation or, on the contrary, in the direction of meaningful rational behavior.

The same is true of affectual conduct. It, too, contains some unintelligible instinctual, sensory, emotional and passionate elements, or else a sublimation which only psychology or psychoanalysis can explain. Affectually determined behavior is the kind which seeks revenge or an immediate sensual gratification, or even a surrender to pure blissful contemplation. Consequently, this type of conduct, too, may cross the line either into the realm of pure psychology or, on the contrary, into that of value-oriented or goal-oriented behavior, or both, so that as an ideal type it can be used to determine to what extent a specific form of conduct approaches either purely psychological or meaningful rational conduct.

Value-oriented conduct is distinguished by the fact that the agent is guided solely by his convictions, without giving a thought to the foreseeable consequences. The value-oriented individual espouses a religious, political, or other value or cause with the feeling that it is an unconditional and personal obligation.

Such conduct is rational in that it is not governed solely by success or lack of it and is not patterned on prevailing customs, but has an inner coherence and expresses itself in acts which are in line with the individual's convictions. Nevertheless, it is irrational in other respects, in that it sets up some one value as its goal without taking other possible goals into account and without giving critical consideration to the appropriateness of the means or to the irony inherent in the foreseeable consequences. That the conduct should be in harmony with the exigencies of the chosen goal is all that counts. Such conduct becomes increasingly irrational as its goal comes closer to being an absolute value. It is, in other words, incapable of consciously recognizing its own irrational elements; this faculty we shall find only in goal-oriented conduct.

It will readily be seen that, at the level of ethics, rational value-oriented conduct corresponds to what, in "Politics as a Vocation," Weber calls the "ethic of ultimate ends," which he opposes to the "ethic of responsibility," whose sociological basis is goal-oriented.[6]

Interpretative sociology gives priority to goal-oriented conduct, as being rationally most accessible to verifiable proof. It may be defined as conduct in which, once the goal has been chosen, due consideration is given to the appropriate means and full account is taken of the foreseeable consequences which may conflict with the line of action decided upon. The verifiability of this type of conduct arises from the fact that it draws on the general rules of experience, not in blind obedience to some intangible criterion, but in order to make a rational projection of future possibilities. Such conduct is not simple adaptation to a given situation, however, for it may on occasion attempt the impossible in order to achieve the possible. In any event, it takes account of conflicting ends and of various and competing means, as well as of possible consequences which may either completely thwart the agent's intention or make his conduct lead to an undesired result.

This is a purely ideal-typical definition, but it, too, allows of certain variations. Thus, the pressure of needs may be such that there is no option but to choose a certain goal; in that case, conduct can be rationally goal-oriented only as regards the choice of means. The choice of the goal may also be determined in terms of value-orientation, although the goal may not be readily attainable and may require a long and sustained effort; in that case, goal-oriented conduct may consist in arranging the means in an order of priority as part of a progressive plan. Rational goal-oriented conduct is thus an extreme case, and at some levels may be related to value-oriented conduct.

The great importance of rational goal-oriented behavior, consequently, is that it is the ideal type of social conduct most susceptible of rational proof; this is true both of the agent who constructs the ideal type of a subjectively meaningful means-and-end relationship and the probable course of events, and of the scientist who makes such a construct in order to clarify the subjective meaning of the agent or agents and to measure the gap between their actual conduct and their original intentions.

A statesman, for instance, will not decide to act unless his action is intended to open up new prospects and consequently has a meaning; accordingly, in so far as his conduct is rational, he weighs the foreseeable consequences and considers those circumstances over which he has no control and which might wreck his projects; in short, he constructs an ideal type of his future conduct in the form of a plan. The only difference between him and the historian and sociologist is that the latter two have the advantage of being able to judge an accomplished action, so that by constructing an ideal type of rational goal-oriented behavior they can determine, within the limitations of their knowledge, whether the agents correctly assessed the available means and foreseeable consequences, and whether they were right in regarding their plan as feasible; in other words, whether or not the actual course of events was in line with their intentions.

An ideal type of rational conduct thus enables the sociologist to evaluate the effect of the intervention of irrational elements, whether accidental, affectual or other, to assess the extent to which they impaired the original plan and to measure the deviation between the actual course of conduct and its subjective meaning.

By way of illustration, we may take two of Weber's own examples.

In order to examine a stock-market panic, it is useful first to construct an ideal type of normal market activity, which will show what course that activity would have taken had certain irrational or unforeseeable elements not intervened; we shall thus be in a position to measure the extent of the disturbance. As we see, the ideal type charts an ideal course of events on the basis of objective possibility with a view to arriving at the most nearly correct causal imputation.

Similarly, if we wish to study a battle or some other military or political undertaking, we construct mentally, in a purely rational way, the ideal type of the battle in order to see how the event would have developed had the actors—that is, the opposing commanders in chief—had complete knowledge of the conditions and situation both in their own and in the enemy's camp and had been as well-informed as the historian is now. Such a Utopian construct enables us to determine, by comparison with the real course of events, what mistakes were made and what part was played by the element of chance and by ill-considered decisions. This example shows, once more, how an objectively possible construct enables us to impute causes, to understand the significance of lack of information or incorrect information, and to assess the qualities of a commander, the extent to which his decisions were prompted by his temperament, etc.

We can now see why Weber should always have denied that he had invented a new methodological instrument in evolving the ideal type; the ideal type is merely a logical development of the device spontaneously practiced by historians and sociologists, who in the course of their explanations constantly refer to an ideal picture of the action under consideration in order to understand what actually took place. We are reminded of Molière's *Bourgeois Gentilhomme*, who was surprised to discover that he had always spoken in prose without knowing it.

The ideal type, then, is a concept with great potentialities, because it combines flexibility in research with scientific exactness. It is possible, for example, to construct the ideal type of a corporate group in general (systematic sociology), in order to treat it as a form of social behavior having its purposes, services, members, an executive committee, enforcement machinery, duration, etc. (as Weber does in paragraph 12 of his *Basic Concepts in Sociology*); or of a specific corporate group (historical sociology), in order to compare the practical and empirical development of such a group with what it was in theory intended to be.

To take other examples, which Weber did not give, we might formulate an ideal type of war in general (as did Clausewitz in describing what he called absolute war) and also of any one particular war. What is Rousseau's *Social Contract* but a Utopian rationalization of the direct government of the people by the people? If need be, the scientist is free to conceive of an ideal type of error, in order the better to see the distance between it and the ideal type of correctness.

In brief, there is no single ideal type of goal-oriented rational conduct, and the sociologist may evolve as many such constructs as he finds necessary in his effort to understand the meaningful relatedness of some particular action involving a means-to-end relationship, in order the better to grasp the contradictions, dissimulations, disturbances, sublimations, tensions and values which were present, although the agents themselves may not have been aware of them.

The range of ideal-typical constructs varies according to the needs of research. It must be pointed out, however, that goal-oriented rational behavior does not necessarily coincide with the ideal type of logical correctness, in the sense of the dogmatically true and correct meaning discussed above. "Correct" rational behavior is merely behavior in which the means are correctly related to the end in a set of given circumstances. Thus a course of behavior may seem eminently rational to a scientist in terms of the goal sought, but have in actuality been based on mistaken assumptions. And a magical rite may have a higher degree of rational goal-orientation than religious conduct which, because of the disenchantment of the modern world, is obliged to tolerate various forms of ideological or mystical irrationality. Moreover, inasmuch as rational goal-oriented conduct implies adequate relatedness of the means to the end, it may on occasion be of practical use to the man of action; but it can never aspire to normative rank.

Whatever use is made of the ideal type, it never rises in validity above a "paradigm," the purpose of which is to enable us to understand a meaningful relationship. In other words, it necessarily departs from empirical reality in order to gain a better theoretical view of it. It is never anything more than a tool. Consequently, it would be a mistake to consider rational conduct the ultimate concern of sociology. As we look at the world around us, the opposite seems closer to the truth, for the major part of actual human behavior demonstrates disregard of pure rationality, inasmuch as irrational, accidental and unintelligible factors abound in it. For this reason, whatever ideal type may be used, whether it is one of traditionalist behavior, affectual behavior, or rational value-oriented or goal-oriented behavior, it is never more than a Utopian schema, a theoretical concept constructed to facilitate research. Its validity is therefore always problematic and its worth is measured only by its usefulness in research.

4. The individual

Since interpretative sociology attaches capital importance to the meaningful relatedness of behavior to the behavior of others, it is bound to regard the individual as the basic unit with which it is concerned. In Weber's view, the collective is not an independent reality in sociological terms.

> Action, in the sense of a subjectively understandable orientation of behavior, exists only as the behavior of one or more *individual* human beings. For other cognitive purposes it may be convenient or necessary to consider the individual, for instance, as a collection of cells, as a complex of biochemical reactions, or to conceive his "psychic" life as made up of a variety of different elements, however these may be defined. Undoubtedly such procedures yield valuable knowledge of causal relationships. But the behavior of these elements, as expressed in such uniformities, is not subjectively understandable. . . . Both for sociology in the present sense, and for history, the object of cognition is the subjective meaning-complex of action.[7]

The reason adduced by Weber in this passage, namely, that only the individual is an intelligible executant of meaningfully oriented conduct, would in itself suffice to justify his position. In order to avoid all possible misunderstanding, however, we shall elaborate on his idea.

All reference to meaning presupposes a consciousness, and consciousness is individual. Weber does not even treat the collective consciousness as a hypothesis, for from his point of view that would be the purest supposition. For the fact is that evaluating the means in terms of the end, choosing that end, foreseeing the possible consequences, reaching a decision, and finally executing it—all the various processes involved in meaningful behavior—are matters for the individual will.

That will is a natural unit, and unless sociology so regards it, incoherence and confusion will result and sociology will seek in vain to affirm its validity as an autonomous science. That the individual is a unit of meaning is a postulate without which interpretative sociology looking for the meaning of social conduct would itself have no meaning.

Interpretative sociology is, of course, no more than one possible approach to infinite reality, but as such it must obey its own laws, or it will become an intellectual game with scientific pretensions. In this connection, collective concepts become sociologically intelligible only in the light of meaningfully related individual behavior. Naturally, there are numerous other approaches, each of which gives rise to an independent science (this is the inevitable subjective moment in all scientific work), but once the approach has been chosen, its conditions must be complied with. This is to say that interpretative sociology in no way excludes other and equally legitimate approaches, including that of purely causal sociology. Weber himself makes this point, justifying the need for interpretative sociology to deal with the individual as the unit of meaningful behavior by comparing this procedure with the methods properly used by juridical science and psychology.

No one can prevent the sociologist from making use of such collective concepts as feudalism, the state, nation, class, or family, to name but a few. That is a matter of current usage, and it would be pedantic not to conform it. Nevertheless, when sociology deals with, say, the state, that concept acquires a meaning other than the one it has in politics or in law. Juridical science sees the state as an autonomous entity with a moral personality of its own, even as it regards the embryo as a legal person, a view very different from that taken by biology or psychology. Hence the state does not have the same meaning for interpretative sociology as it does for law: it is the scene of the meaningful behavior of the persons composing it. Interpretative sociology is concerned with the various forms of conduct which take place in the state, the exchanges which occur and the conflicts which arise in it as a result of the meaningful relationships of command and obedience, power and protection, etc.

Those elements of the collective concept of the state which are important for the jurist are not necessarily so for the sociologist, although it would be a mistake on the latter's part to ignore the former's work entirely. Nevertheless, the sociologist's point of view is quite different, since he is primarily concerned with understanding the subjective meaning which the state has for its members and on the basis of which they accept it as a reality, conduct social relationships and pursue definite activities within it.

The same comment could be made with regard to other collective concepts, such as crowd or nation. The nation depends for its existence on the meaningful intention of those who want to live in such a structure, for, as soon as that intention weakens, the nation disintegrates and may even perish, unless it falls under the domination of a more resolute neighbor. Similarly, charisma presupposes a crowd of followers, but the crowd has no meaning as such, and acquires it only through the meaningful relationships between its individual members and the leader who commands their devotion. In the absence of such meaningful relationships, collective concepts are fit subject matter for analysis only by purely causal sociology.

Are we to conclude from this that interpretative sociology is a branch of psychology, since it too is concerned with the individual? Nothing could be further from Weber's mind, for the point of view from which psychology studies the individual is essentially different from the sociological approach. In fact, Weber's work is permeated with mistrust of psychology, since in his day psychologism was riding high in Germany. Weber felt that psychology was groping in the dark fully as much as sociology, despite the findings of psychophysiology, psychoanalysis and interpretative psychology.

It is not to be denied that, while opposing the psychoanalysts, Weber made excellent use of the results of psychoanalytical research in his interpretative sociology, particularly as regards motivation of action: the man who acts does not always know why his actions are oriented in a certain direction, and often he is not clearly aware of the real meaning of his activity because it is concealed from him by sublimations, pretexts and rationalizations. Furthermore, the same action may be inspired by different motives, to say nothing of the fact that conflicting impulses may cause different persons to react differently to the same situation or make one and the same person adopt an ambivalent attitude to a given problem. Nevertheless, in Weber's opinion such contributions did not go beyond normal interdisciplinary exchange.

Whatever its status, psychology could never serve as the foundation for interpretative sociology. Indeed, the latter is no more closely allied with psychology than with any other science. An adequate level of meaning is not to be achieved by relying on psychic elements alone, although sociology may take them into account as relevant data. Weber's position on this point is very clear, since he goes on to say that the distinction between physical and psychic is alien to sociology and of no importance to the understanding of the objective meaning of a given type of social behavior.

Lastly, the fact that interpretative sociology takes the individual as its basis, because only the individual can create meaningful relationships, does not mean that it is individualistic, as opposed to some other, collectivistic, discipline. Certainly sociology has no intention of affirming the unique worth of dignity of the human person. Such a position is purely ethical, and is in contradiction with that principle of ethical neutrality without which no truly scientific work is possible. Moreover, the fact that sociology uses rational methods and types is no reason for concluding that it is rationalistic. Every science proceeds by introducing rationality into reality in order to explain and understand it; but in so doing it does not engage in rationalism, which is and remains a philosophical conception based on ultimate, personal and subjective convictions and value judgments.

5. Probability and social structures

Social behavior, which Weber also terms communal action (*Gemeinschaftshandeln*), is to him the primary reality with which sociology has to deal. It may be contingent and transitory, as in the case of an unrepeated encounter, a conversation with strangers in a trolley or a discussion among people attending a public meeting, or it may assume lasting forms, which furnish the basis for the majority of social structures. These permanent forms are analyzed in *Basic Concepts in Sociology*.

In order to understand this study, we must become acquainted with yet another concept, which is nearly always present in Weber's sociological explanation, and which is that of probability. This element, which he never strictly defined, although it is of capital importance to his work, is used to show that every sociological construct, no matter how rigorously established, is and always must be essentially probabilistic. This does not mean that social structures themselves are necessarily precarious, but merely that their meaning may alter with time, if men in their relevant conduct should assign another meaning to them under the pressure of necessity, or because of new interests or of technical and rational progress; and if men divest them of all meaning, they will vanish altogether.

To say that a person's behavior is meaningfully oriented to the behavior of another is tantamount to recognizing that he is entitled to expect a degree of uniformity in the conduct of others—in other words, that their behavior allows him to have certain expectations in the light of which he can estimate his chances of success in some undertaking. This is the idea of objective possibility in another form.

Social conduct, then, is characterized by the fact that the agent adjusts his behavior in the expectation that others will behave in a certain way, giving him reason to hope that there is a probability of successfully completing his line of action. This probability may lie in the expectation that the others will respect an existing agreement or will on the average respect it in the way in which the agent himself subjectively understands it. In the absence of an explicit agreement, the agent may expect the others to behave in a certain manner because of rational value-orientation, or out of a sense of duty, by tradition or for the sake of personal dignity.

The same applies to the conduct of a person who proposes to violate a regulation, for he counts precisely on the probability that others will continue to conduct themselves in accordance with their usual rules. From this point of view, a thief, for example, while consciously and in a subjectively meaningful manner violating the law, nevertheless orients his conduct to the law; but he acts surreptitiously, or the violation would not be meaningful.

Probability may thus be taken to mean that, on the average, or in all likelihood, men will orient their conduct to a meaningful precept, which may take the form of a law, a custom, a value or a belief, and which will furnish each of them with reasons for so orienting their behavior. Only where such probability continues to exist will the social structure be stable and lasting. In other words, the probability in itself provides a solid foundation for a social relationship, while at the same time giving it consistency. To say that a regulation is in force, or that a state normally exercises its prerogatives, is to recognize that by and large men obey the regulation and respect the decisions of the government. As soon as the probability is lessened, the continued existence of the social relationship or structure is compromised.

The idea of probability is thus linked with the category of objective possibility, which is to say that under objectively given conditions it is probable that men will act in an approximately foreseeable manner. The concept of adequacy is highly relevant here. Weber calls a social behavior causally adequate (*kausal adäquat*) when, on the basis of past experience—or according to the rules of probability—a certain course of behavior may be expected to result from other types of behavior whose subjective meaning we can approximately assess. Such behavior will be meaningfully adequate (*sinnhaft adäquat*) when, taking such probability into account, it proceeds systematically on the basis of a correct evaluation of the proper means to the desired end.

Starting with this idea of probability, Weber shows how social conduct develops and ramifies, giving rise to other action which furnishes the basis for political, economic, religious and other organizations. He was not attempting to reconstruct a society; rather, he was intent upon isolating the types of structures which have formed the framework of various institutions in the course of history. From the ideal-typical viewpoint, the basic element is the social relationship, that is to say, the behavior of a large number of individuals, each of whom, by the meaningful content of his activities, predicates his conduct on that of the rest. The reasons motivating their behavior (fear, solidarity, desire for protection) matter little; what does matter is that the probability of a meaningful relatedness of their separate lines of conduct should exist and that the individuals should act in approximate conformity to that expectation, it being understood that their actions may

relate to the actual or the merely potential and probable conduct of the rest. It goes without saying that the
meaningful content in question is the empirical content
which the participants actually or usually assign to
their actions, and not a meaning which would be
normatively correct from the logical or ethical point of
view. What, then, are the basic types of social behavior?

(*a*) *Associative behavior* (*Gesellschaftshandeln*).
This type presupposes the existence of rules which the
members have laid down or to which they adhere of
their own free will. Consequently, at the basis of such
behavior is an explicit agreement on a set of regulations. These define the purpose of the organization, its
resources and services, its property, the composition of
the executive apparatus, penalties for violators, prerogatives, method of admission, etc. Generally, the
structure is a permanent one, although with time some
members may leave it and others be admitted, on condition that they accept the rules. This type of structure
is basic for the majority of associations, for example,
sports or philanthropic associations, veterans' associations, political parties and trade unions. An organization of this type continues in being as long as its members find it valuable; in other words, as long as they are
prepared to respect the meaning they subjectively attribute to it, although they may interpret that meaning
in different ways or may change it by common agreement.

(*b*) *Behavior based on mutual consent* (*Einver-
ständnishandeln*). In this case we have a structure which

does not rest on a set of rules; there is no agreement, statute or set of regulations of any kind, but the participants nevertheless act as if they had assumed a definite obligation, because they feel that a meaningful relationship exists. At the lower extreme, such behavior is of very short duration, one instance being that of a man rescuing another from drowning. At the upper extreme, there is a permanent structure, examples of which are a market economy, a racial or national community, or, for that matter, that respect for others which takes the form of politeness. Such mutual consent must in no case be confused with solidarity, for even while complying with the principles of the market or the requirements of courtesy, the participants in this form of relationship may be openly or secretly combatting each other.

(*c*) *Institutional behavior* (*Anstaltshandeln*). In this case there is a set of rules, generally handed down from above; in other words, there are explicitly stated regulations which were not formulated by the members themselves. One does not freely join the type of institution in question, but is either born into it or becomes a member automatically, by education or because of other circumstances. Consequently, no formal expression of will or declaration of intention is required, and yet, because a set of rules exists, the members are subject to official coercion. This type of structure will be found in the family, in political organizations such as the tribe, the city, and the state, and in religious organizations such as a church.

(*d*) *Group behavior* (*Verbandshandeln*). Here we have a structure to which people adhere without being obliged to do so and without being subject to any explicitly stated or definite rules. Nevertheless, it exercises an authority which gives the behavior its meaning, and it may also subject its members to coercion. In this category we find such groups as the master and his disciples, the prophet and his followers, and the charismatic leader and his adherents.

As is true of all ideal types, such structures are hardly ever encountered in all their logical purity. There may be any number of transitional stages between them. Finally, as a rule, the same individual is at the same time a member of all, or at least most, of these structures, toward which his conduct is meaningfully oriented.

6. *Social relationship and basic concepts of sociology*

Social behavior gives rise to various types of social relationships which, as noted above, Weber defines as participation in reciprocally oriented, subjectively meaningful social conduct. Without a minimum of reciprocity, there can be neither a social relationship nor meaningfully oriented conduct; reciprocity is therefore a basic and characteristic element in Weber's thinking.

This does not mean that all those participating in a social relationship ascribe exactly the same meaningful content to it (reciprocity is not solidarity). Reciprocity in behavior is not, in other words, synonymous with reciprocity in the meaning attached to a social relationship. Two adversaries reciprocally orient their behavior toward each other precisely because the meaningful content of their relationship, which is one of struggle, is seen by them in different terms. A social relationship based on attitudes which are completely identical in reciprocity of meaning is an exceptional case. On the contrary, reciprocity may be either positive or negative: men do not participate solely in relationships of friendship, trust and concord; they also engage in various struggles, ranging all the way from armed conflict to rivalry in love and emulation. There is no reason to think that a social relationship must be peaceful; in fact, quite often peace simply means the transposition of a struggle to another plane. Obviously, therefore, the meaningful content of a relationship may change with time; the same participants may pass from solidarity of interests to competition.

Here again, there are many transitional stages, which can be delimited only by the use of ideal types. Starting from his concept of meaningful reciprocity which links individuals together in the course of their action, Weber formulates an exact definiton of those basic concepts which are constantly used in sociological research.

Every lasting social relationship presupposes certain uniformities. At the most immediate level, these are usage (*Brauch*) and custom (*Sitte*). Being careful to avoid ontological interpretation, Weber defines them in terms of probability. Usage is the probability that a uniform conduct will persist in a group whose existence is based on habit. It becomes custom when the habit is of long standing and has become ingrained.

The essential feature of these uniformities is that they are not obligatory, are not enforced by coercion from the outside, but are conformed to voluntarily by the individual for reasons of convenience or practical advantage. Having breakfast in the morning is a matter of usage; but there is no obligation to have such a meal or to have it consist of any particular foods. Generally, men react socially under some more or less consciously realized or perceived form of coercion; in so doing, they submit to a legitimate authority. The probability that an authority will be obeyed is termed its validity. An official who comes to his office on time may do so out of simple habit, or in order to get ahead, but also because there is a valid authority involved, to disobey which might land him in trouble.

Generally, an authority which is accepted as a matter of custom is more stable than one which is merely obligatory, unless it is also legitimate (usually the two elements go hand in hand). Nevertheless, the existence of some form of coercion does not cause custom and authority to coincide. They are two different concepts, as may be illustrated by the case of a man fighting a duel where duelling is forbidden by law: on the one hand, he is of his own free will obeying a custom by engaging in an affair of honor, and on the other hand, he recognizes the validity of the legitimate authority by fighting his duel in secret.

The typical forms of legitimate authority are convention and law. Convention means that uniformity of conduct is guaranteed by the probability that the individuals who depart from or violate it will meet with general disapproval within their group. Law means that the validity of an authority is guaranteed by the fact that there exists an organ set up for the express purpose of exerting coercion on the members of the group and that the violators may be punished. (Weber readily admits that this definition of the law is valid solely for interpretative sociology, and that other definitions may be evolved from the point of view of economics, political science, or juridical science).

Unlike custom, convention presupposes pressure from the group in the form of possible damage to one's reputation; unlike law, this form of coercion is not exercised through a special apparatus. In other words, convention involves "formal" coercion by the group, while the law employs "physical" or institutional coercion. In some cases, the public opinion on which convention rests may be harsher than the law, while in others the law may set requirements which public opinion is not prepared to accept.

The apparatus of coercion, which is essential to the law, may consist in a court of justice, as it does in the rationalized modern societies; in other societies it may be the prerogative of the clan (vendetta, *vheme*) or of the family. The characteristic element of the law is the existence of an official organ of coercion, regardless of the nature and variety of the means it employs. Coercion may, in fact, take the form of fraternal exhortation in a religious community as well as of police measures in an organized state. It goes without saying that coercion, as here seen from the sociological viewpoint, is not to be confused with moral duty, although the two may coincide.

Regardless of the subjective motives for submitting to an authority, the validity of that authority may rest on a variety of foundations. It may be respected as a matter of tradition (that which has long existed is valid), or because of an affectual belief (that which has been revealed, or set as an example, is valid), or by virtue of a value-oriented rational belief (values such as freedom, justice and equality are valid), or again by virtue of a goal-oriented rational belief (that which is legitimate is valid). This last form is the most commonly encountered today, although legitimate authority may either be based on a contract among those who agree to respect it, or be delegated by a man who exercises domination which the others regard as legitimate. The other foundations for legitimacy are mainly of historical interest, although they continue to influence legitimate authority, if only through the recognition of natural law.

Despite its universality, legitimacy raises a number of problems which are far from being resolved. There is, for example, the opposition between contract and delegation, and the relationship between majority and minority, between rule by law and rule by decree, etc., to say nothing of the meaning of obedience, which varies according to the type of legitimate authority selected. In other words, legal and political authority are often irreconcilably opposed.

Under a given system of authority, social relationships are of two principal types: communal and associative. The term "communal relationship" (*Vergemeinschaftung*) designates unified social behavior based on the agents' subjective sense of belonging to the same community. The term "associative relationship" designates behavior unified by a compromise or coordination of interests on the basis of either value-orientation or goal-orientation.

Communal relationships rest on an emotional or traditional factor, which may be religious, domestic, erotic or ethnic (e.g., a religious or national community, the family, a couple in love, a fraternity). However, the existence of common characteristics or qualities does not lead to a communal relationship unless the individuals concerned discover in them a subjective meaning which prompts them to orient their behavior on the basis of common sentiment. Associative relationship rests on a reciprocal agreement entered into on rational grounds (stock exchange, commodity market, association formed to defend the interests of its members, ideological grouping such as a political party, etc.). Both a communal and an associate relationship may be either "open" or "closed," according to whether or not the members freely allow others to join.

Finally, all the participants in a social relationship may be jointly responsible, under a system of definite rules, for the action of each of the members and may also benefit by the advantages which any one member is in a position to procure for them; or they may divide themselves into representing and represented members (*Vertretung*), where the former are responsible for the action of the latter, while the latter profit by the fortunate ventures of their representatives and suffer the consequences of their failures. Representation may consist in a delegation of powers to an individual as such, or it may be conferred on a permanent or temporary basis on one or several individuals in accordance with prescribed standards or under a statute. In either case, representation establishes a hierarchy in social relationships.

The most common form of social relationship is the corporate group (*Verband*), which is characterized on the one hand by being closed—i.e., having regulations whereby the accession of new members is subject to a number of more or less restrictive conditions—and on the other by using a system of representation, since the corporate group has a leadership (individual or collective) and usually an administrative apparatus. One of its determining factors is thus the existence of an authority with more or less clearly defined powers (president, director, prince, magistrate, employer, head of a church, etc.), so that the meaningful orientation of the members' conduct toward one another is accompanied by orientation to the decisions of the authority.

A corporate group may be either autonomous or heteronomous; in other words, it may freely determine its own conduct (for example, the state), or it may be obliged to respect regulations established by an outside authority (for example, an association which must comply with legislation relating to associations). It may also be either autocephalous or heterocephalous, depending on whether it has its own leader (President of the French Republic, for instance) or accepts foreign authority (the appointment of a governor in a British Dominion is an example of heterocephaly). Usually, autonomy and autocephaly go hand in hand, but that need not be so, as demonstrated by the German Federation before 1914, where each member state, Bavaria for one, was autonomous and heterocephalous.

The internal regulations by which a corporate group is governed may be established by the free and mutual consent of the members, or they may be imposed on them by a representative authority. The idea of imposition must be taken in its broadest sense, for a decision by the majority to which the minority must bow falls within this category. In principle, of course, free and mutual agreement presupposes unanimity.

There are numerous varieties of corporate groups, the following being the most important: the enterprise (*Betrieb*), which is a system of continuous activity pursuing a definite goal under the guidance of a higher authority; the association (*Verein*), which is based on common agreement concerning regulations that are valid only for those who join it voluntarily; and the institution (*Anstalt*), which has a delimited area of activity (territorial, pedagogical, or other) under regulations imposed from above. A factory is an enterprise, a club is an association, and a university is an institution. There are of course many transitional forms between these three categories.

Any social relationship may involve a struggle (*Kampf*) and may either provoke it or keep it alive. Struggle is purposeful orientation of an activity with a view to making one's will triumph over the will of others. It may be either war-like or peaceful; in the latter case, it eschews violence. Peaceful struggle, or competition, is an attempt to gain control over advantages which are also sought by others. When competition pursues a definite end, with means which are governed by express provisions, it is called controlled competition. The name "selection" is given by Weber to the (generally latent) struggle for survival in which individuals are opposed to each other in a competition devoid of meaningful relatedness, the participants being concerned only with securing better chances of survival. This form of selection is akin to what in biology is called natural selection.

Between bloody combat, where the aim is the physical destruction of the adversary, and simple controlled competition (such as a sports contest) there are transitional stages of struggle of every variety. Such struggle may take many different forms—political, economic, erotic, ideological, etc. The means used will vary according to the object of the competition (to become a husband, lover, civil servant, deputy, entrepreneur, star), and may consist in physical strength, cunning, greater intellectual ability, sheer lung power, a better demagogic technique, greater ingenuity, flattery, a talent for intrigue, etc. The struggle is eternal and it is inconceivable that it should ever be totally eliminated. The most peaceful regulations can never be more than a way of tolerating certain means and forms of competition, to the exclusion of others.

Struggle is at the heart of various social phenomena, the most important of which are power (*Macht*) and domination (*Herrschaft*). Power implies the existence within a social relationship of the opportunity to enforce one's will against the resistance of others. Power is therefore not merely political; it can be exercised in economic matters, within the family, in religion, and even in teaching. Domination implies that an opportunity exists to have an order of a definite content obeyed by a given group. It is founded on a relationship of command and obedience, and may even rest on the will of a single individual, without the need for any formal association or administrative apparatus. Domination entails a political association when a commanding authority is able continuously to enforce its orders within determined geographical frontiers, if necessary by means of physical coercion. The modern form of political association is the state, which claims a monopoly of the legitimate use of force and physical coercion. An association which is in a position to employ psychic coercion because it can grant or withhold the means of salvation is a hierocratic association. If it can resort to legitimate hierocratic coercion, it is called a church.

Armed with these concepts and with ideal types of human behavior in general and social behavior in particular, Weber undertook in his *Wirtschaft und Gesellschaft* to explain in sociological terms the evolution of such various forms of human endeavor as economics, politics, religion, law, the arts and the sciences. In passing, he analyzed in depth certain structures which seemed to him of particular importance, such as status group and social class, race, nation, market, city and bureaucracy. Unfortunately, death cut short this monumental work, extraordinary both for its intellectual penetration and for its incomparable wealth of erudition. Some chapters were fully completed, others are known to us only through fragments assembled and arranged by a pious hand, while still others never went beyond the planning stage. Nevertheless, the work forms two volumes, amounting to over 800 large pages in small print.[8] To this must be added the *Sociology of Religion*[9]—also uncompleted, despite the three finished volumes, for Weber projected a study of Islam on which he left only notes—and, lastly, the various studies brought together in *Gesammelte Aufsätze zur Soziologie und Sozialpolitik* and his *General Economic History*.[10]

4

Special Sociologies

---·•◦∞◦•·---

1. Historical and systematic sociology

Raymond Aron rightly regards Max Weber's work as "the paradigm of a sociology which is both historical and systematic."[1] At the same time, we have to remember that Weber had no intention of constructing a system of the type constructed by Comte, Marx or Spencer. Nothing was more alien to him, as we have seen earlier, than the establishment of general laws of development which professedly teach us how humanity has passed from one stage to the next before arriving, in an unforeseeable future, at some ultimate stage. Such reflections, although not altogether useless for philosophy and even practical action, are outside the province of science. For science is not intended to lead to unanimity of thought, action and evaluation (that would be contrary to its nature), but rather to agreement on the fragmentary sectors of research which alone are susceptible of demonstration and verification by scientific investigation. Because there is no knowledge that is not hypothetical, it is impossible to construct a scientific system (sociological, historical or other) of humanity and culture. The concepts of humanity and culture necessarily have an axiological significance, since we inevitably relate them to values. Hence the concept of humanity has altogether different meanings in the eyes of, say, Marx or Comte, who started from different presuppositions and developed their theories on the basis of different values, by virtue of which they selected certain aspects of reality and ignored others.

> "Culture" is a finite segment of the meaningless infinity of the world process, [writes Weber] a segment on which human beings confer meaning and significance. This is true even for the human being who views a particular culture as a mortal enemy and who seeks to "return to nature." He can attain this point of view only after viewing the culture in which he lives from the standpoint of his values, and finding it "too soft." This is the purely logical-formal fact which is involved when we speak of the logically necessary rootedness of all historical entities in "evaluative ideas." The transcendental presupposition of every cultural science lies not in our finding a certain culture or any "culture" in general to be valuable, but rather in the fact that we are cultural beings, endowed with the capacity and the will to take a deliberate attitude towards the world and to lend it significance. Whatever this significance may be, it will lead us to judge certain phenomena of human existence in its light and to re-

spond to them as being (positively or negatively) meaningful. Whatever may be the content of this attitude, these phenomena have cultural significance for us and on this significance alone rests its scientific interest.[2]

Elsewhere in his writings, Weber stated his intention of following up this essay with a special section on methodology. Circumstances doubtless prevented him from carrying out his project, with the result that we have to look for his views in various passages in which he set down his thoughts on the subject.

Methodology, in Weber's thinking, would appear to cover three things: the elaboration of concepts that are as rigorous and univocal as possible, for example, in the form of ideal types, so as to avoid all confusion as to meaning and hence all confusion of problems; the analysis of empirical and historical reality by means of this intellectual apparatus with a view to clarifying the singularity of an event or the analogies among different phenomena; the construction of a rational picture of the segment of reality investigated, in order to make the correct and probable causal imputations and elucidate the most adequate meaning. When we study an economic system, for instance, from a sociological point of view, there can be no question of announcing what it should become in a distant future; on the contrary, it must be analyzed systematically, that is, rationally, with a view to discovering its variations, irregularities and irrationalities; in other words, we have to try to understand it better as it exists. Only thus can it furnish the economist with sound data, thereby enabling him to make the most accurate forecasts for the near future.

Such work is possible only if a system is available, that is, a set of clear concepts. In other words, rigorous systematization has a zetetic and possibly teleological significance, but never an eschatological one. Had Weber read Durkheim? We do not know. Although some American and German sociologists (including René Koenig) think they can reconcile the two theorists, it is certain that Durkheim's philosophical position cannot be reconciled with Weber's conception of sociology. Weber would indeed have approved of the conclusion of the *Rules of Sociological Method*,[3] in which Durkheim abandoned the idea of subordinating the science which he practiced to any positivist, evolutionary, spiritualistic or materialistic doctrine; but he would just as certainly have opposed the idea of system in Durkheim's sociology. For according to that idea, it is possible to establish the laws of social development, and thus to forecast, for instance, that, through the play of "wholly mechanical causes," the individual personality will be absorbed by the collective personality, or again, on the basis of a progress which is no more than a metaphysical supposition, to declare that the organization of the Hebrews was less advanced than that of the Salian Franks, or that the Athenian city was inferior to the Roman.

And Weber would also have rejected a sociology founded on the concept of the progress of institutions, as being scientifically undemonstrable. The notion of progress, Weber felt, is all too often wrongly identified with that of the increasing differentiation of human activities. He would have been all the more wary of a sociology which claimed to systematize the future on the basis of a classification as arbitrary as one that takes progress as its criterion. In his view, no science can prove that the diversified society of today is superior to the less diversified societies of former times. All science can say is that the values we believe in are different from those in which our forbears believed; no one can say that our forbears were less well adapted to their circumstances than we to ours, or that they considered themselves more unfortunate than we do. The validity of a value does not detract from that of others, for only a dogmatic system can judge between them.

The fundamental error of most systems, according to Weber, is that they attempt to represent the true course of events; to be the reflection of reality and of its development in the sense of a *ratio essendi*. This applies to liberalism as to Marxism. Some even claim to reproduce reality so to speak without error, on the grounds that they have discovered the "authentic" or "true" causes, or some ultimate cause. Not only do such concepts indicate a misunderstanding of the probabilistic character of historical causality, but they are also in contradiction with the very nature of science, since there is no knowledge without presuppositions.

The only purpose of Weber's methodology, on the other hand, is to serve as a *ratio cognoscendi*. As such, it is capable of discovering the flaws in doctrines which claim to reproduce reality and of determining the distance which separates their conceptual intention from the historical reality which they purport to reflect. When Weber systematized capitalism in a rational Utopia, he was not attempting to account for the totality or for the whole truth of that phenomenon. His purpose was simply to render certain aspects more intelligible, those, that is, which make it possible to elucidate certain meanings in historical events through research within a context of research delimited by value-orientation. He was well aware that law, for instance, could be variously defined, according as it is viewed by the jurist, the sociologist, the student of politics or the economist. All the definitions may be valid, provided that they are systematizations productive for research, that is, provided that they lead to useful analogies and profitable discussion, unfettered by confusion and ideological bias. In sum, Weber rejected any system claiming identity with reality, and accepted the systematic elaboration of concepts only in the sense of tools for probing the meaning of reality.

Sociology can also apply to history. We should make it clear from the start that in Weber's eyes history is a science capable of making objectively valid judgments. In that respect again, his position differed from Durkheim's, for the latter saw history simply as a cluster of successive events among which sociology alone is able to introduce some coherence by establishing the laws of social institutions and development. Weber saw history—like sociology or any other human science—as an autonomous science with its own purpose. He doubtless arrived at that conception as a result of his own experience, since as a professor of political economy he was primarily a historian of economics rather than an economist proper. He thus had the opportunity to reflect on historical method before devoting himself, toward the end of his life, to sociology. Since the latter discipline entails not only causal analysis founded on a generalizing method but also interpretative study, it is not hard to see why Weber was able to transpose the historical method to sociology, with a few modifications.

Thus selection on the basis of value-orientation, the construction of ideal types, and the use of categories of objective probability and adequate causality are equally valid methods in both disciplines. The difference lies only in this, that history is concerned only to explain singular events, whereas the sociology of history, while respecting the singularity of events, seeks in addition to establish patterns. While it examines what is singular in the doctrines of Confucianism, Hinduism or Christianity, for example, it also seeks to determine what analogies there are between these different forms of religious life.

Because Weber's sociology is historical in character, it not only examines the general relations between economics, morals and religion or politics, but it also attempts to understand the various ways in which the different religions have conceived of these relations, their reasons for viewing them thus and the circumstances in which they have come to do so. Without assuming to establish actual laws, we shall be in a position to see why a warrior ruling class is barely compatible with a rational religious code of ethics, or why a political structure based on the masses inclines toward a charismatic authority. Similarly, after elaborating the ideal type of capitalism, Weber could point to the germs of capitalist enterprise in the non-European civilizations and explain why the capitalist structure did not succeed in developing there.

His sociology is historical because it is interpretative. Hence it does not assert that the relation between masses and charisma is a necessary one, but only an adequate one, according to the general rules of experience. For in so far as Weber recognized that an event never has a single cause, he was also obliged to abandon the notion of an initial or fundamental cause. In brief, because his sociology is based on the concept of meaningful individual action and on that of typical modes of behavior, it can help us to understand, in the light of history and general experience, in what sense we may anticipate certain probable consequences rather than others in certain given circumstances.

Here we have to stress the expression, "general rules of experience," because this concept is basic to Weber's thinking. In no case was he referring to the so-called lessons of history, but rather to a knowledge of a nomological nature, developed through humanity's long experience of itself, which probably goes back into prehistory. Weber believed in a human nature capable of all kinds of differentiation—psychological, social, etc.—but whose reason and passions nothing as yet has succeeded in mastering. Man is capable of meaningful recognition of man because his nature has undergone no substantial modification.

2. The singularity of Western civilization

The historical character of Weber's sociology emerges particularly in the construction he himself placed on his studies and which he indicated in the introduction to his *Sociology of Religion*,[4] in which he raised the question of the singularity of Western civilization. How is it that Europe has produced this unique culture, with its virtually universal significance and value? Weber believed the cause to lie in the influence of its rationality.

Rationality, of course, is not lacking in other civilizations, if only because a mode of conduct which adapts the available means to the desired end is rational, and is not reserved to any special category of men. Confucianism, for instance, is in large measure a rational teaching. Even magical rites which seem to us eminently irrational constitute a rationalization by comparison with other, more primitive usages. Similarly, there is rationality in Buddhist contemplation; and many other examples could be cited. Nevertheless, all these forms of rationality have remained static and confined to a certain number of actions, without betraying any internal force of expansion.

To be just, however, it must be added that the notion of rationality is far from being univocal. An action may sometimes be considered irrational in the light of a more rational, external point of view, although it carries its own rationality within it. For an irreligious being, any religious mode of life appears irrational, just as asceticism, whose rationality is indisputable, passes for irrational in the eyes of pure hedonism. The reverse is equally true. In brief, the distinction between rational and irrational is usually made on the basis of certain values which are preferred to others, whereas in fact any idea of value is based on a subjective and irrational factor. That is equally true of Western culture, in so far as it does not call into question the validity of the values in which it believes. This means that not even the broadest or most intensive rationalization ever succeeds in altogether, or definitively, surmounting the original subjectivity of its position.

It remains, however, that the rationality of Western culture presents a number of absolutely distinctive traits, characteristic only of itself, although today they are spreading throughout the world.

Only in the West has science developed in the sense of a body of knowledge possessing universal validity. Elsewhere we find observations of great subtlety, as well as empirical knowledge and profound reflections on life and the universe, and even philosophical and theological insight, but nowhere else do we find rational demonstration on the basis of mathematics or precise experiment conducted in laboratories equipped with accurate instruments of measurement. Only the West has developed a rational physics, chemistry and astronomy; it alone has developed a scientific history (with which the annals of the Chinese scholars are hardly comparable), and a systematic political science, although elements of a Machiavellian doctrine are to be found in some Hindu works.

The rational state, with its specialized institutions, its written constitution regulating political activity, is unknown anywhere else. While other codifications exist here and there, only in the West do we find a rational jurisprudence, heir to Roman law, or again such a structure as canon law. Nor is there any equivalent of the European bureaucracy formed of specialists, jurists and other trained personnel.

Some peoples may possess a more highly developed ear than that of Europeans, yet the latter alone have rationalized music with descant, the simultaneous play of a number of instruments, harmonics, orchestra and a system of notation. The same applies to architecture, in which the West succeeded in solving the technical problems of the Gothic arch or of the cupola. Indeed, the rationalization of art as a whole, as effected by the Renaissance, is without parallel.

Finally, a rational economy in the form of capitalism, with its industries and factories, its bookkeeping, whereby costs and profit can be exactly calculated, its separation of industry from the household and its rational conduct of business, is also characteristic of the West. Even the religions practiced in the West have systematized their dogmas and the benefits of salvation. This rationalization provides historical sociology with a vast field of study and at the same time constitutes an inexhaustible fount of reflection.

The distinctive and fundamental feature of the rationality of Western civilization is that it is not confined to a particular or privileged sector of human activity, but permeates the whole of life. It exerts a permanent action, developing and transcending itself ceaselessly. Far from stagnating, like the rationality of other civilizations, it has renewed itself constantly on the basis of new discoveries whose future dimensions it is hard to foresee, but at the same time intellectuals have been concerned to establish its internal coherence, and this has only expanded its power.

That is another characteristic: the rationality of the West has taken the form of a progressive intellectualization of life; it has tended to strip the world of charm and of poetry; intellectualization means disenchantment. In a word, the world becomes increasingly the artificial product of man, who governs it much as one controls a machine. Hence we need not be surprised at the formidable ascendancy of technology with its corollary, specialization, as a result of the ever-growing division and subdivision of functions.

Weber was so interested in and curious about the specificity of the Western world that we get the impression that his studies of Hinduism, China, the Islamic world and other cultures were little more than counter-proofs, as it were, intended to set off more clearly and more cogently the originality of the West.

We may therefore ask whether the theme of rationality as Weber developed it was not in contradiction with his rejection of any system or philosophy of history. The question is the more pertinent since at the end of the foreword to which we referred above he wonders about the causes of this prodigious rationalization. He regrets the ethnographic lacunae which have forced him to assess the meaning of other civilizations solely by comparison with the West. Then he turns to the anthropological problem. Since so typical a rationalization is constantly to be found in the West, and only there, we have to consider whether this originality is not to be imputed to hereditary qualities. And Weber adds: "The author admits that he is inclined to think the importance of biological heredity very great." But he is careful to follow up this statement immediately with the remark that

> In spite of the notable achievements of anthropological research, I see up to the present no way of exactly or even approximately measuring either the extent or, above all, the form of its influence on the development investigated here. It must be one of the tasks of sociological and historical investigation first to analyze all

the influences and causal relationships which can satisfactorily be explained in terms of reactions to environmental conditions.[5]

These passages have given rise to some misunderstandings. Weber felt that studies dealing with racial and hereditary characteristics have significance and utility in so far as they achieve scientifically verifiable results; as such they can serve as indices or data for sociology. In no case did he espouse racism; such a position would have conflicted with his fundamental principle of axiological neutrality. In other words, he believed that the misuse of racism as a conception of the world cannot discredit a positive science dealing with race, just as moral turpitude cannot discredit morality. In any case, there is nothing scientific about racism, since its evaluations are based on unknown data. Similarly, it would be premature in the present context to draw certain conclusions from studies on heredity and race to explain civilizations, since such a science is still at an embryonic stage.

Although an occasional passage may appear ambiguous, it is certain that Weber never attempted to make Western rationality the basis of a world view. The phenomenon was one which he was content to note as a fact of history and which occasioned his surprise, but he was careful to avoid giving it any prophetic significance whatsoever. It was for him an essential element of foresight; it could not serve as material for predicting the future. At most, he saw it as a factor of progressive differentiation (without equating progressiveness with improvement), but he never regarded it as progress in the axiological sense of the term.

In a word, he accepted rationalization as a fact, irreversible perhaps because historical; he did not seek to legitimize it or to justify it as an advantage. We have already seen that in his opinion a man could have just as good subjective reasons for condemning the artificiality of modern living and preaching a return to nature (a Utopian attitude, no doubt, but an understandable one) as for magnifying the benefits of rationalization. In any event, we obviously cannot assert that rationalization will make man happy. It is true that the Mormons transformed the area around Salt Lake, but were they happier than the Indians who had lived there before being driven away? Do we not sometimes prefer the solitude of an arid and infertile spot to the comforts of a modern city? The theme of rationalization could have served as a pretext for a system or a philosophy of history had Weber attached a value to it, either in the sense of progress or in the sense of ethical improvement. But this he refused to do. Indeed, he could not do so, since he regarded science and the rationalization which it entails as an indefinite research whose consequences may be good or disastrous—one cannot know which.

In so far as Western rationalization means the disenchantment of the world, it also reflects man's almost unreasoning confidence in his own works. In that sense, it is correlative to the growing importance assumed by the technology and invention of which man is master, as opposed to natural phenomena. As Weber remarked, such confidence need not be based on real knowledge; sometimes it is even the counterpart of ignorance. For the man who lives in a rationalized civilization generally has no accurate or even approximate knowledge of the various instruments, devices and machines surrounding him, nor of the composition of the products he absorbs (foodstuffs, medicines), nor finally of the apparatus of society, administration or the economy. He is content with appearances and with the assumption that these artificial things are ordered and controlled by specialists and that, were he prepared to take the trouble, he might be able to understand them, provided he was given appropriate explanations.

Consequently, increasing rationalization is by no means the same thing as a clearer understanding or a growing knowledge of the conditions under which we live. For the ordinary person it means that humanity has succeeded to a point in exorcizing mysterious, blind forces, thanks to its capacity for foresight. Altogether, while rationalization is positive in its achievement, it promotes in man a negative attitude of laziness and sheer pragmatism.

In his analyses, Weber did not disdain the use of a method similar to Marx's, and even certain Marxist concepts, though in ideal-typical form, without attaching to them any metaphysical or other value. This did not prevent him, however, from pointing out the conflicts that can be touched off by social relationships within a civilization. But while he refused to make value judgments in the course of purely scientific studies, he took a clear stand on rationality in his public lectures and in his specifically political writings, in an endeavor to clarify the dialectics between knowledge and action. Rationalization he accepted as a datum, together with its consequences, such as specialization, juridical legalism, etc.; at the same time he demanded freedom of choice in accents reminiscent of Nietzsche's, on the grounds of the irreconcilable antagonism between values. The most far-reaching rationalization is incapable of surmounting the conflicts arising out of the multiplicity of evaluations and possible goals, since it is impossible once and for all to identify truth, justice, goodness, beauty, freedom, equality and usefulness in a definitive doctrine.

Weber was appalled at the thought that rationalization, which controls the sphere of the external relations among men, might enslave the soul to bureaucratization or purely technological utilitarianism. This fear he expressed in particular in the face of socialism, which tends toward a functionalization of the whole of human life, so that rationalization could become more burdensome to man than the situation which it purports to remedy. He was also wary of scientism, which tends to subject the human being to a servile concept of science, whereas science, he felt, is essentially the activity concerned with a perpetual calling into question. He did not expect miracles from any political doctrine, but he believed man capable of putting himself at the service of a cause, especially if he deliberately succeeds in breaking the determinisms which constantly threaten him. Rationalism, then, cannot really escape the conflicts and antagonisms which it seeks to resolve. It does not dispense man from remaining lucid.

It would be useless to go into greater detail concerning Weber's stands on practical issues, since only his conception of sociology is at issue here. The fact remains that the confrontation of the various civilizations in the light of their varying degrees of rationalization gives his sociological studies a certain unity. We find this theme in his sociology of economics as in his sociologies of politics, law, religion and art. For this reason, it is sometimes difficult to classify certain works under one or the other heading. His *Protestant Ethic and the Spirit of Capitalism* belongs to both the sociology of economics and to that of morals and religion. The same is true of the volumes devoted to the sociology of religion, as is evident from the subtitle, "The Economic Ethics of the World Religions." Solely for convenience of presentation, and taking account of the considerations which we have just mentioned, we divide his sociology into different sections.

[A]

THE SOCIOLOGY OF ECONOMICS

1. The various orientations of economic sociology

Weber's economic sociology was based in large measure on his youthful studies, which had borne on the most varied subjects (agrarian problems of antiquity, medieval trade relations, with particular reference to the economy of the Italian cities, the position of agricultural workers in eastern Germany, workers' conditions in modern factories, the phenomenon of the stock exchange, etc.). For everything relating to economic and social questions, as well as others, he displayed a boundless curiosity, based on an almost encyclopedic knowledge, but central to his concerns was the phenomenon of capitalism.

Weber always refused to consider capitalism from the narrow standpoint of the ideologies in vogue, and regarded it as an economic system which would long continue, in different forms, to direct world economy. Capitalism, as Weber saw it, is a system which cannot be destroyed by a revolution, however radical, since some aspects of it correspond to the needs of economic rationalization, and will continue to influence the new social structures which men may establish. Value judgments and purely ethical disapproval are powerless in the face of the necessity of the facts.

The notion of economy in everyday language takes on a variety of meanings, some of which have no connection with a social relationship nor with what is signified in our day by the term "economics." It may, for instance, signify the organization of the elements of a whole, in the sense in which we speak of the general economy of a book or a chapter, of the general economy of a situation, or again of the economy of thought as a method, in the manner of Mach. The term may also designate the principle governing the arrangement of means with a view to achieving the best technical results, whatever the sphere of human effort. This sense belongs to the general philosophy of success, of which goal-oriented activity is the most adequate form. These different meanings must nevertheless be ruled out of a sociology of economics.

For Weber, economic activity in the specific sense of the term means the human relationship based on a need, or a complex of needs, requiring to be satisfied, while the means and services capable of satisfying them are limited either by scarcity, or by poverty, or by lack of purchasing power. In so far as a conduct is oriented in consideration of such factors, it is called economic. Nevertheless, this definition, as such, is still too narrow for sociology, since it places the accent only on the notion of consumption, and hence on the relationship to objects capable of satisfying needs. But economic activity expresses not only a human but also a social relationship. In that sense, it implies, in addition, a meaningful relationship to others, as evidenced by the fact that the acquisition or use of objects desired for the satisfaction of wants gives rise on the one hand to exploitation in the form of production or organized work and, on the other, to economic provision in the form of reserves, profits or, more generally, power of control and disposal (*Verfügungsgewalt*).

Economic activity may therefore be envisaged from two essential standpoints. First, from the point of view of satisfying individual wants. These may lead to the pursuit of all possible goods, from basic food requirements to religious edification, provided that in the latter case their satisfaction is not thwarted by a limitation of the means and services for procuring the desired goods. Economic satisfaction is thus not necessarily purely material in character, since prayers or Masses can become the subject of an economic relationship if the administration of the desired goods presupposes qualified persons (priests) who have to be remunerated in cash or in kind—a condition which introduces the characteristic limitation to which we have just referred. The second point of view is that of labor and of its product, and involves the exploitation of the limitation of goods and services in order to secure a profit or an advantage conducive to the free control and disposal of the goods concerned.

Economic activity is thus a social relationship in so far as the participants direct their conduct in the light of a subjectively viewed goal for the purpose of satisfying wants or engaging in work which will enable them to acquire the necessary goods. This behavior is at the basis of the economic community, whose purpose may be either the satisfaction of wants and work or the utilization of economic means to achieve other purposes of an extra-economic nature. '

Cultural phenomena concern economic sociology from a threefold point of view. First, because they are purely economic events, standards or institutions. This applies to the stock exchange and banks, which are first and foremost economic institutions established to that end. These will be termed economic phenomena proper. Secondly, because certain aspects may be economically important—religious institutions, for instance. For obvious reasons, they do not interest the sociologist primarily from the standpoint of their economic importance or by reason of it, but because some of their aspects may in certain circumstances acquire economic significance, since they produce results which are important from an economic point of view. There is no doubt that churches have been and remain sources of considerable economic phenomena. Finally, because of the economic conditionality of certain institutions or events. Thus, the artistic taste of a particular period is not an economic phenomenon, but some of its aspects may have been conditioned or influenced by economic activity, if only through the social circles interested in art.

One and the same reality may sometimes be studied from all three angles. Thus the state, for instance, appears as a properly economic institution in so far as it controls the public finances or nationalized enterprises. It is an economically important phenomenon in certain of its non-economic aspects when it intervenes in the life of the society through legislative measures which, even without being directly aimed at the economy, may have implications for the economy. Finally, its non-economic decisions on education, public security or military organization may be conditioned by economic motives or factors.

For all these reasons, it is clear that, while the sector of economic phenomena is fluid and difficult to delimit precisely, the economic aspects of a phenomenon are never exclusively conditioned by the economy, just as the effects to which they give rise are never purely and solely economic in character. In other words, a phenomenon concerns economic sociology in so far and for as long as the investigator's curiosity, determined by his value-orientation, bears solely on the influence which it has had or continues to have in the struggle for material existence.

Thus, while accepting the Marxist dialectical relationship between economic activity and other human activities, Weber rejected the metaphysical and ontological basis of that philosophy; if science implies open research, it cannot reduce the explanation of all cultural phenomena to an economic substratum. It is of course possible and even useful, in certain circumstances, to put a unilaterally economic interpretation on phenomena; such a method may, on occasion, open up new perspectives. Nevertheless, this interpretation is based on an arbitrary a priori selection based on value-orientation, so that it is never more than a partial view of reality and a preparatory step to the historical interpretation of civilization as a whole.

2. The economic group

The economic group has the same characteristics as the group generally, which we studied earlier. In particular, it can constitute a closed or an open relationship. By reason of competition, which is the driving force of the economy, the economic group tends to develop in the form of a closed relationship, on the basis of a community of interests, possibly entailing rational and juridical regulation, especially in cases where the group possesses property or intends to act as its defender. The nature of the property matters little; it may take the form of movable or immovable goods, but also of the privileges of a religious order or of a category of officials, or of acquired rights. The existence of the property prompts the economic group to constitute itself a monoply, which may in its turn be applied to every conceivable object—fishing rights, game preserves, the appointment to certain jobs only of persons with specific diplomas or of members of a particular party, protectionism for a country, etc. Examples of monoply are as diverse as they are hard to enumerate.

The idea of monopoly, therefore, should not be taken in the current polemical and ideological sense, as used by those whose purpose is to discredit a certain form of capitalism. For the trend toward monopoly is not bound up with any particular historical economic and social structure, but is inherent in the development of economic activity. Socialism, for instance, is hostile to some forms of monopoly and favorable to others which it regards as more just from the subjective viewpoint of its own theory. The distinction it makes is thus based purely on an ethical valuation which can be justified only in terms of the ever controversial belief in a particular goal, but it is of no value to a sociological analysis of the economic structure of a group. Monopoly exists as soon as a group imposes a closed-door policy, within variable limits, in order to enhance its opportunities as against those on the outside.

The reasons for the closed-door policy may be very varied: to protect the unity of a group from which all internal competition has been banished against external competition (as in a career service or a state monopoly of education), or to provide more opportunities for internal competition among members of the group by eliminating external competition (in this case, the group is closed to the outside and open to the inside). The relationship between monopoly and competition constitutes the whole dialectic of appropriation. Seen more closely, the system based on the exclusive rule of collective property appears as a closed relationship, whereas the system which accepts private property is an open one, since it is founded on the principle of the possibility of a change of ownership. In that sense, socialism is the present type of the closed economic group, while capitalism is the relationship offering the greatest possible number of opportunities.

In general, monopoly or the closed system is the defender or initiator of privilege. The trend toward monopoly may of course take different forms according to the social structures involved, depending on whether it promotes the privileges of an order, of a corporation, of a social class, of a category of officials or employees, of a social stratum (peasants, notables, traders, liberal professions), or of a religious fraternity of an ascetical or other nature.

The typical form of the closed relationship of earlier times was the guild (*Zunft*). Its essential feature was that it constituted a monopoly of a vocational nature which engendered a characteristic approach in that it subjected the enjoyment of economic, cultural and social goods to very strict rules entailing duties as well as rights. The corporation, indeed, required of its members a form of novitiate (apprenticeship, companionship), a qualifying test (master work) and also all kinds of duties, services and even burdensome obligations within the system.

Although corporatism ultimately proved a stumbling block in the way of the development of a dynamic society, we should not forget that, sociologically, it was a rational form of organization. It was supplanted by capitalist enterprise, whose characteristic feature is to produce a more open economic group, offering free scope to both internal and external competition. However, precisely by reason of such competition, it has also come to create other monopolies (licenses, patents, manufacturing secrets), and in certain cases has led to industrial concentration and has even revived protectionism, no longer at the level of a particular branch of business but at that of the wider grouping of the state. In theory, however, the capitalist enterprise tends to be an open relationship, as is clear from the fact that anyone is free to take part in the ownership and profits of a firm by becoming a shareholder.

From a strictly sociological point of view, we have to recognize that it may be to the advantage of an economic group, depending on circumstances, to form either a closed or an open relationship. Both such forms of organization have their technical advantages and disadvantages, their strength and their weakness. What is out of the question is that sociology should be able to decide, as a science, whether an open relationship is preferable to a closed one, or the reverse. The debate would be endless, since it would remain at the level of pure evaluation. Consequently, a comparative sociological analysis of capitalism and socialism must confine itself to noting that, from an economic point of view, socialism tends rather toward the closed group and capitalism toward the open one (from a political point of view, the position may be otherwise, taking into account the internationalist vocation of socialism). Such a finding, however, does not imply any judgment as to the respective merits of one or other form of organization from the point of view of justice or, more generally, of ethics.

The economic group possesses its own specific characteristics by reason of the autonomy of economic activity, which cannot be identified with other types of activity, such as politics, science, law, etc. Moreover, because of the diversity and disparity of needs, any attempt to reduce them to a common denominator must fail, although such attempts constantly recur. There thus exists a specifically economic activity, in the sense defined above. However, just as the direction of economic activity can be influenced by other activities, so the direction of these other activities can be influenced by economic activity, that is, obey economic motives while pursuing an aim other than an economic one. We might cite science, politics and technology as examples. Because economic activity is based on need, it is oriented toward objects, but such orientation has none of the objective or logical necessity about it which characterizes science, for instance; it is a matter of subjective necessity based on urgency, and may entail a hierarchy of priorities according to the imperatives of demand and prevision. For this reason, economic objects are termed "goods" and not "truths." Economic activity is thus, in itself, primarily a practical activity and not a science; it seeks not objectivity but satiety.

These considerations, however, do not stand in the way of the establishment of a science or sociology of economics, along the same lines as a science of politics or of law. From that point of view, Weber welcomed the importance assumed by mathematics in economic research, so long as this collaboration did not become a pretext for confusing economic science with practical economic activity, as he pointed out in his inaugural lecture on "The National State and Economic Policy."

For economics is an "international" science, that is, it tends to establish propositions of universal validity when it explains either the economic phenomenon in itself or the objective conditions of a historical economic situation. As thus defined, it can make no value judgments in the manner of those who see economic activity as a cohesive force or as a condition of peace or social justice. Such evaluations belong to economics in the sense of a practical activity, with a definite goal and the means capable of achieving it. In that case, it is no longer an object of cognition but is at the service of a specific intention concerned to resolve a particular problem under given historical and empirical circumstances. To resolve the difficulties involved, it may take account of scientific elements as well as of ethical factors without thereby becoming a science or a system of ethics.

If any activity whatsoever may be influenced by economic motives, then the violent activity of war must clearly be one such activity. Here, then, in an extreme case, the problem is raised of the connection between economics and politics. It has rightly been asserted that political means should be contrasted with economic means, and that the latter lead by preference to a peaceful struggle, which today we call competition. Economic activity is not belligerent in itself. From this correct observation, however, the erroneous conclusion has been drawn that economic activities are essentially peaceful, as a number of nineteenth-century authors believed, following Benjamin Constant.

Politics constantly uses economic means and, conversely, economic activity can use political means. Such collaboration does not mean, however, that economic activity might one day replace political activity; that would be a second error. In theory, of course, we might conceive of an economy from which all political intervention was ruled out, but in practice, and at all times, whether under a tribal system, a patrimonial system or a system of state control, economic activity has required of the political authority that it ensure the ownership of property by means of legal constraint. This applies as much to a socialist economy based on collective property (for the state guarantees the status of such property) as to an economy based on private property. Possibly, even, a planned economy has more need than any other of state protection. This observation disposes of a third error; the fact that economic activity is protected by state power, even violent, in no wise implies that it is itself an expression of violence.

Finally, economic and social problems have today assumed overriding importance, to the point where the state is itself transformed into a series of economic enterprises. This development has been facilitated in part by modern wars, which have placed all the levers of economic control in the hands of the statesman. The consequence is that politics leans increasingly on economic factors to achieve power or to preserve it. Nevertheless, the fact that this development has become so widespread does not mean (a fourth error) that economic activity could become no more than a means in the service of a purely political end. Regardless of all confusions, economic action retains its autonomy.

Another phenomenon which has developed on a formidable scale in our day is technology. Because production and labor have become key issues, must we identify technology with economy? Rational technique is the organization of means in view of an end which it does not itself determine. There is consequently a technique of every type of action—administration, cognition, research, trade, education, eroticism, art, prayer, asceticism, etc. In other words, the question of technique arises as soon as there is doubt concerning the most rational and appropriate means to be used to achieve a particular end. Therefore, although technology in our day plays an ever larger role in the economic sector, it is not logically more closely linked with economic action than with any other.

One of the principles of a rational technique, of course, is to achieve maximum efficiency with a minimum of resources. Such economy of means, however, has nothing to do with economic action as we understand it here. We may ask whether, from a technical standpoint, it is preferable to use platinum or iron in a particular instrument or machine. This purely technical question becomes an economic question only if the problem arises: shall we be able to find platinum in sufficient quantities? And again, shall we have the financial ability to pay for this technological advantage? In a word, a technological problem becomes an economic problem when the question of relative scarcity and cost arises. We must therefore not confuse technological efficiency with economic viability.

3. Fundamental economic concepts

The foregoing remarks sufficiently indicate the possible area of research of the sociology of economics. To avoid ambiguities and misunderstandings, some of which we have pointed out, Weber sought to define the fundamental concepts of economics as rigorously as possible. That was his aim in the lengthy second chapter of *Wirtschaft und Gesellschaft.*[6]

It is hard, in these pages, to give any adequate idea of the impressive subtlety of the concepts which Weber developed in that work, with its numerous divisions and subdivisions, explanatory notes, provocative commentaries and detailed analyses, especially since his method was to cumulate definitions without placing the connecting thread of his thinking in the reader's hands. It is debatable whether all the notes belong to the sphere of sociology as such or rather to the methodology of economic theory. We have to remember, in any event, that Weber, the sociologist, was by profession an economist.

The difficulty seems greatest in connection with his economic typology. Faithful to his concept of the ideal type, Weber constructed innumerable such typologies in response to the needs of his research, now to study medieval trade and the urban economy of the cities, now to clarify the concept of the artisanate, etc. In addition, he elaborated various overlapping typologies on the basis of often heterogeneous principles. As a result, his economic typology lacks the clarity and simplicity which we find in his sociology of law or politics. At the same time, some of the criticisms of his work have been too sharp, since they ignore the fact that death prevented Weber from completing it. The editor of *Wirtschaft und Gesellschaft* collected the fragments without concealing repetitions and deficiencies, so that rough drafts appear side by side with completed chapters. When criticism takes issue with the accidents of fate, it becomes mere foolishness.

In this presentation, we confine ourselves to those basic concepts which directly concern sociology, to the exclusion of those which are more closely related to finance and other economic specializations.

By "utilities," Weber meant "the specific and concrete, real or imagined advantages [*Chancen*] or means for present or future use as they are estimated and made an object of specific provision by one or more economically acting individuals. The action of these individuals is oriented to the estimated importance of such utilities as means for the ends of their economic action."[7] Such utilities comprise both goods and services. In the economic sense of the term, a "good" is not the object as such (e.g. a horse, an iron bar), but the possibility of using it for economic ends, as constituting, say, a power of traction or of support. The same principle applies to property, mortgages, clientele, etc. "Services" are the operations of specific economic action or of labor.

Typical measures of rational economic action are the following: (*a*) the systematic distribution of utilities available to the agent, for whatever reason, in the present or in the future (savings); (*b*) the systematic distribution of available utilities in the order of their manifold potential uses; (*c*) systematic action designed to produce or to use utilities, in so far as the agent possesses the means of obtaining them by his own efforts; (*d*) the systematic acquisition of such utilities which are in the control of a third party. In the last-mentioned case, acquisition may take the form either of a sharing of resources and utilities through the creation of groups (cooperatives, mutual aid societies, etc.), or of exchange.

By exchange we should understand a compromise of interests between economic agents, in the course of which goods or other advantages pass reciprocally from the control of each to that of the others. Anything—even future services—may become the substance of an exchange, provided that the parties place the same value on the equivalence. While the parties believe that such transfer will be to their advantage, exchange does not necessarily presuppose the idea of gain or profit. Everything depends on the estimation which each forms of the objects of the exchange; the exchange may therefore be based on irrational motives. A rational calculation of profit comes with a market situation, but this also brings with it a struggle for trade, or competition.

A market situation occurs whenever a number of economic agents speculate, be it only on the part of one of the parties, on the possibilities of profit afforded by trade in a context of competition. It is conceptually immaterial whether the "market" is a purely local one, a fair, a stock exchange or commercial relations among states. Two things are sociologically important: on the one hand, the reciprocal yet discontinuous character of the market relationship, since the relationship ends with the transfer of goods; on the other hand, the continuity of the process, since in theory those who make an exchange count on the fact that others will do the same under similar conditions.

Underlying the process, therefore, is a sort of dialectic between the discontinuity of market relationships and the continuity of prevision, which necessarily leads to regulation. Hence, at the market level, trade is altogether different from barter, precisely because it presupposes prevision and regulation.

A sociological analysis of the market is possible only if we take account of two basic conditions. First, in contrast to barter, the estimation of the values exchanged on the market is not subjective and qualitative in character, because the exchange takes place on the basis of a quantitative element, namely, money. Considered from that point of view, the market relationship is the most impersonal one that exists among men since, through the money element, they can keep in communication at a distance without the parties having to know one another personally. Secondly, because it presupposes regulation, the market is—or rather, has been

—a determining factor in the rationalization of economic action, since such regulation implies, in addition to continuity of exchange, legal and, indirectly, political safeguards, in so far as the political authority is in a position to regulate the flow of trade. Without monetary quantification and legal regulation, there could be no market.

Leaving aside the question of law, which transcends the purely economic sphere, it is necessary to look more closely at the concept of monetary quantification. Not only does money make it possible to measure the quantity of work and production, but it is above all the most rational "formal" means of economic orientation. What is important is not so much the use of money but the calculations which it makes possible, both within an economic unit and among several such units. Without quoting Aristotle on chrematistics, Weber believed that the introduction of money had caused economic activity to pass from the purely household phase to what might be termed the political phase. Money radically transformed the concept of acquisition because it added to the mere satisfying of wants the concept of profit, and indirectly that of capital, in so far as capital consists in the accumulation of wealth for undetermined uses.

Acquisition may thus be defined as economic action oriented according to the possibilities of gain (single, repeated or continuous), offering various alternative ways of controlling particular goods. It may take a variety of forms: interest lending, saving, profits from competition, etc.

The antithesis of a monetary economy is an economy based on payments in kind. The latter concept is far from being univocal; such an economy may involve no exchange at all, and it may also involve exchange with the use of money. It would be of no account today were it not that socialism is haunted by an economy from which the expedient of money is banished.

The real economic problem today is that of the opposition between a market economy and a planned economy. The former is based on financial calculation and on the distinction between household and business budgets. The planned economy, by contrast, tends to exalt payments in kind, although in reality it is oriented according to the decrees of an administrative general staff which itself is sometimes the instrument of dictatorship. A market economy entails risks for the worker and for the producer; a planned economy does away with the autonomy of both.

While the crucial difference between these two forms of economic activity might seem to lie in prevision, in the sense that a market economy is less rational than a planned economy, it is in fact primarily a political difference, as we can see from Lenin's writings. Fundamentally, it is the irrationality of politics which threatens to upset the rational calculations of a plan. What must be rejected is the claim of the advocates of a planned economy that such an economy is more altruistic or more scientific. No science can determine which of these economic forms is preferable; all it can do is to indicate the consequences involved in the choice of one or other of them.

Whatever the type of the economy, we have to deal with the problem of labor, or rather, with that of the division and coordination of activities oriented toward the acquisition of goods. Such division and coordination may be of a technical character, depending on whether a person is called upon to perform a single task (specialization) or several, and whether the activity is one of direction or of execution. They may also take on a social character by reason of the distribution of goods, according to the various possible definitions of the notion of property. But what is basic to an understanding of the economic phenomenon and its development from the beginning is that it gives rise to a perpetual tension between appropriation and expropriation, the forms of which vary according to the periods and the given circumstances of those periods. This constant alternation of appropriation and expropriation is what gives meaning to the historical development of economic action.

4. Economic typology; capitalism

Weber supplemented this analysis of sociological concepts with a typology which, as we said earlier, is far from being as thoroughly worked out and as coherent as that of his political sociology. Rather than types, we should speak of ideal types, most of which have no more than a provisional character in the context of research; for instance, the type of urban economy, or of the artisanate, to which we referred before. Some of his explanations are very summary, for example, those concerning classes, doubtless because his *Wirtschaft und Gesellschaft* was never completed.

The class, according to Weber, is an associative relationship based on interest arising out of the situation in which individuals find themselves; these individuals regard themselves as having a common position in relation to those outside their class, as well as a common destiny, because they control—or do not control, as the case may be—economic goods. Weber distinguished between three types of classes: the property class, characterized by the possession of a monopoly; the acquisition class, whose common bond is its desire to do business in the various sectors of commerce, industry or agriculture; and finally the social class, which is defined primarily by its rank in the social hierarchy (working class, middle classes, etc.). There will be status (*Stand*) when an associative relationship of individuals is based on privileges involving a positive or negative difference from the standpoint of respect and social prestige. While status constitutes at least an amorphous community, the class is never a community.

Weber's most fully worked out typology is certainly that of cities. Sociologically, the city is hard to define. Neither the quantitative criterion (large area where houses are clustered, but lacking vicinage), nor the qualitative criterion (area whose inhabitants engage in commercial, artisanal or industrial rather than in agricultural activities) is really adequate. Definitions will vary according as sociology takes the political, the economic or some other aspect as a starting point.

Generally speaking, however, the combination of political and economic aspects makes it possible to describe these realities sociologically. From a political and administrative standpoint, the city may be said to have been constituted through the presence of a prince or a garrison, or because it was a fortress; economically, its chief feature was the regular rather than sporadic market if offered. And the inhabitants of these areas had a specific status, that of bourgeois. Where the political factor predominated, we may distinguish various types: the princely city, the plebeian city (controlled by a people with revolutionary leanings), or the patrician city (of which Venice, among many others, is a characteristic type); or, taking the economic structure as the basis, we may distinguish other types: the city which is a consumption unit (such as health resorts), the city which is a production unit (industrial cities), and the commercial city (of the Hanseatic or some other type). Maritime-type cities may also be distinguished from inland-type cities. This typology is in reality dependent on the nature of the sociological investigation undertaken, and may vary with the necessities of the study.

On the more general level of the historical development of economic action, we can elaborate other economic types. While variations in Weber's thinking may be noted depending on whether we refer to his *General Economic History*, his *Wirtschaft und Gesellschaft*, or other works or articles, it is nevertheless possible to trace a general pattern in his typology, even if he rejected any systematic classification.

Without pronouncing on the truly primary character of the household community, Weber nevertheless regarded it as a most characteristic type in the historical development of economic action. He particularly stressed the sexual element in explaining the various household economic systems—based on promiscuity, patriarchy, matriarchy, etc.—while at the same time recognizing the religious and political factors. Historically, the types of system varied according to peoples, from the narrow group which, like the Slavic *Zadruga*, comprised father, mother and children, to the wider forms embracing some of the kin and servants. Obviously the economic role of the family would vary according to its structure. The importance of marriage, Weber felt, may not have been sufficiently emphasized; its whole significance lies in its contrast with irregular, ephemeral and irrational sexual relationships; it introduced a rationality into society whose repercussions have been expressed in habitat, property, inheritance, or, again, in internal solidarity in the form of a family communism. The economic role of the family may be illustrated by an example with which we are fairly familiar, that of the autarchy of the Greek *oikos*.

The second type of community is that of vicinage, to be found principally in regions of agrarian economy. It was based essentially on regular mutual assistance in work, on solidarity in case of trouble, or, again, on common defense against external threat. This type of relationship did not necessarily imply equality. On the other hand, while it constituted a fairly amorphous community, it could adopt the form of a closed or open relationship according to circumstances. A community based on vicinage was generally at the origin of the formation of villages, which subsequently assumed a political character—the commune—or a religious one— the parish.

Another type of historical community is that of the *Sippe* (a term hard to translate; perhaps the word "clan" would serve). It constituted a discontinuous, essentially extra-household associative relationship; its members sometimes did not know one another personally, and their relationships might not lead to any genuine action, but merely to tolerance or abstention from action. Its main feature was that it gave rise to ways and customs based on fidelity to certain forms of living.

The Greek *oikos* type was succeeded by various types of economic organization. In the rural areas, manorial properties were constituted by a military—and usually also administrative—chief (Roman *patronus*, Merovingian *senior*) with the ability to protect the population of the surrounding area in time of war, invasion, raids, etc. This type gave rise to the feudal system. Parallel with it there emerged the type of the demesne or landed property, usually involving, at least at first, forced labor, performed either by slaves or by serfs. Weber regarded this as one of the origins of agrarian capitalism, going back to Carthaginian and Roman times. It developed the most varied structures, according to the country concerned, in Italy, Spain, England, France, Germany and Russia, up to its most recent forms in the southern states of the United States, or the South American pampas, not to mention the plantations of the colonial era.

The cities generally produced other types of economy, based on the processing of raw materials: on the one hand, the first forms of an industrial economy (mining, manufacture), and on the other craft corporations and merchants guilds. In all these forms a common tendency was apparent, namely, the creation of monopolies.

The type to which Weber gave most attention was capitalism.

> Capitalism is present wherever the industrial provision for the needs of a human group is carried out by the method of enterprise, irrespective of what need is involved. More specifically, a rational capitalistic establishment is one with capital accounting, that is, an establishment which determines its income-yielding power by calculation according to the methods of modern bookkeeping and the striking of a balance. The device of the balance was first insisted upon by the Dutch theorist Simon Stevin in the year 1698. It goes without saying that an individual economy may be conducted along capitalistic lines to the most widely varying extent; parts of the economic provision may be organized capitalistically and other parts on the handicraft or the manorial pattern.[8]

Capitalism existed in embryonic or other forms in the ancient East as in the ancient West. What we have to understand first and foremost is modern capitalism as we have known it for some three centuries past.

The most general presupposition of modern capitalism is that rational calculation is the norm of all large production enterprises concerned with the supply of everyday wants. This rationality presupposes, in its turn: (*a*) the appropriation of all the material resources (terrain, plant, machines, tools, etc.) as the undisputed property of private and autonomous production enterprises; (*b*) a free market, instead of the irrational restriction of the flow of trade; (*c*) a rational technique, giving rise both to prevision and to considerable mechanization, both in the area of production and in that of the distribution of goods; (*d*) a rational legislation, which can be clearly evaluated; (*e*) freedom of labor, in the sense that individuals who sell their abilities do so not merely out of legal obligation but for economic reasons; (*f*) the commercialization of the economy, including the opportunity for all those who so desire to participate in the enterprise as shareholders. Without entering into details which pertain to history rather than sociology, we should note that Weber insisted on the dual nature of joint stock companies, in that they facilitate the financing of an enterprise and that they play an anticipatory role which promotes speculation. The joint stock company should not be regarded as a cause of capitalism, however, but rather as a consequence.

Capitalism was really a consequence of the growing rationalization of Western civilization from Greek times. This rationalization reached one of its summits in medieval monasticism. "In that epoch," Weber wrote, "the monk is the first human being who lives rationally, who works methodically and by rational means toward a goal, namely, the future life . . . The economic life of the monastic communities was also rational."[9]

One of the foundations of modern rationalization was asceticism. With the Reformation, asceticism became secularized, while everyday life was rationalized, in the sense in which Sebastian Franck could say, "You think you have escaped from the monastery, but everyone must now be a monk throughout his life."[10] We shall come back to the importance of asceticism in connection with the sociology of religion, in analyzing how a particular economic ethos, together with rational conviction, could prepare the ground for the acceptance of capitalism.

Weber denied that the population increase of the eighteenth century was the determining cause of capitalism, since an identical increase in China at the same period served to impede capitalism rather than promote it. He also disputed Sombart's theory, in *Der moderne Kapitalismus*, that the cause was the influx of precious metals; just as he disputed the role which Sombart ascribed to the Jews. While it was true, Weber maintained, that the Jews had fostered existing capitalistic enterprise, they had not created that economic form, since their particular ethics were not compatible with the capitalistic structure. The Jews, he said, were "virtuosos" of commerce but their activity in this area was rather a "capitalism of pariahs" in reflection of the situation which had been theirs during the Middle Ages. At the same time, Judaism had indirectly contributed to the development of capitalism, by bequeathing to Christianity its hostility to magic, which everywhere else had stereotyped technique and economic action. This hostility to magic, and also the fact that, in contrast to the Oriental religions, Christianity was a plebeian religion, led to the process of disenchantment of the world which became ever more widespread with the movement of secularization at the close of the Middle Ages.

In his *Wirtschaft und Gesellschaft*, Weber pointed to a more immediately economic origin of capitalism. With the decline of the corporations, the need to separate "household" from "trade" became increasingly apparent. This separation, which originally was purely spatial in purpose, subsequently assumed a juridical character and encouraged the development of specialization. This development, in any event, was peculiar to Western civilization, and should therefore be classified among the various phenomena which qualitatively characterize the uniqueness of modern capitalism. Thus capitalism cannot be said to have had a single cause; it had several. In particular, a thorough analysis will take account of the position of the Italian cities from the time of the Renaissance, since their banking system was sufficiently developed for each bourgeois to be able to open his personal account. What seems to matter, therefore, is not so much the more general utilization of currency than before, but the fact that it was rationally used.

The complexity of the causes of capitalism, as well as that of the factors which constantly intervened in the course of its historical development, sufficiently indicate that there is no single form of capitalism which can be reduced to a definition or a slogan. It is a basic movement in world history which must be approached otherwise than merely aggressively. For this reason, and in order to give an at least formal unity to this vast economic development, so varied according to countries and eras, Weber usually preferred to refer to the "spirit" of capitalism. For the same reason, he counseled the sociologist to elaborate as many ideal types of the phenomenon as possible, in order to avoid hasty generalizations or the pitfalls of abstraction, and to make it clear in every case, according to the needs of the investigation, to which form of capitalism he was referring. The same counsels applied to the analysis of socialism.

[B]

THE SOCIOLOGY OF RELIGION

1. The area of the sociology of religion

Sociology is not required to study the essence of the religious phenomenon, but only the behavior to which religion gives rise because it is based on particular experiences and specific conceptions and goals. Thus it is the meaningful behavior of the religious being which the sociologist must study. This does not involve speculating on the respective merits of dogmas or competing theologies or philosophies, nor even on the legitimacy of belief in the hereafter; it does involve studying religious behavior as a human activity in this world (*diesseitig*), meaningfully oriented according to ordinary ends. Nor is there any question of adopting a positivist approach, which is generally based on the negation of or contempt for religion; the sociologist must try to understand the influence of religious behavior on other activities—ethical, economic, political or artistic—and to identify the conflicts which may arise from the heterogeneity of the values which each of them claims to serve.

Thus defined, sociological studies of religion become at the same time sociological studies of economics or politics, and particularly of morals. Although Weber began his sociological career by reflecting on economics, it would seem, judging by his works as we know them, that the sociology of religion was central to his studies in his later years.

What Weber studied primarily was the influence of religious behavior on ethics and economics, and secondarily on politics and education. Religious or magical activity is at least relatively rational, not so much in regard to the relationship of means to ends, as in the sense of reliance on the general rules of experience. That is why there is no reason to exclude it from the series of regular goal-oriented activities.

There is nevertheless an important distinction to be made between the religion of conviction oriented to salvation, which is generally hostile, in some respect, to the world, and the purely ritual or legalistic religion which accepts the world and seeks to adapt itself to it. The most characteristic type of the latter is Chinese Confucianism and, in some ways too, Talmudic Judaism, although the latter possesses an inner morality of the community and another, laxer one directed toward the outside world. These are religions of order and stereotyped conventions; the law is "sacred," although it sometimes rests on extraordinarily subtle reasoning. Adaptation to the world may lead to a purely bureaucratic form of morality, of which Confucianism is the most striking example, since it comes ultimately to forget all transcendency. The force of tradition is such that it confines moral conduct to a series of purely practical precepts and rules. The problem of the meaning of the world becomes secondary, and pragmatism prevents all asceticism as well as all mysticism. Some salvation religions follow a similar pattern when they descend to the level of a mere religiosity of humanist intellectuals, or when they lose all prophetic and charismatic character, under the guidance of priests

who have become functionaries of a hierocratic authority, of the established order and of a code of ethics
which conforms to that order.

The salvation religions are at the service not of a
"sacred law" but of sacred conviction. Hence, on the
ethical level, they very often act in a revolutionary
manner by reason of the element of prophecy and
charisma which sustains them. The manner of life has
no significance in its own right, but solely in terms of
the meaning which religion confers on the world. Beings who live this type of religion of faith usually do
not enjoy inner repose, because they are constantly in
the grip of inner tensions. These beliefs can give rise to
simple salvation religions such as Buddhism, or they
can be soteriological, when they preach belief in a
savior.

In the former case, the influence on moral behavior
depends on the works which are regarded as susceptible of contributing to salvation. They may consist of
(*a*) purely ritual acts or ceremonies, capable of raising
the being possessing the personal charisma to mysticism; the importance attached in this case to the sacred
causes ritualism to turn its back on rational action; (*b*)
social works, prompted for example by love of others;
in certain circumstances, they may lead to an ethical
systematization of "good works"; (*c*) individual perfection, according to a method of salvation which may
lead to a form of personal deification of the believer, in
so far as he believes himself capable, through ecstasy,
euphoria or orgy, of incarnating the suprasensible
being.

These are extreme cases growing out of the desire
of the religious soul to "possess" the divine. In general,

a religious man will seek merely to be "God's instrument," or "filled" with God, and this will prompt him to despise what is not divine, and consequently the ordinary things of life, to the extent that they separate him from the deity or stand in the way of the deity's approach. The systematization and rationalization of salvation thus lead to a rigorous separation between ordinary life and extraordinary religious life. The great problem, in this case, is to resist the pull of the mundane and find a way of remaining in a permanent state of grace.

The influence of such beliefs on moral conduct clearly becomes very great, according as one does or does not consider salvation assured. The sense of certainty very often leads to a distinct religious designation; in some cases, it will produce "virtuoso ethics" (*Virtuosenethik*), such as those of the Buddhist monk, the Pharisee, the Moslem of Omar's day, the Protestant ascetic or a man like St. Francis, with his unworldly goodness.

The same features are to be found, of course, in the soteriological religions, but belief in a savior adds a distinctive feature. The savior declares himself to be the supra-terrestrial intermediary between the human and the divine, usually identifying himself with the divinity. Here the phenomenon of mystery assumes its fullest significance, for the savior is the dispenser of grace. And faith, rather than merely the concept of the sacred, becomes central; it no longer rests on sacred learning or *gnosis*, but on an authentic *pistis*, a confidence in the revelation of the savior and in his promises. Whatever the nature of the faith, whether it is based on tradition, a text or dogmas, it will always consist in the belief in the meaning which the believer inwardly attaches to life and to the world in the light of an accepted knowledge, in accordance with which he directs his conduct. We shall return to these points later.

Weber focused his main attention on the problem of the tension between religion and other activities; he dealt with it at length in his *Wirtschaft und Gesellschaft*, and especially in his essay "Religious Rejections of the World."[11] Such tensions are rarely found in purely ethical religions of adaptation, but they become acute in those of conviction, based on the idea of salvation.

Because of the prophetic character of the latter type of religion, the first aspect of this tension must necessarily be conflict with existing communities. Thus Jesus declares, for example, that whosoever is not capable of leaving father, mother and family to follow him cannot become his disciple. A salvation religion nearly always assumes the character of a social revolution, in so far as it aspires to a new community founded on a principle, or on new standards. Thus Christ taught his disciples a universal charity which abolishes the dualism of internal and external ethical codes, whatever the group concerned. In the light of charity, one's neighbor is every human being as such. This unworldly communism of love embraces not only the suffering and unfortunate, but also enemies. The revolutionary character of this precept is indisputable, and its unconditional character threatens to call in question all social structures whose basis is local or regional.

The second aspect of this tension is conflict with the economic factor. This has taken various forms: opposition to interest and usury, encouragement of alms-giving and of a style of living reduced to the strict minimum of need, hostility to commerce which cannot "be pleasing to God"; but especially there is a latent opposition between the unworldly principle of love and the modern rationalization of economic life based on business undertakings. For modern economic life is a rivalry of interests, and without the conflict represented by the market, rational calculation is not possible. Indeed, the very concept of capitalism may be said to conflict with the contemplative and ascetical tendencies of salvation religions, inasmuch as pursuit of profit deflects the religious being from the interior life. Even so pragmatic a religion as Confucianism was an obstacle to the development of rational capitalism. While religions have generally reached an accommodation with economic forces—an institutionalized Church inevitably becomes a force of this kind itself—only Puritan ethics succeeded in overcoming the contradictions in any consistent fashion, by abandoning the universalist principle of love and turning work itself into a service of God.

The tensions with the political factor are just as pronounced, since politics challenges the fraternity preached by very many religions. Both Buddhism and Christianity preach non-resistance to evil; and general experience, for its part, teaches that violence breeds violence and accompanies even the noblest movements of reform and revolution, so that the struggle for justice ultimately leads not to the establishment of greater justice, but to the acquisition of greater power. For the success of force depends, whether we like it or not, on the balance of power and not on the ethical value of right. Hence genuinely mystical religiosity is nearly always apolitical if not antipolitical.

Here again, ambiguities and compromise often reinforce tensions, not only because religions sometimes become in some respects political powers, but especially because their relationship with the state is difficult to define clearly. Even in the early days of Christianity, for example, extremely diverse attitudes prevailed, from rejection of the Roman Empire as the handiwork of antichrist or indifference to practical political realities to a positive assessment of the concept of authority. Such contradictions have been equally apparent in times of national wars, when the clergies of the various belligerent countries have called upon the same God to protect the respective warring armies. History shows us yet other such problems, with the Moslem "holy war," the crusades, and the wars of religion following the Reformation. Doctrinally, Luther's position differed from Calvin's, for while the former rejected the idea of war in defense of faith, the latter was prepared to countenance recourse to violence to defend the faith against a tyrant. But in any event, the theoretical universalism of a salvation religion is hard to reconcile with the particularism of political action.

Another form of tension is that arising out of the relationship of religion to art. Magical religiosity is generally closely related to esthetic phenomena such as dancing, singing, music, idols—in brief, whatever can serve to generate ecstasy, exorcism or orgy. Other religions also attach great importance to art in the most varied forms: rites, ceremonies, services, churches built on certain architectural principles, music, statues, vestments, etc. It might therefore be conceded that a basic affinity exists between religion and art.

The nature of the problem changed, however, with the emergence of the notion of art for art's sake, as a rationalized and intellectualized civilization became aware of the specificity of art as a human activity. Art now became suspect to religion, especially with the appearance of rigorist sects which regarded purely external esthetic phenomena as pertaining to the sphere of idolatry. This hostility was reflected in the distinction made between meaning and form, the latter being regarded as a yielding to the accidental and artificial at the expense of the profound reality expressed by the religious act. The tension was further aggravated when art became an autonomous and self-conscious phenomenon and sought to create values of its own which might bring salvation to the individual in the form of an interior liberation; art was now deemed a "divinization of the creature," a deceitful and even blasphemous rival power, usurping the prerogatives of religion.

It should nevertheless be added that this anti-esthetic position is more characteristic of aristocratic religions, for mass religions usually tend to be sensitive to the esthetics of ceremony, services, rites and other artistic media. The problem is one of special concern to Christianity, which has always claimed to be a religion of the masses.

Weber gave a prominent part in his sociological expositions to sexuality, as one of the most irrational forces in life. It is therefore not at all surprising that he should have regarded it as a fifth cause of tension with religion. At the level of magic, a profound affinity is observable between the two domains. Sexuality is at the origin of many extremely important symbolical phenomena, of certain rites (phallic, bacchic and others), and of ecstasies and orgies, including prostitution within the precincts of temples and other sacred shrines. And there have been gods and goddesses of love. Moreover, mystical love of the creator may sometimes be a sublimation of sexuality. Religious asceticism, by contrast, is fundamentally hostile to eroticism and makes the renunciation of sexual relations a condition of self-control. Hence many religions have sought to regulate marriage as strictly as possible. Catholicism, incidentally, is by no means alone in deprecating sexuality, for instance by prescribing clerical celibacy; the renunciation of sexual relations is just as characteristic of Buddhism, and even Confucianism condemns sexual irregularities. From a sociological standpoint, all these problems clearly affect the always controverted position of woman in society.

The final tension which Weber analyzed relates to learning. There again, we find that at certain periods of history priests have been the agents and even the initiators of culture, either because they were the element capable of reading and writing which the political leaders needed, or because they held a kind of pedagogical monopoly. Moreover, in proportion as a religion abandons its magical and mystical aspects and becomes a "doctrine," it tends to develop as a theology or a system of apologetics. But with the development of the positive sciences, based on mathematics, and especially with that of an independent philosophy, a radical change set in. Religion could make shift with metaphysics; it was much harder to find an area of agreement with disciplines which strip the world of all enchantment, not only because such disciplines are usually indifferent to the problem of meaning, but also because they give rise to a purely mechanical technique and to a rational approach to problems, so that religion is increasingly relegated to the irrational or antirational forces which require a "sacrifice of the intellect." The religions have sought to retort that the knowledge peculiar to them is on a different level from that of purely scientific knowledge, and that they are based on intuition or charismatic illumination more than on argument.

The problem of theodicy, however, assumes a different character with the development of culture in the direction of human progress and perfectibility. The central problem ceases to be that of suffering and evil, and centers instead on the imperfection of a world doomed to sin. This has led some religions to launch a veritable assault on culture and in the process to challenge some of the noblest human values. It is a fact that, with the emergence—since the eighteenth century —of world views which seek to interpret historical development, religion has lost its monopoly on the interpretation of the ultimate "meaning" of existence.

Without going into details, we should note that Weber was much preoccupied with the problem of theodicy; in addition to the numerous passages in other works in which he raised the question, he devoted a special chapter to it in his *Sociology of Religion*.[12] He believed that the question of theodicy had become central to the monotheistic religions; it is at the root of most messianic eschatologies, of notions concerning rewards and punishments in the hereafter, of dualist theories according to which good and evil remain in conflict until the definitive triumph of good at some undetermined time, and also of belief in predestination.

2. *Concepts and their evolution*

Weber approached the sociology of religion through the concept of the divine, which he felt was more fundamental than that of the divinity. There are magical or animist religions which do not recognize God, but only benevolent and maleficent spirits—generally material yet invisible beings, impersonal and yet possessing an efficacious will which expresses itself through the course of events. Major salvation religions, such as Buddhism, are similarly unaware of the idea of a divinity. As for gods, they may be nameless and no more, according to Usener's dictum, than "gods of the moment"; that is, man believes in their intervention at the time of a specific event, but may forget them later unless some happening of the same kind recalls them to mind. Gods may have a universal significance or be merely local or special divinities, peculiar to a city. A religion may also be polytheistic or monotheistic. In the former case, the pantheon may be populated by an undetermined number of gods, sometimes subject to a superior being which, for its part, is not necessarily the most effectual or the most important in men's belief. Gods may be creators or themselves subject to the cosmic order. According to Weber, there are only two strictly monotheistic religions, Judaism and Islam. For lack of space, we shall not enter into his analysis of the various types of gods in any detail.

What is important for the sociology of religion is man's religious activity, or conduct, in relation to supernatural forces. Since these forces are outside the field of normal observation, man has had to create symbols in order to enter into contact with them, to portray them to himself and to understand their action. For if one believes that behind the things of everyday are hidden forces which do not reveal themselves directly, means must be found to give them significance; those means are symbols. And since the divinity manifests itself only indirectly, symbols become the only means of communicating with it, reality being wanting in this respect. In other words, symbol is the instrument of a wordless language which enables men to understand the will of beings who do not speak. It should not be forgotten, in that connection, that the first paper currency served as a symbolical method of payment to the dead, not to the living. It is therefore understandable that analogy, and especially parable, should be the basic expression of religious language.

Just as important for the analysis of religious behavior is the "competence" attributed to the divinity, or divinities, for quite astonishing specializations are observable in this area. (The same applies to the saints.) The classic example is that of the Hindu pantheon. Brahma, or the "lord of prayer," was as it were monopolized by the Brahmans, with the result that, thanks to the priests, he came to monopolize all supernatural efficacy and to become, if not the sole god, then at least the highest and most important one. On the basis of this specialization and apportionment of capacities, the believer each time addresses himself to a different god, whom he hopes to be able to influence more easily. What is necessary, therefore, is each time to find the most appropriate charismatic means, and especially a means more powerful than the god in question, since the object is to move his will in the direction of the believer's desires. In this sense, "divine service" (*Gottesdienst*) often becomes an "obligation imposed on God" (*Gotteszwang*).

Magical elements nearly always survive in prayer and sacrifice, particularly in ordinary practice. According to some conceptions, prayer must be accompanied by gifts in order to please God and therefore to influence him more effectively. Like the minister of supernatural powers (sorcerer or priest), God appears to have every interest in confirming his power, save that the priest can shift responsibility for failure onto the divinity; on the other hand, his prestige will ultimately decline along with the divinity's.

These, of course, are anthropomorphic religious conceptions; but because they hold currency at any time, they are essential to a sociology of religion. And while Weber was thinking mainly of the irrational religions of the past, some of his examples show that he was also taking account of practices current, perhaps, in every age.

Specialization introduced a qualitative differentiation among the gods, which had various repercussions on the manner of life of believers. Some gods, for instance, acquired a moral character denied to others. Let us consider the introduction of law. Neither Varuna in India, nor Maat in Egypt, nor Dike or Themis in Greece and Italy were originally major gods in the pantheon. They became patron divinities of law not because they were believed to possess any special moral virtues, but because they were the patrons of a specific activity which assumed increasing importance during periods of peace, such periods being character- ized by a more rational economy and a more balanced regulation of men's relations with one another. They became major gods because man had become more clearly aware of the meaning of certain obligations which had assumed the character of ethical and juridi- cal duties. Any morality presupposes an order and standards, and the increasing aspiration toward this order conferred on these gods an importance which they had lacked at first.

The need for order also explains the concept of the taboo. In his brief analysis of this concept, Weber ig- nored its religious significance as something sacred, and considered only its moral and indeed pragmatic features. Essentially, he saw the taboo as reflecting a process of rationalization on the economic and social level, since the basic purpose of the prohibition was the protection of the forest and hunting grounds, or health, or the family and other institutions. In a word, the taboo in his view was a secondary phenomenon from a religious standpoint, its purpose being mainly eco- nomic, pedagogical and pragmatic. Similarly, Weber saw in totemism a symbol of fraternity, and denied it the status of a universal principle explaining all religion and all association; in so doing, he was disputing a theory much in vogue among the sociologists of his day.

With the rationalization of beliefs, the idea of the possibility of constraining God declined, to be super- seded by adoration of the divinity through worship. The result was a greater emphasis on the ethical character of religion, since actions contrary to the pre-scribed norms came to be regarded as infringements of the divine will. Whence the idea of sin, which had been virtually without importance in the magical and irrational religions (the concept was alien to the Greeks and Romans, as it was to Confucius).

The concept of sin brought with it a major change: the failure of prayer and sacrifice could no longer be imputed to God's impotence, but to the wrongful actions of men which anger God and call down his wrath. The prophets of Israel ceaselessly un-covered yet further sins committed by the Jews, point-ing to them to explain why God had abandoned his people. The idea of moral culpability awakened men's consciences and contributed to a different apportion-ment of good and evil, of the important and the second-ary, at the same time opening men's eyes to the tragic aspects of life. It was in this context that a religion of conviction—and not merely of ceremony—as well as a salvation religion could come into being.

With religions of conviction come disciples, com-panions and apostles, attached to the cause of the prophet or savior, in contrast to the impersonal associa-tion produced by the older religions. At the same time, religious activity assumes a new character: it becomes missionary, that is, its object is no longer to form a sporadic association but rather a permanent one in the form of a community, or later of a parish. The aim of such communities is to inject the message, or new promise, into the life of every day, and thus to ensure the perpetuation of grace, ultimately through economic means.

Thus a new associative relationship developed

alongside the charismatic promoters of the faith—that of the laity. It was the laity which produced a communal religious sentiment and, in so far as that sentiment gave rise to action, or resulted in active participation, it led to the formation of permanent associations. The contours of these communities were originally fairly fluid, both in the East and in Islam, and even in the medieval Church, and only much later did they establish themselves as territorially circumscribed groups, under the jurisdiction of a priest. With the emergence and proliferation of sects, these groups became closed and specifically local associations. However, communal religious sentiment led to a diversity of relationships between clergy and laity, the minister finding himself obliged to compromise with the faithful, according as the community tended more to traditionalism or to reform or sometimes, even, to prophecy. Generally speaking, the establishment of religious communities led to the bureaucratization of religion, which became in part an administrative affair with its own regulations and procedures.

Once a new religion takes hold, the clergy's task is to promote a better understanding of the new doctrine, to assert it as against rival prophecies and to define the respective spheres of the sacred and the profane. This development generally leads to the elaboration of canonical writings and the affirmation of dogmas. Here we have to discuss the distinction which we encountered earlier between sacred knowledge (*heiliges Wissen*) and faith (*Glaube*). Sacred lore generally means a knowledge of sacred texts and canonical writings, as well as of dogmas, the former containing the revelation and sacred traditions, the latter defining the interpretation of the writings as understood by the priests or hierarchy. Sacred lore may also have esoteric and exoteric aspects. Whence, in the former case, the need for a charismatic training with its attendant novitiates, trials, dignities and degrees in ordination or consecration; the result is generally a very marked separation between clergy and laity. In the latter case, religion remains essentially based on sacred texts, which serve as the foundation of the education of both priests and laity. This may lead to a decline in the charismatic aspect, and a pedagogy founded on sacred texts may eventually develop into an education of a purely literary and scholarly character.

In addition to the interpretation of texts and the duty of combatting rival doctrines, the clergy has also to prevent the laity from falling into indifference. In our day, this duty generally takes the form of preaching and pastorate (*Seelsorge*). Preaching is collective instruction on religious and moral themes. It is peculiar to prophecy and the revealed religions; in other contexts it is mere parody. It assumes more importance in proportion as magical elements lose theirs; this is particularly apparent in Protestantism, where the emphasis is on the word. The pastorate is the individual care of souls, and as such is also a product of the revealed religions. It consists in practical counselling in case of doubt concerning duties, in comforting and giving spiritual aid. Preaching is most effective in periods of prophetic agitation, and its efficacy declines when it becomes an expression of everyday religious life. The pastorate, on the other hand, is the priest's most effective means in ordinary times, and its scope broadens as religion becomes more ethical in character. Both elements, however, tend to clash with lay rationalism in consequence of the decline in the charismatic element.

Faith, too, is a lore, but of a very particular type and peculiar essentially to the soteriological religions. Theoretically, it has nothing to do with submission to practical norms, but is rather an acceptance of revealed truths and dogmas. This means that it is not in the nature of demonstrable or purely rational knowledge. In addition, it confers a power on the believer, in the sense of the dictum about faith moving mountains. With increasing intellectualization, it tends to lose its force and to become, in part, a theological faith.

Essentially, however, faith is something different from mere comprehension or acceptance of the truth of theological dogmas; it has a personal note which makes it more than a form of learning—a confidence in God's promises in the sense of the fullness of faith shown by Abraham. We find the same note in St. Paul's writings, although his Epistle to the Romans, for instance, has constantly given rise to differing interpretations. To some degree, faith may be characterized in the well-known phrase, *credo non quod, sed quia absurdum est,* in that it implies unconditional abandonment to the providence and goodness of God.

3. *Religious types*

As everywhere else, Weber sought to isolate the characteristic types of religious activity. First, that of the sorcerer, who remains a typical figure even in our own day. However, Weber did not study the sorcerer in his own right, but in comparison with the priest. We shall follow the same course.

There are various ways of distinguishing priest from sorcerer. The latter acts on demons by magical means, while the former is by vocation the minister of a cult intended to honor the divinity. This criterion is a relative one, however, for in some religions the priesthood includes magical elements. We might also distinguish them by saying that the priest is a functionary of a permanent, regularly constituted undertaking, whereas the sorcerer's activity is discontinuous, since it is exercised for individuals in individual circumstances. Or again, we might say that the priest is a functionary of an associative group—whatever the structures—comprising members and an administration, whereas the sorcerer exercises his profession freely. These distinctions remain tentative, and are subject to many variations when transposed to the level of reality.

Finally, we might distinguish them by saying that the priest is an intellectually qualified person in the service of a specific body of knowledge and of a conceptually elaborated doctrine. There are, of course, very learned sorcerers, and priests with very little learning, but this criterion seems more satisfactory than the preceding ones, although it does not cover all categories of priests.

Taking the last criterion as our starting point, while retaining whatever is valid in the others, it is possible to establish a sociologically adequate differentiation. For while the sorcerer's knowledge is empirical in character, and relates to irrational means, the priest's education is based on a rational discipline, on a rational system of religious thought and on a systematized ethical teaching.

This distinction has a bearing on religious activities. The priest is the minister of a cult practised by specific persons, having its own rules and assembling its members at stated intervals and in specific places. There is no priesthood without a cult, although there may be cults without a specialized clergy. However, in cults without priests or religions without worship—such as those in which the sorcerer holds sway—one element is generally lacking, namely, a rationalized metaphysics and a specifically religious ethics. Moreover, where there is no organized clergy, there is no rationalized religious life either.

The third figure is that of the prophet. By "prophet," Weber means the absolutely personal bearer of a charisma who in virtue of his mission announces a religious doctrine or a divine command. It is essentially immaterial whether he announces an ancient revelation, or one regarded as ancient, in a new manner, or delivers an entirely new message; he may be the founder of a religion or a reformer. Nor is it conceptually necessary that his action should give rise to a new community or that his disciples should be personally attached to him, or to his teaching alone. The determining factor is his personal vocation.

In this, he differs, first of all, from the priest. The priest is at the service of a sacred tradition; the prophet is the man with a personal revelation, who claims authority in virtue of a new law. It is seldom, moreover, that the prophet arises from the ranks of the priesthood; he is usually a layman. Further, while the priest carries out responsibility entrusted to him by the associative salvation enterprise to which he belongs, the prophet acts in a purely charismatic fashion, like the sorcerer, in virtue of a personal gift. The prophet differs from the sorcerer, however, in that he announces a revelation whose content does not consist of magical practices but of a doctrine or an obligation. The sorcerer may of course use oracles and divination, and the prophet may resort to this or that magical practice to impose his authority, but there is one feature that is absolutely fundamental: the prophet promotes his idea for its own sake, and never against remuneration of any kind. His activity is wholly gratuitous.

Depending on circumstances, the prophet may assume the character of a law-giver or simply that of a teacher of doctrine (*Lehrer*). In the former case, his action is intended to influence social relations through the creation of a new kind of law. He may even usurp political authority, in the manner of a tyrant, to establish a new system, as did Mohammed. In the latter case, he is principally the promoter of a new way of life or a new code of ethics, but not in the manner of the founder of a new philosophical school, for he remains the herald of a truth of salvation by virtue of a revelation. From this point of view, Hindu reformers like Shankara or Ramanuja, or European reformers like Luther, Calvin, Zwingli or Wesley, were not really prophets, since they did not speak in the name of a new revelation nor even on the strength of a special commission from God, in contrast to the Jewish prophets or the founder of the Mormon Church. We may also distinguish between ethical prophecy (Zoroaster) and exemplary prophecy (Buddha), depending on whether the prophet merely urges others to live a new life or offers himself as an exemplary figure. Finally, prophecy may degenerate to the type of the mystagogue.

Religious activity may also lead to typical virtuoso phenomena: that of asceticism and that of mysticism. Asceticism is an ethical and religious activity accompanied by the consciousness that God directs this activity, so that the individual feels himself to be the instrument of the divine will. Weber recognized that the term might have other meanings too, but he held to this one in his writings. Asceticism, further, may assume two forms. On the one hand, it takes the form of flight from the world, cutting all ties with family and society, and renunciation of all personal possessions and all political, artistic and erotic interests, so that the individual concerned may be at the service of God alone. This Weber calls an asceticism which renounces the world (*weltablehrende*), on the pattern of the Catholic monk. The other form is the asceticism practised within the world (*innerweltliche*); like the Puritan, for example, the individual concerned will consider creatures too as instruments of God, and will seek to glorify God through his professional activity, by an exemplary family life, by the strictness of his conduct in every area of life, and by carrying out all his functions as duties willed by God. On this theory, provided one strictly observes the precepts of religion, success in business and professional ventures become signs of divine approval and even of election.

The mystic regards himself less as an instrument than as a vessel (*Gefäss*) of God. Here, there is no longer any question of engaging in worldly activities in conformity with the will of God, but of achieving a condition akin to the divine. In consequence, the individual will renounce the world and turn his back on its attractions. Only if all creature interests are silenced will God be able to speak to the soul. It is much more a matter of renouncing the world than of fleeing from it. The aim is to find rest in God. All this will obviously be accompanied by asceticism, but of a particular nature, since the individual must refrain from all activity, and ultimately from thought, in order to create an emptiness in himself concerning all that is worldy, and thus to achieve the mystical union which brings with it a new and different knowledge.

The more profound this knowledge is, the more incommunicable it becomes; yet it claims to be knowledge. It consists not in the discovery of new positive data but in the perception of the univocal significance of the world and, as such, it even claims to be what mystics call a "practical" knowledge. Pure contemplation appears to flee the world, but only the better to master it. Nevertheless, it must not be regarded as abandon to sheer fantasy, for it requires extraordinary concentration on truths other than those which are merely demonstrable.

Apart from the fact that the ascetic regards himself as an instrument and the mystic as a vessel of God, asceticism and mysticism are opposed in a variety of other ways which Weber subjected to analysis. To the ascetic (of the Puritan type), mystical contemplation is a form of indolence and self-indulgence, unproductive from a religious standpoint and to be condemned as idolatrous pleasure-seeking; instead of working for the glory of God and seeking to carry out his will, the mystic is concerned solely with his ecstasies. To the mystic, on the other hand, the ascetic who lives in the midst of the world dooms himself to useless tensions and conflicts and perhaps to compromises which separate him from God. While the mystic is never certain of his salvation, the ascetic is assured of his, so long as it is confirmed by success in business.

It may thus be said that the ascetic's view is circumscribed as far as the meaning of the world is concerned; while that meaning, on the contrary, is what preoccupies the mystic, although it cannot be comprehended by rational means, since it is situated beyond the realities of the senses. In point of fact, neither the ascetic nor the mystic really accept the world; for the former, it is merely the scene of a success for which the credit is not his, while for the latter worldly success has no bearing on salvation and may even become a temptation which deflects man from salvation. Finally, while the ethical demands which motivate the ascetic may lead him to prophecy and to a revolutionary overturning of social conditions, the mystic who takes the same road generally becomes a mystagogue or the exponent of a millenaristic doctrine of revolution.

Just as we may regret that, in connection with the analysis of religious concepts, Weber neglected to investigate so important a relationship as that of the sacred and the profane, so we many deplore that his typology contains only a few allusions—with a few scattered remarks in other works—to the typical figure of the religious reformer. We may understand why he should have shown little interest in the activity of men like St. Benedict, Bernard of Clairvaux or Ignatius of Loyola, but it is less understandable that he should not have attempted a conceptual and systematic characterization of figures such as Luther, Calvin or Wesley, with whose activity he was very familiar. His sociology of religion, it is true, remained unfinished, and therefore, perhaps, his typology too.

4. Attitudes of different social strata to the religious phenomenon

Weber constantly returned, in his analyses, to the problem of the laity; he even devoted a long chapter to the subject, in which he considered the attitude of the various social classes to the religious phenomenon.

Because the peasant is in what might be called immediate and constant touch with nature, he appears more susceptible to supernatural forms of a magical character. But the notion of the peasant as a pious man and well-pleasing to God is a quite recent one; that privilege was his only in one or two ancient patriarchal-type religions, or in Zoroastrianism. Buddhism, on the other hand, treats him with suspicion. For primitive Christianity, the rustic (*paganus*) was simply the heathen. Religion in general was an essentially urban affair.

A military caste is on principle hostile to religion, and concepts such as sin, salvation or humility tend to be alien to it. A real relationship between the military and religion came into being with the religions which proclaimed wars of faith, especially when the adherent of another confession or the unbeliever could be regarded as political enemies. This transformation may be credited principally to Islam. The concept of a holy war was not altogether unknown in ancient Greece, but it did not really gain acceptance until the advent of the salvation religions.

A bureaucratic caste, too, is generally indifferent to religion; this follows from its rationalism. Religion takes on importance for it only as an element of the social order and a subject of legal regulation. The pietism of the German—or rather, Prussian—functionaries of the last century does not invalidate this statement.

The attitude of the commercial class offers more contrasts. By its nature, their activity is quite far removed from preoccupations other than those relating to the things of this world. And it would seem that, the more powerful a commercial patriciate becomes, the more indifferent it should be to the problems of the hereafter. History, however, shows the contrary to be true. The bourgeois used, as a rule, to be the most pious of beings, and this piety was only accentuated with the emergence of capitalism and the increasing emphasis on ethics in religion. The most characteristic illustration of this is the correlation between the sectarian spirit and the commercial and industrial development of the past centuries, on the impetus not only of Calvinists or Puritans, but also of Baptists, Mennonites, Methodists, Quakers, Pietists, and so on. There is thus an affinity, as we shall see later, between the Protestant ethic and the spirit of capitalism. Similarly, the lower middle classes and the artisanate have generally been drawn to religion, perhaps in a not very orthodox fashion, for from these circles there arose the most diverse religious trends and currents of thought.

The lower social strata of slaves or workers have never, thus far, produced a specific religious sentiment, perhaps because the circumstances of their lives have prevented the constitution of communities. Much has been made of the importance of slaves in primitive Christianity, but judging by the facts and documents it would seem that the phenomenon has been deliberately exaggerated. The modern proletariat is characterized by almost total indifference to the religious phenomenon, if not by outright rejection of it. This is doubtless because religion has so frequently been used to legitimize the position of the upper classes. Thus, while the lower classes might have seen in the salvation religions a possibility of liberation, they have generally found in them only a pretext for resentment.

Finally, there is the intellectual element. The destiny of the religions has undoubtedly been strongly influenced over the centuries by the various developments in the intellectual sphere. So long as the intellectual caste was made up almost exclusively of priests and monks, who were concerned not only with theology and morals but also with metaphysics and science, intelligence and religious sentiment were closely linked. With the greater independence and increasing secularization of that element, it is only natural that the relationship should have taken the most various turns: either tolerance of all beliefs, on humanist lines, or indifference or even aggressiveness toward religion, as in the time of the Enlightenment. Two new phenomena still further complicated the situation: on the one hand the emergence of a proletarian intellectual class, and on the other the concern of many scientists and writers to interpret the meaning of the world quite independently, on the strength of their own reflections. We should note, however, that, while turning their backs on religion and even displaying sometimes violently anti-religious sentiments, intellectuals continue to be indirectly haunted by these problems, particularly by eschatological questions, very often under a revolutionary guise.

5. Protestantism and capitalism

Weber's best-known work on the sociology of religion remains his *Protestant Ethic and the Spirit of Capitalism.* We shall not go into the endless controversy, polemics, disputes and refutations to which this book has given rise in the past half-century, not so much in regard to the method used as in regard to certain explanations and conclusions; instead, we shall endeavor to present the theme of the work and Weber's intentions as clearly as possible. It would nevertheless seem useful to warn the reader against simplistic interpretations which imply that Weber regarded Protestantism as the sole cause of capitalism. His book is in part a reaction to the Marxist metaphysical assumption that all the events of civilization are reducible to a single cause, namely, the economic substratum. So one-sided a theory, Weber held, is incompatible with scientific research, which should not impose conclusions in advance of analysis.

Capitalism existed in embryo in the Babylonian, Roman, Chinese and Indian societies, but nowhere did these elements lead to the rationalization which characterizes the development of modern capitalism. That phenomenon is peculiar to Western society. The question is why these embryos developed into the modern form of capitalism only in the West, and nowhere else. An explanation in terms of the internal dynamics of economics is unable to account for this peculiarity. It is necessary to take account of the specific ethos of the first European capitalistic entrepreneurs, and realize that this was precisely what was absent in other civilizations.

To avoid misunderstandings, Weber specified that the causal relationship between Protestantism and capitalism must not be taken in the sense of a mechanical relationship. The Protestant ethos was one of the sources of the rationalization of life which helped to create what is known as the "spirit of capitalism." It was not the sole nor even a sufficient cause of capitalism. "The question of the motive forces in the expansion of modern capitalism," he wrote, "is not in the first instance a question of the origin of the capital . . . but, above all, of the development of the spirit of capitalism."[13] In other words, Protestantism was an element which, were it to be theoretically excluded as one of the categories of objective probability and adequate causality, would doubtless not have prevented the development of capitalism, but would have made it necessary to view that development differently.

R. Aron makes Weber's position extremely clear when he writes:

> Protestantism is not *the* cause, but *one* of the causes of capitalism, or rather, it is *one* of the causes of *certain aspects* of capitalism. . . . The starting-point of a search for causal relations is not a historical phenomenon such as capitalism, considered as a whole, but only certain unique features. In the case of capitalism, Weber selected the characteristics which seemed to

him peculiar to western capitalism. . . . It is evident that the cause of capitalism will differ according to the concept of capitalism which is employed.[14]

What, then, is the background to the ideas which contributed to forming the spirit of capitalism? For Weber, it lay in certain Protestant groups—Calvinists (mainly Dutch), Pietists, Methodists and Baptists—whose manner of life was characterized by an asceticism which has been called by that "highly ambiguous word," Puritanism.[15] While the theological dogmas of these various churches differed, their ethical maxims were more or less the same. What interested Weber was not the theoretical and official teachings contained in the manuals of moral theology—they might be important for other aspects of research—but the psychological motivations which had their source in religious beliefs and practices.

Weber elaborated those motivations in the form of an ideal type which should be as coherent as possible, without aspiring thereby to reflect historical reality. He sought, by means of this rational Utopia, to understand how these motivations operated in actuality to form the spirit of capitalism. Consequently, when Weber referred to Calvinism, he was thinking only of the ethics peculiar to certain Calvinist circles at the close of the seventeenth century, and certainly not of the doctrine taught by Calvin himself, who had lived some 150 years earlier. It is therefore quite useless to cite Calvin's own writings in refutation of Weber's thesis; to do so would be to stray outside the subject of his discussion.

The ideal type of the ethos peculiar to these

groups may be summed up as follows. Underlying everything is an interpretation of predestination; hence a religious conviction. Since God's decrees are as impenetrable as they are irrevocable, so that it is as impossible to lose grace once it has been bestowed as it is to gain it if it has been refused, the Protestant concerned is necessarily thrown back on an interior life, for it is in his own mind and not through the agency of another human being that he must understand the word of God and the sign of his election. This explains the rejection of the sacred and particularly of the sacraments which might help him to find, or to rediscover, grace. This conviction leads to the elimination of all magic, and to a disenchantment of the world through a growing rationalization.

But how is a man to know whether he belongs to the category of the elect? What is the sign of election? Because true faith may be recognized in the type of conduct which enables the Christian to increase God's glory, he believes that it is to be found in a personal life rigorously subject to the divine commandments and in a social achievement corresponding to the will of God. This social achievement includes success in one's professional activity. Thus the most effectual work manifests the glory of God and is a sign of election based on an ascetic way of life. In other words, business success strengthens a man's personal vocation and may be interpreted as a proof of election, since only the elect truly possesses a *fides efficax*. Salvation may therefore not be bought by good works or the sacraments; a man acquires certainty of salvation through the efficacy of his faith, which is attested by the success attendant upon his industry. Social achievement, in such circumstances, could only reinforce the strictness of his personal conduct and make of asceticism the method assuring the state of grace. Thus it is not by renouncing the world in the manner of the contemplative that a man puts his faith to the test, but by exercising a profession in the world.

Asceticism contributed to a rational molding of every aspect of life, which was seen as related to the will of God. Constant self-control through a systematic effort of will resulted in a rationalization of individual conduct, even to the conduct of business. Thus the Puritan became particularly adept in organizing undertakings and at the same time in rationalizing economic action. But since business success is generally reflected in growing affluence, which is contrary to the rigor of a life subject to God's commandments, was not the Protestant of this type guilty of inconsistency? Not at all. What is reprehensible is not the acquisition of wealth but repose in possession and the enjoyment of the things that money can buy, with the idleness, temptations of the flesh, and so on, which they bring in their train. A man must not waste time, therefore, since work contributes to glorifying God, and on the other hand he must take from his assets only what is absolutely necessary for his personal subsistence, for a life of sobriety and obedience to the divine law.

Thus the greatest possible productivity in work and the rejection of luxury led to a style of life which directly influenced the spirit of capitalism, by creating the right atmosphere for its development. The fact that present-day capitalists have broken with this kind of morality does not change the fact that Protestant asceticism, acting in the world, was in its origins hostile to the enjoyment of riches, while on the other hand freeing morality of its traditional strictures against acquisitiveness and desire for profit. In order that work might retain its character of manifesting God's glory, profits must be used for necessary and useful purposes, that is, put back to work in the form of investments. Thus the Puritan came to accumulate capital without cease.

Here, then, we have not the cause of capitalism, but one of the fundamental elements of the *spirit* of modern capitalism, based on a rational conduct and organization of business.

The Puritan ethos is merely one of the factors which help to explain the development of capitalism in consequence of the climate which it introduced into the economic sphere. To make clear his intentions in writing *The Protestant Ethic and the Spirit of Capitalism*, Weber wrote in conclusion:

> It is, of course, not my aim to substitute for a one-sided materialistic an equally one-sided spiritualistic casual interpretation of culture and of history. Each is equally possible, but each, if it does not serve as the preparation, but as the conclusion of an investigation, accomplishes equally little in the interest of historical truth.[16]

For a thorough understanding of the significance of this work, we have to bear in mind the theory of one-sidedness which Weber developed in connection with his explanation of the concept of the ideal type. There is no objection to a sociologist's viewing a question from a one-sided point of view, whether materialistic, spiritualistic or any other. Sometimes such a method is not only useful but also necessary. But it is scientifically valid only provided that the sociologist is aware of its relative nature and realizes that it has a purely methodological validity in the sphere of research. It is therefore no more than an approach to truth and not a full description of the real course of events.

There is another point which Weber sought to clarify in the light of this analysis: just as a dogmatism which subordinates religion or politics to economics, or the reverse, has no place in an empirical discipline, so the sociology of religion cannot confine itself to a strict explanation of the religious phenomenon in itself. Its object is to find out how religious conduct orients or influences in part other human activities, and is influenced by them. The same applies to the sociologies of economics, politics, law, etc. For in real life ethical conduct, for instance, is never a closed activity alongside political or economic behavior. Quite the reverse; one and the same behavior reflects correlations, reciprocities or conflicts with all types of activity. The analysis of the relations between Puritanism and capitalism is really only a thought-provoking illustration of that fundamental fact, for it shows how an attitude whose origins are religious determines a form of moral conduct which, in its turn, is practiced in the sphere of secular affairs.

6. *The economic ethics of the world religions*

Max Weber returned to the same theme in his monumental work on the economic ethics of the world religions. By world religions, he meant those which have succeeded in gathering a mass of believers around a central religious idea or morality: Confucianism, Hinduism, Buddhism, Christianity and Islam. He added Judaism to the list on account of its influence, although the Jewish people have always constituted a minority, and often a people of pariahs. This work on world religions also remained unfinished, for Weber did not have the opportunity to write the study on Islam; all he left on the subject were innumerable but formless notes.

We cannot of course go into this immense work in any detail; all we can do is to indicate its general lines. And in the first place, we have to make Weber's intention clear. His object was not to set out the moral theology of these religions, but to understand the psychological and pragmatic factors which serve as practical motivations in men's activities in general and in their economic activities in particular. He states in the introduction that an economic morality does not depend simply on the forms of economic organization, and on the other hand that it has never been conditioned solely by religion. This means that, among the factors which have determined such a morality, the manner in which religion has conditioned modes of living is one factor among many others. There is no question, therefore, of explaining economics solely in terms of morality or religion, nor religion solely in terms of economics or morality; the intention is to understand the interaction of the various elements of human conduct without reducing all factors to a single one, metaphysically regarded as determinant.

It follows that sociological research does not confine itself to the study of the religious phenomenon. In analyzing Chinese religious sentiment, Weber made a lengthy and detailed study of the material conditions of life—financial institutions as well as the urban phenomenon and the position of peasants or traders. He made a close study of the character of the feudal administration, of the structure of the state as well as of the relations between the central government and the local governors, the constitution of the army, and the nature of the bureaucracy. He reviewed the various reforms. At the same time, he always related the social structure which he was studying to the relevant religious conceptions, whether of a magical, charismatic or rational nature, especially in view of the importance which the scholars enjoyed in China. He insisted on the ritualistic and technical character of the humanism of these scholars; on their pacifist orientation and their traditionalism. The Chinese bureaucracy was able to endure because it was hierarchical, but also because that hierarchy had a hierocratic aspect. That aspect was all the more necessary since the conventional culture was devoid of any doctrine of natural law, any coherent system of logic and any positive scientific body of thought.

While examining the influence of these structures on the daily life of the Chinese, Weber also emphasized the conflicts which disturbed the apparent harmony or "stupor." Those conflicts were between heterodox Taoism and the sects of a more or less mystical character on the one hand, and external influences, particularly that of Buddhism, on the other.

Still on a strictly sociological basis, Weber studied the religious sentiment of India, going into detail on Hinduism with its doctrine and rites, the position of the Brahmans and the organization and discipline of the castes. And since the work was also intended as a comparative sociology of religion, he compared the Brahmans with the Chinese and Greek intellectuals. But here again, what interested him was heterodoxy, as a factor more capable of explaining the moral conduct of individuals as well as their aspirations and desires. He went into the phenomenon of Djanaism; and he discussed Buddhism and the importance of sects such as Mahayana, as well as Lamaism, Vishnuism, and the mystagogy of the *guru.*

He dealt in similar fashion with ancient Judaism. After analyzing the geographical and climatological conditions, he studied the cities, the position of the peasants, the legal institutions, the form of worship, sacrifices and the problem of the Levites. He made a thorough analysis of the situation prior to and during the captivity. After the captivity, profound internal transformations took place as a result of the emergence of sects, among them the Pharisees and the Essenes, and particularly as a result of the growing influence of the rabbis. The characteristic feature of Judaism was its hostility to magic, which paved the way for the rationalist movement of future centuries. Weber would undoubtedly have made as attentive a study of Islam had he been able to write his projected work on the subject.

But what interests us in the first place is the questions which Weber raised in connection with all these sociological analyses. For there exist other works, often remarkable ones, on these religions, as well as on the comparative sociology of religions, but few have so penetratingly raised the overall question of the cultural significance of these historical phenomena, in the sense of what Weber called the ethos orienting the conduct of life.

Initially Weber's objective seems to have been twofold. On the one hand, to examine, in the light of religions other than Protestantism, the influence of the material situation on religious convictions and thought, and conversely, the latter's influence on moral conduct and thus, indirectly, on economic orientation. (Space does not permit us to go into his analyses in any detail.) On the other hand, to confirm, indirectly, the uniqueness of Western civilization which alone has produced a rationalized economic action, a rational jurisprudence, a rational art, etc. Not that rationalization has been lacking in other civilizations, but it has proved incapable of forging the technical tools and providing itself with the spiritual equipment needed for further development. However, one thing to be avoided at all costs is the snare of evaluation. When Weber pointed to the singularity of Western rationalism, he had no intention of asserting its absolute superiority.

For the concept of rationality is simple only in appearance. In fact, nothing is irrational in itself, but only in relation to a given rational point of view. For the hedonist, ascetism is irrational; and the ascetic views hedonism in the same manner. Rationality, here, should rather be considered as a "historical concept" which must each time be clarified in contrast to a given irrationality or another type of rationality, for the conduct of life may be rationalized in accordance with the most diverse ultimate ends and in equally diverse directions.

As his sociological investigations advanced, Weber

came to emphasize other phenomena, some of which foreshadowed the central problems of contemporary philosophy. Discussing the theodicy of suffering, he explains how this problem should have given rise to a sense of guilt, the happy man being rarely satisfied with the possession of happiness, feeling as he does the need to justify, to legitimize his right to happiness. He generally finds this justification in the criteria of the social stratum to which he belongs, since legitimization involves not only religious but also ethical and especially juridical considerations. As a result, the dominant classes tend to monopolize not only the good things of society but also the spiritual benefits and, in order to consolidate their power, to impose on the rest a certain type of moral conduct and, more generally, a manner of life.

The universal phenomenon of struggle thus has its place in the religious sphere too, whatever the original purity of the intentions underlying the doctrine or of the convictions. Thus, to maintain their preponderance, the Confucianist writers had to combat sorcerers, Taoist mystics and Buddhist monks; the Brahmans had to challenge the claims of Djanaism, Buddhism and other sects; while the Jewish prophets had to battle with the *nabis*, soothsayers and certain groups of Levites. And all these different religious sects or groups were defending material and spiritual interests in addition to their particular religious convictions. This struggle for the monopoly of legitimacy is even more characteristic of the salvation religions, which specify "from what" (*wovon*) and "for what" (*wozu*) the faithful are, or might be, delivered.

All these latent or open conflicts show that religious conviction is at the service of individuals ceaselessly working, struggling, resigning themselves or aspiring to other things. This struggle, precisely, is what gives the world its meaning from a religious point of view, and when the intellectuals of the various social strata endeavor to rationalize the conduct of life, they are really endeavoring to consolidate that meaning. Thus, in the various religions too, Weber found that tragic paradox of the consequences, the sense of which marks his political conceptions and his vision of history; he saw that the result achieved by religious beings is often contrary to their original intention. Every choice has a price; it entails the sacrifice, for the sake of estimable values, of others just as estimable. The Confucianist cult of tradition blocked economic development; the Protestant produced a constantly increasing wealth of which, basically, he disapproved.

This paradox of the consequences is inherent in every struggle, whatever the sphere in which it occurs. As the struggle develops, it eventually shifts the meaning of the values which it was intended to defend. Because it requires a preliminary act of adherence, its development sometimes brings men to adopt a course of behavior contrary to their conviction or to their original intentions. For they very seldom draw the logical conclusions from the causes which they champion, and they try to achieve accommodations, theoretically in order to safeguard the validity of their convictions, but in practice often unconsciously jettisoning them.

Weber also saw a very profound tension within religious activity itself. Because it is oriented toward goals which are not empirically real and because the powers to which it appeals are neither natural nor habitual, it involves an opposition between the ordinary and the extraordinary and operates a cleavage between everyday life and the exceptional phenomena of religious life. This tension is aggravated by the fact that all individuals are not equally qualified to fulfill the optimum conditions required for salvation, so that a vast gap often exists between the religious practice of ordinary believers and that of the virtuosos (ascetics, mystics and other persons endowed with a religious charisma). The consequence, as we have seen before, is a difference in men's religious designations, so that there is a constantly widening distance between everyday life and the demands of religion. And since economic activity belongs to the sphere of the everyday, we can more easily understand why the virtuosos depreciate it, to the point of sometimes regarding it as the source of sin and of the fall.

What, in these circumstances, can be the real action of the religious phenomenon in the secular world? Do not the virtuosos sometimes convey the impression (perhaps a false one) that they are more concerned with themselves than with others? Charisma, indeed, is as ancient as the religious life and will doubtless accompany it always. Nevertheless, the separation which it establishes between everyday life and the loftiest religious experience explains, at least partially, the religious indifference of many individuals, except when religion turns into a moral rationalization of conduct. And this is possible only provided that contemplation is not regarded as the highest good of salvation and that the means of grace are stripped of their magical and sacramental character. That was the achievement of certain Protestant circles. It should be noted, however, that this asceticism remained a secular one, that it did not prompt the individual to flee the world, in the manner of the mystic, but to renounce some aspects of the world, while remaining in it. Secular asceticism accepted everyday life and banned only the luxury immediately contrary to the divine commandments. The glory of God thus becomes the pretext for a rationalization which, like every choice, sacrifices certain human values to others.

Whatever the alternatives offered, the religious life necessarily moves between the ordinary and the extraordinary, but with the possibility of adopting all kinds of transitions and combinations. For men are not only logical or psychological beings, but above all historical individuals of flesh and blood. A rational conduct which accepts all the consequences of its premises is more the exception than the rule. This applies also to the salvation religions which set particular store by the charismatic traits of the virtuosos. That is why a sociology of religion cannot exactly render empirical reality; it is obliged by the force of circumstances to characterize certain phenomena as typical according to the one-sided point of view imposed by the nature of the investigation undertaken. History is always richer than any systematization, so that the point of view selected here —that of the economic ethics of the world religions—is merely one sociological approach to the religious phenomenon.

[C]

THE SOCIOLOGY OF POLITICS

1. Politics and the state

What we shall discuss here is Weber's sociology of politics, and not his practical and personal stands on German and, ultimately, international policies. The reader wishing to acquaint himself with Weber's personal views may consult his *Gesammelte politische Schriften*, or Mommsen's *Max Weber und die deutsche Politik*.[17] Here we confine ourselves to Weber's sociology of politics as set out, in particular, in his *Wirtschaft und Gesellschaft*. It may be summarily described as a sociology of domination (*Herrschaftssoziologie*).

Politics is a common activity of human beings; it fills human history. It has assumed different forms over the ages; it has been based on different principles and has produced the most varied institutions. This is the aspect which interests the sociologist. Thus defined, political action is obviously not to be confused with the state, which is only one of its historical expressions, and precisely the one corresponding to the trend of modern civilization toward rationalization. There have been political units other than states, from cities to empires. Politics thus predates the state, even if in our day political activity tends to be reduced to state action or to pattern itself on certain aspects thereof.

Weber defines the state as the political structure or grouping which "successfully upholds a claim to the monopoly of the legitimate use of physical force in the enforcement of its order."[18] That is its specific character, to which must be added others. On the one hand, it implies a rationalization of law, with consequences such as specialization of the legislative and judicial powers and establishment of a police force responsible for protecting the security of individuals and ensuring law and order; on the other hand, it is dependent upon a rational administration, based on explicit rules, which enable it to intervene in the most various areas, from education to health, economic action and even culture; finally, it possesses a virtually permanent military force. In Weber's view, a socialist state favoring systematic state planning is not an original structure, save perhaps by reason of the charismatic character of the revolution which brings it into being, for in all other respects it does no more than carry the rationalization of political society a step further. Basically, socialism is merely a typical form of the modern state.

Weber observed an analogous development in the structures of the churches as hierocratic powers which, like every other power, use psychic coercion and claim a monopoly thereon in the form of an institution which dispenses or refuses the spiritual benefits of salvation. Hierocracy is characterized by spiritual domination; to put it another way, the churches assume the character of an undertaking based on rational rules and an administrative authority.

Weber was less concerned, however, to analyze the historical structure of the state than to clarify the nature of the political phenomenon in general. For the legitimate use of violence has belonged to other groups than the political unit: to kinship groups, to corporations or again to feudal lords. The political organization is thus far from having always possessed the institutional rigor of the modern state; in earlier times, it was sometimes no more than an amorphous structure, or even an occasional and ephemeral association. Weber puts this idea in yet another form: the political unit has always constituted a grouping (*Verband*), and only in our own day has it assumed the character of a rigid institution (*Anstalt*). We therefore have to explain the specific nature of the political group if we wish to understand the political phenomenon as such.

Political activity is characterized in the first place by the fact that it takes place within a circumscribed territory. Its frontiers do not have to be strictly established; they may be variable; but without the existence of a territory individuating the group, there can be no politics. A consequence is the characteristic separation between internal and external, regardless of the form of the internal order or that of the external relations. This separation is inherent in the concept of territory.

Secondly, those who live within the frontiers of the group adopt a form of conduct meaningfully oriented in relation to that territory and the corresponding community, in the sense that their activity is conditioned by the authority responsible for maintaining order, involving the possible use of coercion and the obligation to defend their integrity as a community. At the same time, the members of the political group find within it a number of specific advantages which provide new opportunities for their activity in general.

Thirdly, the instrument employed by political action is force, and potentially violence. Of course, it also uses all other conceivable methods to bring its undertakings to a successful conclusion, but, in the event of the failure of other methods, force is its *ultima ratio*, its specific means. It follows that domination (*Herrschaft*) is central to the political phenomenon and that the political group is essentially a group exercising domination. Political action may consequently be defined as the activity which claims the right of domination on behalf of the authority established in a territory, with the possibility of using force or violence in case of need, either in order to maintain internal order and the advantages which it entails, or to defend the community against external threat. In a word, politics is the process which ceaselessly aims at forming, developing, obstructing, shifting or overturning the relationships of domination.

Domination is the practical and empirical expression of power (*Macht*). Weber defines power as "the probability that one actor within a social relationship will be in a position to carry out his own will despite resistance," and domination as "the probability that a command with a given specific content will be obeyed by a given group of persons."[19] Neither of these is peculiar to politics alone, since there exist other circumstances or necessities (economic, pedagogical, etc.) where men also have to assert their will. They become political when the will is meaningfully oriented in relation to a territorial grouping with a view to achieving a goal which is meaningful only through the existence of that group. There is nothing political in putting power at the service of a strike with a view to obtaining material advantages (better pay or other conditions of work) so long as such action is not aimed at the domination of the territorial group as a whole; in other words, so long as it is respectful of established authority and regulations.

Underlying all political domination is the fundamental relationship of command and obedience. Provided the order is carried out, the person in command possesses authority, regardless of the reasons which prompt the members to submit (fear, respect, advantage, expediency, tradition, etc.). Obedience signifies that the members of a political unit act as persons who regard the content of the command as the precept governing their individual conduct, simply because they formally recognize its necessity, independently of their personal opinions on the merits or demerits of the command as such.

The exercise of authority is by its very nature the factor of organization of the group; in our day, it is generally exercised on the basis of a highly structured organization, thanks to the existence of an administration, a permanent apparatus of coercion, rational regulations, etc., which serve as safeguards of the continuity of political activity. This situation, however, is characteristic only of the modern state and not of politics in general, for political groups have existed without any established administration, or where the political functions were performed by slaves or individuals personally attached to the sovereign.

The relationship of command and obedience means that any domination will be exercised by a small number—a minority which in one way or another imposes its views on the majority. There is no government of all by all, nor even of the minority by the majority. The democratic system may make it appear that this is not so, thanks to the elective process and other forms of majority consultations, but in fact it is always a minority which decides and which orients the general political activity of the group according to its views. From this, there follows a second consequence: in so far as the apparatus of domination succeeds in securing its continuity, it tends inevitably to wrap its intentions and some of its actions and decisions in a cloak of secrecy. This is an indispensable condition of all coherent and effective political activity. While the nature and the number of actions which governments conceal may vary from one system to another, or from one state to another, it remains that there is no form of domination which does not remain secret in some essential points.

2. *Prestige and other concepts*

The power exercised by a political group is generally accompanied, even among its members, by a sentiment of pride and arrogance which may, in given circumstances, assume an aggressive character. Some political units—generally small nations like Switzerland or Norway—while forcefully expressing their pride, generally relate that sentiment merely to their autonomous status, being jealous only of their independence, of the exemplary character of their institutions or simply of their history. Political pride may also assert itself in the play of foreign relations, as in the overbearing attitude of the country which pursues policies of "greatness," "honor" and power in the world; then we have desire for prestige. This latter concept is fundamental, in Weber's view, because it throws light on certain political phenomena such as that of "great power," nation, or imperialism. It undoubtedly implies an irrational aspiration; nevertheless, without it, some international relationships, such as hegemony or colonialism, would be incomprehensible. Desire for prestige appears as a dynamic factor of politics.

Theoretically, every political power is a potential aspirant to prestige; because of the competition and rivalry between political units, whether on commercial, ideological or any other grounds, it is natural that each should seek to play a historical role in which it can take pride, or champion a solution which it regards as preferable to those presented by other countries. To seek to influence international relations, whether for purposes of annexation or aggression or in order to contribute to pacification, is to assert the will to prestige. Clearly, therefore, the "great powers" which in our day hold the key to peace or war are actuated by this motive more than the rest. The economic capabilities of those countries are of course a major factor, but without the specific passion for prestige—in other words, if we do not take account of the role which they desire to play—the motivation of most of their actions will remain incomprehensible.

Changes of system do not affect this fundamental attitude. Thus while the economic factor, for instance, has rightly been regarded as one of the constituents of imperialism, Weber rejected the exclusively economic explanation in vogue in his day, particularly among Marxists, and maintained that imperialism is also in large measure the expression of a desire for prestige. States with a feudal structure are perhaps least drawn to this form of political expression. On the other hand, since the socialist countries constitute merely a particular type of the modern state, they too will display imperialistic tendencies. Indeed, it is hard to see why their attitude toward weaker states should differ from the familiar attitude of the great powers in that respect; moreover, because of its internationalist vocation, socialism presents itself as a victorious idea aspiring to the widest political propagation and expansion.

In common parlance, "national state" in our day means simply "state." But what is a nation? Is it an ethnic reality based on racial community? This definition does not correspond with the facts; many examples, including that of Alsace (annexed by Germany at the time when Weber was writing his *Wirtschaft und Gesellschaft*), belie that notion. For we see that the bond created between the Alsatians and France through their participation in the historical destinies of the French Revolution, and their consequent contribution to the overthrow of feudalism, is stronger than the one existing between the Alsatians and Germany by reason of a common racial origin. The criterion of linguistic or confessional community is equally inadequate.

The nation is primarily the expression of power based on the passion for prestige. Neither politically nor conceptually is it a univocal term (national sentiment is variously expressed by the English, the Americans, the Russians, the Germans or the French); an analysis could be developed in this connection of the attitude peculiar to each nation. Because it is based on prestige, the nation is an emotional reality belonging to the sphere of evaluations and faith. It is therefore highly probable that nationalism will continue to be a determining political factor, particularly since the prestige

of power and that of culture usually go hand in hand—
although it cannot be said that such concomitance
serves the cause of cultural development.

Notwithstanding the humanitarian and egalitarian
program of certain parties, they too are power organizations. Weber defines the party as "an associative type
of social relationship, membership in which rests on formally free recruitment. The end to which its activity is
devoted is to secure power within a corporate group for
its leaders in order to attain ideal or material advantages for its active members. These advantages may
consist in the realization of certain objective policies or
the attainment of personal advantages or both."[20] Unlike social classes, parties are always associative relationships, because they have specific goals, such as the
execution of a program or the attainment of lucrative
positions. They thus constitute an apparatus, or an
undertaking, based on power and intended to procure it
through the domination which they claim to exercise.

It is possible to develop an analysis of parties
(which Weber was content to outline) according to
whether they constitute permanent or ephemeral organizations, whether they are based on patronage, class
or ideology, or again, whether their structure is juridical, traditionalist or charismatic. Weber laid particular
emphasis on the role of large-scale contributors to party
funds, which is often neglected. Contrary to what
might have been anticipated, parties based on class
ideology do not reject such patrons, as we see from the
German Socialist party, which was financed by Paul
Singer, or again from the Russian revolutionary parties.
Another point which the sociologist must examine is
that parties are combat organizations and that their

efficacy in the rivalry for power depends in large measure on the prestige of their leaders. There may even be
a contradiction between the apparent internal democ-
racy of a party and the devotion of the activists to the
person of the individual who has succeeded in gaining
control of the apparatus. In general, organizations intended simply to advance the material interests of their
members display more hostility to the charismatic
leader than do ideological parties.

At the time when Weber was writing *Wirtschaft
und Gesellschaft*, the racist ideology was beginning to
gain ground in Germany, under the cloak of a so-called
science of anthropology. As early as 1910, Weber took a
clear stand against the movement at a congress of the
German Sociological Society, explaining that race is an
ambiguous concept which remains undifferentiated,
and therefore cannot be used scientifically, but only
evaluatively. Hence, from a strictly sociological point
of view, statements such as "the vigor of a society depends on the vigor of the race" or "the race reacts in a
given manner," or again, the expression "racial unity,"
are devoid of meaning.

In *Wirtschaft und Gesellschaft*, Weber approached the problem quite differently, concentrating
on the ethnic rather than on the anthropological aspect.
The sociology of politics, in so far as it aspires to the title
of a science, must not issue value judgments or condemn a political opinion, but must seek to understand
the political choices and the value judgments made by
political leaders or groups. The racist ideology must
therefore be recognized as a power phenomenon. Biology, clearly, can no more be regarded as the foundation
of the sociology of politics than can economics, psy-

chology or religion. Nevertheless, because certain political parties or structures base their action on the ideology of race, sociology has to take account of it.

A closer look at racism shows it to be an essentially subjective and negative concept, since it asserts the superiority of blood without valid reason, and leads to a segregation based on contempt and superstition. In addition, the meager results culled by the science of race are all debatable. Nevertheless, racism is a determining factor of power and therefore of prestige, particularly since the concept of nation introduces ethnic factors, even if the latter do not constitute criteria for its definition. The race concept, then, plays or may play a determining political role to the extent that the idea gains credence that a common existence (*Gemeinsamkeit*) within the confines of specific frontiers is founded on a community (*Gemeinschaft*) of race.

Weber mentions numberless other political concepts, without going into them all and sometimes without giving them so much as the briefest analysis. The concept of collegiality he treats at somewhat greater length, but without introducing any novel insights by comparison with what may be found in other works devoted to the theory of the state. The same applies to his treatment of the concepts of the separation of powers and representation, save that he sought to make his typology more rigorous. The main emphasis in his sociology of politics is on a particular aspect of domination —that of legitimacy, and particularly on the types of legitimacy, that is, on the various possible ways of conceiving the relationship between command and obedience.

3. *The three types of legitimacy*

No form of authority is satisfied with an obedience which is merely external submission on grounds of common sense, expediency or respect; it seeks further to arouse the members of the group to faith in its legitimacy, that is, transform discipline into adherence to the truth which it represents. Weber conceived of three types of legitimate authority. The first, which he called "legal authority," is rational in character; it is based on belief in the rationally established laws and in the legitimacy of the leaders appointed in accordance with the law. The second, or "traditional authority," is based on belief in the sanctity of traditions in force and on the legitimacy of those who are called upon to exercise power. The third, which Weber called "charismatic authority," is based on the members' abandonment of themselves to an individual distinguished by his holiness, his heroism or his exemplariness. Legal authority is the most impersonal; the second is based on piety, and the last is in the realm of the exceptional. Weber makes it clear from the outset that he is referring to ideal types—hence to forms which are seldom if ever encountered in their pristine purity in historical reality; for charismatic authority, for instance, is not wholly lacking in legality, and traditional authority has certain charismatic and even bureaucratic aspects.

The effectiveness of legal authority, Weber says, rests on the acceptance of a number of interrelated ideas. First, that any given legal norm, whether established by agreement or by imposition, is valid on grounds of expediency or rational values or both. Secondly, that every body of law constitutes a system of technical prescriptions or norms; justice consists in the application of general rules to particular cases, while the purpose of the administrative process is to protect people's interests within the limits laid down by legal precepts, through agencies established to that end. Thirdly, that the legal chief, or the highest authorities, including the elected president, are subject to an impersonal juridical order to which their actions are oriented. Fourthly, that the members of the group obey only the law; they are citizens. This means that there is an obligation to obedience only under conditions provided by law.

Legal authority, finally, is a continuous organization of official functions bound by rules and divided into specified spheres of competence. The application of these innumerable rules demands a qualified administrative staff who work entirely separated from ownership of the means of administration, and without appropriation of their positions. On the other hand, they are protected by specific rules in the exercise of their functions. The administrative procedure is based on the principle of documents and records which are preserved; all decisions, orders and rules are formulated in writing. The most typical form of legal authority is bureaucracy.

In the case of traditional authority, power belongs not to a leader chosen by the inhabitants of the country, but to a man who assumes office by virtue of custom (primogeniture, family seniority, etc.). He therefore reigns in his own right, so that obedience is addressed to his person and becomes an act of piety. The governed are not citizens, but peers (in the case of a gerontocracy) or subjects, obedient not to an impersonal norm but to a tradition or to orders legitimized through the traditional privilege of the sovereign. According to the latter's mood, a man may obtain his favors or fall into disgrace. In general, the traditional chief is guided by the customary laws of equality and moral justice, or by personal expediency, not by fixed and formal principles. However, tradition is not to be identified with arbitrary rule, for if the sovereign violates it he is liable to provoke a resistance aimed not, indeed, at the system but at his person or at his favorites. In such circumstances there is clearly no question of creating a new type of law; in case of difficulties, men must rely on prudence, through the interpretation of precedents or prejudices.

The persons who assist the traditional chief in his government are not officials, but servants recruited, as the case may be, from slaves, freedmen, dependents, members of the family, vassals or benefice-holders who owe their wealth to the sovereign's good pleasure and are therefore loyal to him personally. History offers many and varied examples of this type of authority.

What is absent in such an administration is a clearly defined sphere of competence subject to impersonal rules, technical training, a rational administrative hierarchy including a regular system of promotion and often financial remuneration, for the sovereign's aides either share his table or obtain a variety of benefices.

The most primitive types of traditional authority are gerontocracy, where control is exercised by the eldest in years, and patriarchalism, where authority devolves on an individual designated by a definite rule of inheritance. Both types are characterized by the absence of any organized machinery of government, even personal; furthermore, the governed are peers and not subjects. It is otherwise in the two more common types, namely, patrimonialism and "sultanism." In the case of "sultanism," the governed are subjects; the sovereign has a personal guard and governs only through his favorites. We shall return later to patrimonialism, since Weber regarded it as the most characteristic type of traditional authority, just as bureaucracy is the most characteristic type of legal authority. Moreover, patrimonialism is the form best known to us, since most of the old European monarchies come under that heading.

Charismatic authority is the exceptional type of political power, not because it rarely occurs but because it sets aside the usages of normal political life. Weber describes charisma (a term he borrowed from Rudolf Sohm) as the exceptional quality of a person who appears to possess supernatural, superhuman or at the least unaccustomed powers, so that he emerges as a providential, exemplary or extraordinary figure, and for this reason is able to gather disciples or followers around him. Charismatic behavior is not peculiar to political activity alone, for it may be found in other areas, such as religion, art, morals and even economic life, although, according to Weber, one of the features of charisma is that it remains alien, if not hostile, to the normal economic processes. In the political sphere, this type of authority assumes a variety of forms—that of the demagogue, the social dictator, the military hero or the revolutionary.

All charismatic authority implies men's whole-hearted devotion to the person of the leader who feels himself called to carry out a mission. Its foundation is therefore emotional rather than rational, since the whole force of such activity rests on trust, mostly blind and fanatical, and faith, unrestrained and usually completely uncritical. Charisma means a break with continuity, whether legal or traditional; it overturns institutions, it challenges the established order and customary restraints and appeals to a new concept of human relationships. It is both destructive and constructive. The boundaries and norms it sets are those established by the leader on his own authority, by virtue of the demands made by what he believes to be his vocation; thus the leader draws his legitimacy from sources within himself, independently of all external criteria, and is prepared to repudiate or eliminate those of his followers who refuse to follow him in the path whose direction he alone may specify.

The influence of the charismatic leader is proportionately greater as he places himself outside any political grouping, despises the powers that be and tears men from the routine and boredom of everyday life by exalting the irrational aspects of life. A charismatic policy is thus an adventure, not only because it courts failure, but also because it is constantly obliged to discover a new impetus, to provide new motives for enthusiasm to confirm its power. Clearly, therefore, such authority is radically opposed to legal as well as traditional authority, which are both limited by respect for law or custom, or by the obligation to take account of the established administrative processes or of the privileges of orders and various social groups. Theoretically, the charismatic leader's horizons are unlimited, at least so long as his followers remain loyal to him and their number continues to increase, for as soon as doubt assails them, his power collapses.

It is therefore difficult to speak of law in connection with such authority, which recognizes neither institutions, nor rules, nor customs nor precedents. It is a law unto itself and the word of the leader is sufficient reason for obedience, or for the assumption of an obligation. Nor are there servants or officials in its scheme of things, but only apostles, followers or disciples, whence the often disorderly and haphazard, but also surprising and sometimes impressive character of the administrative measures introduced by a charismatic leader who assumes power. The important element in such cases is not stability but movement, and even upheaval, in imitation of the leader who is the embodiment of an ideal and not of a law or a regulation. Charismatic authority leaves no room for political representation; it is its whole self at every moment or, to use Weber's own term, its own "epiphany."

4. Bureaucracy, patrimonialism and the problems inherent in charismatic authority

Bureaucracy, as we have seen, is the most typical example of legal authority. It is based on the following principles: 1. The existence of specific services and hence of spheres of competence strictly defined by law or regulations, so that offices are clearly divided and apportioned, as are the powers of decision required for the performance of the relevant functions; 2. Protection of officials in the exercise of their functions under specific regulations (irremovability of judges, for example); in general, officials have life tenure, so that the public service becomes a principal career and not a subsidiary occupation alongside some other profession; 3. The hierarchical organization of functions, i.e., the administrative system, is strongly structured in subordinate and executive posts, with provision for appeal from the lower to the higher authority; in general, this structure is monocratic rather than collegial, and displays a tendency to increasing centralization; 4. Recruitment on the basis of competitive examination or diplomas attesting qualification; thus specialized training is required; as a rule, the official is appointed (seldom elected) on the basis of free selection and contractual relationship; 5. Regular remuneration of the official in the form of a fixed salary and a pension once he retires from the public service; salaries are graded according to rank in the administrative hierarchy and responsibility; 6. The right of the superior to regulate the work of his subordinates, if necessary through the establishment of a disciplinary committee; 7. Promotion opportunities for officials on the basis of objective criteria and not at the discretion of the superior; 8. Complete separation between the office and the incumbent, for no official may appropriate his position or own the means of administration.

This description applies, of course, only to the state as organized in modern times, for the bureaucratic phenomenon is of much more ancient date; we find it, for instance, in ancient Egypt, in the period of the Roman principate, particularly after the reign of Diocletian, in the Roman Church after the thirteenth century, or in China after the Shih Huang Ti period.

Modern bureaucratic administration developed under the protection of royal absolutism at the beginning of the modern era. The old bureaucracies were essentially patrimonial in character, that is, the officials did not enjoy real statutory guarantees nor did they receive payment in coin. Bureaucratic administration as we know it developed with the modern financial economy, although no exclusive causal relationship can be established between them, since other factors are involved: the rationalization of law, the importance of the phenomenon of the masses, growing centralization in consequence of improved communications and the concentration of industry, the extension of state intervention to the most dissimilar areas of human activity, and particularly the development of a rationalized technology.

Sociology is concerned with the transformations which bureaucracy has introduced in modern societies. It is generally agreed that democratization and bureaucratization go hand in hand. In France or England, for example, democratic progress has been correlative with the expansion of bureaucracy; although this was not true of Germany. Yet it cannot be affirmed that, in the first two cases, the people succeeded in achieving autonomy, nor even in diminishing the prerogatives of the central authority; on the contrary, it continued to be ruled as before. By democratization, we should understand, rather, the progressive elimination of the influence of local notables in favor of the impersonal powers of officialdom. We thus have a trend toward equalization resulting from the very broad recruitment of officials from all social strata on the basis of rational selection.

Moreover, because offices have become increasingly important, they have not necessarily succeeded in taking over real power within the state. They certainly possess the technical means required for the operation of a modern state; nevertheless, the administrative process remains in the service of the government, that is, of the program of the party in power. It may influence the executive, since a senior public servant usually knows the problems of a ministerial department better than does the minister, but the decision rests in general with the latter and with the government. The millions of officials in the public service are no better placed to decide on general policy than are the millions of proletarian workers in the country concerned.

All things considered, it may be said that there is no specifically bureaucratic system of government, since the administrative process has developed on more or less the same scale in countries where constitutional rule prevails and in those under absolutist government. At the same time, we should stress the tendency of every bureaucracy to operate behind the scenes, away from the spotlight and particularly out of reach of public criticism. This is because every official believes that, as an expert, he is better equipped to resolve political problems than the layman.

The development of the educational system in Western Europe, especially of secondary and higher education (high schools, colleges, universities, technical schools, institutions for advanced studies, etc.) is doubtless to be credited to the constant increase in the number of public servants and the demand for specialized training. Bureaucracy has thus had a decisive influence on the orientation of culture. The same applies to the influence of the basic principles of bureaucratic administration, by reason of the financial security which it provides or the qualities it requires of the official, such as exactness, the study of records before embarking on action, rational calculation, etc. In addition, with the growth of the bureaucratic apparatus, political, economic and other problems have become increasingly technical and formally rational, owing to the specialization of the offices responsible for resolving, supervising or directing them. Weber thus regards bureaucratic administration as one of the sources of the modern Western state:

> The development of the modern form of the organization of corporate groups in all fields is nothing less than identical with the development . . . of bureaucratic administration. This is true of church and state, of armies, political parties, economic enterprises, organizations to promote all kinds of causes, private associations, clubs, and many others. . . . However many forms there may be which do not appear to fit this pattern, such as collegial representative bodies, parliamentary committees, soviets, honorary officers, lay judges, and what not, and however much people may complain about the "evils of bureaucracy," it would be sheer illusion to think for a moment that continuous administrative work can be carried out in any field except by means of officials working in offices. The whole pattern of everyday life is cut to fit this framework. For bureaucratic administration is, other things being equal, always, from a formal, technical point of view, the most rational type. For the needs of mass administration today, it is completely indispensable. The choice is only that between bureaucracy and dilletantism in the field of administration.
>
> The primary source of the superiority of bureaucratic administration lies in the role of technical

knowledge which, through the development of modern technology and business methods in the production of goods, has become completely indispensable. In this respect, it makes no difference whether the economic system is organized on a capitalistic or a socialistic basis. Indeed, if in the latter case a comparable level of technical efficiency were to be achieved, it would mean a tremendous increase in the importance of specialized bureaucracy.[21]

In this work which, from the internal evidence, would appear to have been written in 1919 or 1920, Weber repeatedly returned to the future of Soviet socialism. While basing his study solely on an analysis of the bureaucratic phenomenon in a modern industrial society, and without seeking to play the prophet, he foresaw the part which bureaucracy would inevitably play in a socialistic system. Such a system, he believed, would have to establish a far more rigid bureaucratic administration than that of capitalism. Weber's perspicacity was not hindsight.

Along with the tendency toward "leveling" and plutocracy, which renders bureaucracy particularly suited to mass democracies, Weber adds other traits: the impersonality of such a system, since the official must perform his work *sine ira et studio*—without love or enthusiasm; its essentially formalistic spirit, since it is available to all, without distinction, to whom the regulations apply, such regulations having to be carried out on the basis of the provisions they contain and not of the subjective demands of individuals; finally, the tendency of officials to treat matters from a utilitarian point of view.

Patrimonialism is the most common form of traditional authority. It bears a resemblance to bureaucracy because it too rejects the exceptional and is a permanent and continuous institution, save that the preexisting norm to which it refers is not rational or technical in character, but possesses a practical content, namely, the validity of custom considered as inviolable by reason of the sanctity of what has always been. Its unity does not depend on some constitutional code or other; the person of the sovereign perpetuates the "eternal yesterday." Obedience to his orders, therefore, is not submission to a general principle out of discipline and duty, but subjection and fealty, that is, loyalty to the chief based on piety. Authority, here, is fundamentally personal and independent of any objectively rational goal. The sovereign is lord and not magistrate; power belongs to him by virtue of personal attributes; it is not conferred upon him on the basis of external and formal criteria defining his office.

History shows that patrimonial authority possessed no administration in the modern sense of the term. As we have seen, the sovereign recruited his aides from among his servants, his feudal vassals or the local notables or, if he employed the services of persons outside the patrimonial sphere, he chose men who were attached to his person because they were dependent upon him for their fortune. The continuity of the system made it possible, ultimately, to establish a more highly structured administration, having some analogy with modern bureaucracy. However, office-holders were usually owners of their positions, or at least of the means of administration, particularly when they exercised authority in the provinces on the king's behalf.

What was absent in such a system was any separation between the private and the public spheres, that is, any distinction between the personal interests of the administrator and the public interests attached to the position he occupied. In any case, administrative ability was rarely a factor in the selection of office-holders. No other criterion existed, in fact, than the confidence which the sovereign placed in his favorites. To put it another way, a patrimonial system was blind to ideas of competence and specialization and considered only the honor of "individualities." We should therefore speak of dignitaries rather than officials, as we are reminded by such titles as "constable," "marshal," "seneschal," etc. The personalization of the administration extended to every area, including the army, which was devoted to the person of the king or feudal lord, because the latter was personally responsible for equipping it, and maintained it out of his private purse, increasing or reducing its numbers according to the state of his finances.

Law, too, was regulated by custom, and its place was generally taken by the king's "good pleasure." Subjects, therefore, did not properly speaking possess rights; in case of dispute, all they could do was have recourse to the discretionary power of the representative of the patrimonial authority and, if necessary, appeal to the sovereign's good pleasure. In a word, the basic characteristic of patrimonial authority is that "all governmental authority and the corresponding economic rights tend to be treated as privately appropriated economic advantages."[22] Such appropriation should not, however, be identified with arbitrary power, save in some extreme cases, such as the authority of the Turkish sultan, for it was generally modified or limited in practice by institutions such as parliaments, courts of justice, municipal privileges or again the existence of estates. Historically speaking, a purely patrimonial state, in the ideal-typical sense of the term, has never existed.

Weber's theory on charismatic authority has sometimes been misinterpreted; some have tried to see in it a prefiguration of the Nazi regime. Weber has even been pictured as a precursor of Hitler, although he confined himself strictly to the sociological and ideal-typical analysis of a form of authority which has existed in every age. There were charismatic regimes before Hitler and there have been others since, as for instance that of Fidel Castro. Assuming even that the Weberian analysis helped the Nazis to gain a clearer awareness of their position, the accusation is no less absurd, since it amounts to making the doctor responsible for the disease which he diagnoses. And in that case a sociology of politics should turn itself into an affair of pious sentiments, give up the idea of examining certain phenomena objectively and finally repudiate itself as a science in order to utter condemnations pleasing to those who reduce thought to mere ideological evaluations.

Such an attitude is contrary both to the distinction which Weber always made between empirical observation and value judgment and his principle of axiological neutrality in sociology, and to the obligation which he imposes on the scientist never to shirk the examination of realities which he personally finds unpleasant. In addition, Weber's censors missed the whole point of his conception of the charismatic type. Instead of seeking in it the principles of a particular historical movement which he never knew, they would have done better to read the pages devoted to that type of authority; they contain his explicit thinking on the revolutionary phenomenon, for in writing them he was thinking mainly of Lenin or Kurt Eisner (the latter he mentions by name).

All revolutions are not charismatic, of course, nor are all charismatic authorities revolutionary (as shown by the historical examples of Cleon of Athens or the Dalai Lama); nevertheless most modern revolutions, beginning with Cromwell's, generally had that character. There is no doubt that what is called nowadays the "personality cult" comes under the heading of charismatic phenomena. Weber also noted the tendency of modern political parties to take the same course in regard to their internal structure, save in the case of groups of prominent persons attracted purely by electoral interest or patronage. In these circumstances, it is easy to understand the growing importance of the principle of plebiscite in contemporary societies.

Charismatic authority is above all the most common means of overthrowing or eliminating a traditional and legal system, which indicates that it is a revolutionary or, as the case may be, pseudo-revolutionary or simply seditious force. The aspiration toward change which animates it may be conditioned by the external situation (political or economic), or by a transformation of attitudes (in the religious or intellectual sphere). Reason has thus been a revolutionary force which engendered charismatic regimes at a time when some countries were passing from the stage of patrimonial to legal authority.

However, since charisma creates an exceptional situation, the very principles of its authority become a source of difficulties if it is to produce anything more than an ephemeral revolt. For how is such an authority to be kept in being once the charismatic leader has disappeared? How are people to be brought back to a normal, stable, everyday existence? For such is the fate of any authority of this kind; sooner or later, it returns to a traditional or legal form of government. These questions are more central to Weber's thinking than is his conceptual analysis of the notion of charisma.

Thus the great problem of charismatic authority is that of succession. For how is the system to be perpetuated after the death of the leader, since the charisma can neither be learned nor taught, but is aroused and experienced, and since both followers and the leader's staff have a material and ideal stake in having the regime endure? The difficulty lies in the fact that the followers' obedience is pure devotion to the person of the leader and lacks the continuity which makes the strength of tradition and legality.

Weber examined the various alternatives at length. One is to discover another bearer of charisma possessing characteristics similar to those of the deceased (as in the case the Dalai Lama); the consequence of this procedure is to found a tradition. Another is to trust in revelation, oracles, fate, divine judgment or some other irrational criterion; in such cases, the path leads more or less slowly in the direction of legal authority. Or the leader, during his lifetime, himself appoints his successor with or without the approval of his followers. Or again, the appointment is made by the charismatic general staff; this procedure rules out election by majority vote, for, if the notion of charismatic rule is to be upheld, what matters is to find the right man. Or again, if blood is regarded as the determining factor, then the charisma may become hereditary.

Selection based on charisma may involve ordeals, in the process of which a jury, or the people as a whole, seek to detect the signs of election of one or other candidate. Generally, however, the succession gives rise to a more or less open struggle, and the fact of winning serves to reveal the charismatic qualities of the victorious candidate. Where all claimants feel themselves equally strong, the initally authoritarian charismatic rule is frequently transformed into a non-authoritarian structure and develops in the direction of a rational system. One indisputable fact remains: unlike other forms of authority, charisma is particularly susceptible to Utopian thinking.

[D]

THE SOCIOLOGY OF LAW

1. Aims of the sociology of law, and definition of law

Weber's sociology of law is better evidence of his encyclopedic learning than any of his other sociological studies. In addition to Roman, Germanic, French and Anglo-Saxon law, he treats of Judaic, Islamic, Hindu and Chinese law, and even of Polynesian customary law. Some passages are extremely technical and may baffle the reader who is not very familiar with legal theory. It should not be forgotten that Weber was a lawyer by training. The governing thought here, as in all his other studies, is the same: to indicate the phases and factors which have contributed to the rationalization peculiar to Western civilization. To that end, Weber studied the influence of politics, religion and economics on the development of law, without disregarding the work of lawyers, jurists, legal honoratiores and in general all the professionals of the law.

A distinction must be made between legal doctrine and a sociology of law. The former endeavors to establish, in theory, the intrinsic meaning intended by a legal rule or law, and to ensure its logical consistency in relation to other laws, or even to a whole code of law. The sociology of law, on the other hand, aims at understanding the meaningful behavior of the members of a group in relation to the laws in force and to determine the nature of the belief in their validity or in the order which they have established. It therefore seeks to determine the extent to which the rules of law are observed, and how individuals orient their conduct in relation to those rules. Legal doctrine holds a rule valid once it is established or appears in a code; sociology seeks to determine the bearing of that rule on the social activity of individuals, for an established law is far from commanding universal respect.

The mass of the people will often orient their behavior unconsciously, out of habit, in accordance with legal prescriptions, without any knowlege of their content or precise meaning; they may even be unaware of their existence. Weber remarks, in his essay on some categories of interpretative sociology, that it is possible to have different approaches to law, according as one is suggesting the establishment of a regulation designed to protect a particular or general interest, or interpreting or applying the provisions it contains, or deliberately seeking to infringe it, or complying with it no more than approximately, in accordance with its generally accepted meaning.

His principal criticism of Stammler was that the latter disregarded this essential distinction between what is and what ought to be, and completely misread the Marxist thesis, which emphasizes the gap between the formal character of laws and the practical application of provisions, the latter often contradicting the theoretical intention. The increased rationalization of law is not necessarily accompanied by a growing acceptance of its normative validity. It is this gap which the sociologist must point out. And Weber notes that society could be reorganized along socialist lines without the amendment of any article of the existing code; the code would remain in force, and would simply be interpreted in the light of the changed situation.

Many misunderstandings have arisen as a result of the identity of the terms used by the various disciplines. The jurist and the sociologist, for example, both use the terms "association," "feudal system," "state," etc., but with different meanings. Thus the jurist treats the state as a moral entity, in the same way as an individual or even a human embryo. Given the particular character of his investigations, he is entitled to consider things from this point of view. The sociologist, for his part, is equally justified in considering the state from the point of view of men's practical approaches to it: they may be hostile toward it or take pride in it; or they may hope to secure certain advantages by orienting their conduct in conformity with what they believe to be the government's wishes.

The grammatical structure of sentences is even

more productive of misunderstandings than words themselves. The simple proposition, "x is a valid law," takes on a wholly different meaning for the jurist, the statesman, the sociologist and the man who seeks to infringe it. This being the case, it is easy to see that the concept of law will not have the same meaning for the jurist, the student of politics and the sociologist.

How does sociology view this concept? Weber writes:

> A system of order will be called *convention* so far as its validity is externally guaranteed by the probability that deviation from it within a given social group will result in a relatively general and practically significant reaction of disapproval. Such an order will be called *law* when conformity with it is upheld by the probability that deviant action will be met by physical or psychic sanctions aimed to compel conformity or to punish disobedience, and applied by a group of men especially empowered to carry out this function.[23]

Thus the existence of an apparatus of coercion is decisive for a sociological definition of law; but other definitions may also be envisaged from other points of view. Thus the jurist will speak of a law of nations despite the absence of any authority with power to compel obedience—although Weber was doubtful of the validity of any international system of law. However this may be, we have to speak of law in connection with an apparatus of coercion. This apparatus of coercion does not have to resemble the court of law familiar to us. A clan or a family could formerly serve in this capacity (in the case of a vendetta or *vheme*), if the action was subject to rules recognized as valid by the members of the group. Similarly, the rules governing student organizations come under the heading of law, as do the rules of the hierocratic authority known as canon law, because they are based on a discipline guaranteed by an authority established to ensure their implementation.

Convention, as we saw above, also involves obligation, but without any apparatus of coercion. In other words, it involves sanctions, but these are a matter for the group as such, and not for an institution. Thus no one is entirely free to observe a convention or not, and sometimes a violation is punished more severely than by an apparatus of coercion, as for instance in the case of a social boycott. Under the heading of conventions we may mention the protocol governing official receptions.

Conventions, for their part, should be distinguished from such other rules of social conduct as usage (*Brauch*) and custom (*Sitte*). Usage consists in the "probability of a uniformity in the orientation of social action" in practice. "Usage will be called 'custom' [*Sitte*] if the actual performance rests on long familiarity."[24] Neither usage nor custom is mandatory, nor do they entail any external sanction. No one, therefore, may be required to conform to them. It is customary, for instance, every morning to eat a breakfast conforming to a certain pattern, but there is no obligation to do so; it is a rite which may be dispensed with.

As always, where sociological concepts are involved, the transition between the various types of conduct remains fluid. One type may more closely resemble convention or custom, usage or law, and it is not possible to describe it otherwise than ideal-typically. Again, it is hard to tell whether some action conforms solely to juridical norms or to ethical obligation, owing to the impossibility of distinguishing between external influence and internal motivation, particularly since other factors may intervene, such as religious devotion. It is therefore vain to attempt to explain everything in terms of sociology or any other discipline. As regards sociology, the most it can do is to refer in any particular case to the conception of morality generally and effectively held to be valid in the group concerned. The complexity of human relationships and modes of behavior forbids any one-sided interpretation, save on ideal-typical lines, in which case we deliberately fashion a Utopian construct designed to facilitate an understanding of the human reality as far as it is possible to do so, and in as coherent a manner as possible. Knowledge is never commensurate with reality, whose variations are both extensively and intensively infinite; it can only offer guidelines to facilitate understanding.

2. Four distinctions

Weber's sociology of law is based on a number of distinctions which we must now clarify. Like the authors of most legal studies in Germany, he begins by examining the value of the classical distinction between private and public law, and concludes that, while the distinction is often useful, it rests on no satisfactory legal or sociological criteria. Using one criterion, we might define public law as "the total body of those norms which regulate the activities of the state as such," and private law as the totality of norms regulating conduct other than state activity.[25] Using a second criterion, we might define public law as "identical with the total body of . . . norms which only embody instructions to state officials as regards their duties."[26] According to a third criterion, private law covers all matters in which the parties concerned are legally on an equal footing, while public law covers those which involve a hierarchical relationship of command and obedience, domination and subordination.

It may be argued that areas exist which are outside this hierarchical relationship and which nevertheless come within the purview of public law, or again that certain rules of public law create subjective rights. Is it not true, for example, that private law too is guaranteed by the public authority? Moreover, there are private forms of administration, as in the case of business undertakings; and even government administration was formerly a private affair, since it was in the hands of servants attached to the person of the sovereign. Consequently, by reason of its inherent ambiguity, this distinction between the two categories of law is not calculated to facilitate a sociological analysis of law, even if methodologically it may be of service to the sociologist.

Another common distinction is that between positive and natural law. Sociology, by definition, should in theory concern itself only with positive law, since this alone gives rise to institutions which may be scientifically observed and analyzed. In this respect, the positivist sociologists of the nineteenth century were right. However, such a prohibition cannot be imposed on an interpretative sociology of law, as defined above. Sociology cannot ignore natural law, if such law can serve as a guide to the meaningful conduct of men in specified collectivities. It does not, of course, have to make a judgment on the validity of such law, but only understand the extent to which beliefs of this kind have influenced men's legal dealings. Any sociologist who fails to take account of the natural law must necessarily fail to grasp the meaning of, for instance, religious action oriented according to the rules of canon law, or the revolutionary activity of the late eighteenth century—to say nothing of the fact that belief in a natural law contributed to the rationalization of modern law. Consequently, to disregard this law means taking sides with a particular theory against a sociological science of law.

Two other distinctions constitute, as it were, the structural foundation of Weber's sociology of law. The first is the distinction between objective and subjective law, although he never gave any very precise definition of these two concepts. By objective law, Weber meant the totality of rules applicable indifferently to all members of a group, to the extent that the group comes under a general legal system. As Grosclaude remarks, his conception of subjective law was fairly similar to that described by Jellinek in his *System der subjektiven öffentlichen Rechte* (1892). In Weber's view, subjective law implies the possibility for an individual to appeal to the apparatus of coercion for the protection of his material and spiritual interests. In other words, subjective rights confer security upon persons possessing power over other individuals or over things, such as property; they authorize these persons to impose, prohibit or permit others to behave in a specified manner.

It may seem surprising that Weber should have attached so much importance to these types of rights, which are really no more than legally protected interests, whether we are dealing, for instance, with an employer's right to hire whomsoever he pleases or the worker's right to choose his employment freely. But we must not forget the general pattern of Weber's sociology of law: on the one hand, he was seeking to show the various processes which led to the rationalization of modern law, and, on the other hand, to illustrate once more the singularity of Western civilization. And subjective rights constitute a fundamental aspect of that civilization, because they have played a decisive role in the private transactions which have contributed to the development of modern capitalism.

This category of rights includes, on the one hand, rights to freedom, that is, provisions guaranteeing the security of the individual against the intervention of others, including the state (for example, freedom of conscience, or the right to the free use of one's property), and, on the other hand, provisions authorizing individuals to regulate their mutual relations freely and completely autonomously, by means of legal transactions (contractual freedom). Weber points out, however, that contractual freedom is not unlimited, since what is guaranteed is not so much the freedom of individuals as such as the contracts which they make with each other, and under certain specific conditions. Consequently, contractual freedom derives not from law but from the public authority, for a socialist government is liable to curtail it very severely, either by limiting the operations of economic exchange, or by restricting the freedom of workers on the labor market.

The distinction between formal and material law appears more important, since it directly conditions the rationalization of law. By formal law, Weber means the legal provision which may be logically deduced solely from the presuppositions of a specified legal system. Formal law is thus the totality of the system of theoretical law all of whose rules are based solely on legal logic, without reference to any considerations extraneous to law. Material law, by contrast, takes account of extra-juridical elements and refers, in its judgments, to political, ethical, economic or religious values.

Whence two ways of conceiving of justice: one is to confine oneself exclusively to the rules of jurisprudence, holding that what is established and in conformity with the letter or the logic of the system is right; the other is to take account of circumstances, of the intentions of individuals and of their general conditions of existence. Thus a judge may pronounce a verdict either simply on the basis of the letter of the law, or after searching his conscience in order to determine what, to him, is the most equitable solution.

Thus the rationality of law may itself be either formal or material, which means that it will never be perfect, for all legal conflicts have their source in the insurmountable antagonism between these two kinds of law. Legality and equity may both serve as criteria of meaningful legal action, and both may be either arbitrary and irrational or rational. Obviously, an exclusively material justice would lead, ultimately, to the negation of law. On the other hand, a purely formal justice, which dispenses with any consideration extraneous to law, has never existed and doubtless never will.

Weber's annotators generally distinguish four ideal types of law: 1. Irrational and material law, where the legislator and the judge base their decisions on purely emotional values, without reference to any norm, and consult only their own feelings. This type is not to be found in unalloyed form, any more than the other types, although the justice meted out by a despot comes close to it. The same might be said of the cadi, or Moslem judge, seated in the market-place, who appears to base his sentences purely on his own feelings. (This is deceptive, Weber remarks, for the cadi actually refers more or less implicitly to the religious or political notions current among the people.) 2. Irrational and formal law, where the legislator and the judge are guided by norms outside the purview of reason, because their decisions are based on a revelation or oracle. 3. Rational and material law, where legislation or verdict refers to a sacred book (e.g. the Koran), the policies of a conqueror or an ideology. 4. Rational and formal law, where law and sentence are established solely on the basis of abstract concepts of jurisprudence.

Unlike formal law, which tends to systematize legal norms, material law remains empirical. Nevertheless, both types of law can be rationalized, the former on the basis of pure logic, the latter on that of utility. Yet despite the increasing rationalization, both retain irrational elements, such as, for example, the oath. Moreover, the jury as an institution of penal law is the most manifest sign of the persistence of irrationality, as we see from the attacks made upon it. Some view it as an instrument of class war, others as an opportunity for the jurors to give free reign to their resentments, their instincts or their complexes, others again as an anachronism which challenges progress—progress being understood as a rationalization of the juridical sphere. In a word, it is regarded as a sort of irrational oracle in the hands of laymen, class enemies or "evil-doers." All these strictures, theoretically justified by the goal of greater rationality, are themselves challenged by a new phenomenon: the emergence of the psychiatrist, whose explanations introduce a previously unknown extra-juridical factor which lays claim to scientific validity.

Whatever the terminology employed to replace the concepts of formal and material law—for example, the opposition between subjective belief and objective situation—the antagonism between legality and equity remains irreconcilable. For as soon as the influence of religious elements appears to have been left behind, economic factors frustrate pure rationality. And no sooner has their action been measured than political or ideological factors proceed to disturb the serenity of legal norms. In short, there is no absolute concordance between abstract juridical technique and moral justice, if only because the latter is the constant object of inevitable conflicts between politics, art, economics, religion and science.

3. From irrational to rational law

Should the growing rationalization which we find in the juridical order be regarded as progress, or simply as an improvement in legal technique? Sociology does not really have to concern itself with this question; its task is to interpret the trend to rationalization, without making any value judgment.

Law probably did not emerge of itself, but was a response to political, economic (but not exclusively economic, as some have thought), and especially religious preoccupations. Every human group, if it is to subsist, requires of its members that they conform to common rules, and it will force them to do so if necessary. These usages of a coercive character, benefiting the common activity of the people concerned, were the source of law and continue to render it indispensable. The fact that in our day legal regulation is based on recorded legislation does not affect the substance of law. Written law is the relatively new technical tool of a much older process. It is therefore untrue to say that law derived, by slow stages, from inveterate custom. Custom was law, as our enacted legislation is today, provided that its object was the common activity of the people concerned, and provided that it included coercive measures—these two conditions being of the essence of all law. An interesting illustration comes to mind. Islamic law was divided into four schools: the Malekite, Hanefite, Hanbalite and Shafiite. Only the Hanefite law survived, because it made provision for religious and political constraint, whereas the others withered away.

On the subject of the development of law, Weber wrote:

> From a theoretical point of view, the general development of law and procedure may be viewed as passing through the following stages: first, charismatic legal revelation through "law prophets"; second, empirical creation and finding of law by legal honoratiores, i.e., law creation through cautelary jurisprudence and adherence to precedent; third, imposition of law by secular or theocratic powers; fourth and finally, systematic elaboration of law and professionalized admin-

istration of justice by persons who have received their legal training in a learned and formally logical manner. From this perspective, the formal qualities of the law emerge as follows: arising in primitive legal procedure from a combination of magically conditioned formalism and irrationality conditioned by revelation, they proceed to increasingly specialized juridical and logical rationality and systematization, passing through a stage of theocratically or patrimonially conditioned substantive and informal expediency. Finally, they assume, at least from an external viewpoint, an increasingly logical sublimation and deductive rigor and develop an increasingly rational technique in procedure.[27]

On the strength of numerous historical documents, Weber felt able to assert that primitive law was generally of a charismatic nature. It was the subject of divination on the part of soothsayers or law prophets who interpreted the divine will, so that the mandatory force of the law was a matter not of man's will, but of the divinity's. Fear of the divinity lent force to a legal decision. The Decalogue is an example, as is the law of the Koran. According to Caesar, Diodorus of Sicily and Strabo, the Druids in Gaul performed a legislative or judicial function. A similar phenomenon is to be found in the Germanic countries, where the presiding officer of the court was not entitled to state the law; that was the duty of charismatic soothsayers—*rachimburgi, lag sagas* and other *Gesetzsprecher*. In African societies, the priest or charismatic chieftain state the law, even when magical conceptions have lost currency. We should also mention oracles, *ordalies*, etc.

The charismatic and irrational character of law persists, if in an attenuated form, in the Anglo-Saxon countries. For example, Blackstone in his *Commentaries on the Law of England* (1765) refers to the English judge as a living oracle. The same applies to the American judge, whose sentence is a true creation, to the point that his name is attached to his decision. On the whole, too, the continued existence of the jury is a survival of the irrationality of the law.

Primitive charismatic law was by definition formal in character, not in the sense of the application of a general rule to a particular case, but in that of a decision in a form appropriate to the case considered, independently of individual interests or any subjective sense of justice. The formalism was thus a logical but external one, in that the validity of the prouncement of the law depended on the performance of certain ritual actions. Under the Roman *mancipatio*, for instance, the person who acquired an object must touch it with his hand. In other cases, under the magical processes used, a question could not be answered unless it was correctly formulated, so that the smallest error in the form of words brought with it the failure of the legal measure and sometimes of the suit, or voided the action. That was the case, for instance, in the Roman *legis actiones*.

Primitive formalism aimed less at establishing proof through legal processes (it was not concerned whether an action was just or unjust, true or false) than at establishing which of the parties was entitled to ask the supernatural powers whether it was in the right. Whence the irrational character of the verdict; it was not based on logic or evidence, but was a reply to a question worded in the recognized forms. Very often, an appropriate legal formula existed for each question.

This discontinuity, however, was often offset by the existence of a tradition understood as follows: since the particular question at issue has always been settled in the manner ordered by God, it is necessary to settle it in a similar way. Under this definition, formalism necessarily led to the establishment of certain technical legal concepts, in response to the need for a precise formulation of the question which might be addressed to the gods, or to the law prophets, failing which the procedure would be void. This rudimentary technique in fact contained an equally rudimentary element of rationality, which was strengthened as law prophets tended to become officials, or at least official authorities.

This was one of the causes of the progressive rationalization of law. For in becoming an official figure, the law prophet became a personage who could be consulted, and who was in fact consulted. He was thus often obliged to indicate solutions beforehand, and therefore to coordinate his replies. He had no advantage in contradicting himself; it was rather to his advantage to find at least an empirical standard which might be applied in more or less similar cases. His best safeguard then was to refer to currently held religious notions. The result was the creation of a kind of tradition which, in itself, was already a rationalization. Law continued, of course, to be the subject of revelation or of divination, but at the same time it assumed a more practical character, which inevitably promoted the process of rationalization.

Let us take the example of Rome. The administration of justice comprised two phases: the first, termed *in iure*, was under the responsibility of the magistrate (*praetor*), who organized the suit and specified the rules and procedure to be followed; the second, termed *apud judicem*, involved the intervention of the judge, a private personage, who examined the facts and the evidence and handed down a ruling. The *praetor*, like the judge, sought the advice of jurisconsults, who traditionally included one or more pontiffs. Up to a very late date, the *responsa* of the jurisconsults were delivered as oracles. In addition, the jurisconsults could help citizens by enlightening them on legal procedures and adjustments; finally, although they were not entitled to argue a case—that was the role of the *oratores*—they could advise the parties to the suit. The jurisconsults thus became what Weber called "legal honoratiores," or experts. It is true that the oldest extant documents are mere collections of replies, with no general or logical theory underlying them, so that Weber felt that Roman law had perhaps been less rational than we are accustomed to believe. Yet these collections had an analytical character transcending mere casuistry, with the result that, under the empire, the legal experts had no difficulty in distilling from them abstract concepts capable of facilitating the systematization and rationalization of the pandects.

Space does not permit any detailed discussion of the other types studied by Weber; of his comparisons between the Roman jurisconsult and the English lawyer of the Inns of Court engaged in a casuistic practice, or the theologian-*cum*-jurist who sought to rationalize the law on the basis of sacred texts in a purely theoretical and logical fashion, independently of any practical consideration; or of the correlations and differences which he established between the replies of the Roman jurisconsult and the *fetwa* of the Islamic mufti. What must be borne in mind is that during the second phase, characterized by the emergence of legal honoratiores and more or less secularized legal experts, the process of rationalization and systematization became more marked, although the formal as well as the charismatic features subsisted. It should also be noted that other factors, of a non-formal nature, contributed to the process of rationalization; these were the material conditions of existence of collectivities, such as the increasing complexity of economic exchanges and the development of contractual procedures, as well as the upheavals resulting from wars and the situation arising in connection with the pacification of occupied territories, etc. In a word, the material aspect assumed increasing importance, from an ideal-typical point of view, especially under the pressure of the political or theocratic authority.

Here we should say, at the risk of repeating ourselves, that Weber's analysis must be viewed as ideal-typical in character. The phases to which he referred are not to be interpreted in the sense of a chronological succession of events, but in that of an internal development of law, as indicated by the analogies between the Roman jurisconsult, the English lawyer, the theologian and the Islamic mufti. Weber's typology, therefore, cannot be confused with the succession of stages described in the works of Auguste Comte or Marx.

For reasons of order and efficiency, the political or hierocratic prince came inevitably to intervene in a purely formal legal procedure operating as a closed system and governed solely by its own internal logic. Legal formalism generally afforded the best guarantee of freedom in the defense of individual interests, but often at the expense of the interests of the collectivity and sometimes of those of the state, which was responsible for law and order. It was therefore natural that the public authority should have done everything in its power to counteract a judicial system capable of challenging its decisions, and to establish as reasonable a balance as possible between individual and social interests, based not merely on legal justice but also on ethical, economic or social justice. What the patrimonial princes and hierocrats sought was the development of a system of law corresponding to material and practical conditions, even at the sacrifice of a purely formal legality.

That was the underlying meaning of the efforts of the Athenian demagogues, of the *ius honorarium* and the praetorian measures of Roman procedure, of the capitularies of the Frankish kings, of the changes introduced by the kings of England and the Lord Chancellors, of the inquisitorial procedure of the Roman Church, of the operation of royal absolutism in France or, to cite a more specific case, of Frederick the Great's action in the case of Arnold, the miller.

The intervention of extra-juridical elements of a political, economic, social or ethical nature, far from halting the rationalization of law, merely contributed to its progress, though no longer in the direction of formal, but rather of material justice. The process was in fact speeded up in proportion as the prince's administrative apparatus was itself rationalized, with the emergence of more and more specialized officials. Without wholly eliminating the charismatic and irrational elements (sometimes diverting them to the prince's advantage), the political *imperium* also tended toward a greater systematization of material law, under the pressure of the requirements of order and political unity. One of the princes' first concerns was to codify penal procedure, and then civil law, although the latter operation came much later than the former, as we shall see below. The result was a secularization of law, and this was much more pronounced in the West than in other regions of the world, where the tradition of magic, together with religious rules, constituted effective barriers to secularization.

There is no doubt that the survival of the spirit of Roman law, with its distinction between *fas* and *ius*, between religious duties and legal obligations, strongly influenced the rationalization of Western law, although we should not understimate the influence of canon law, that most rational of all systems of sacred law, since it was founded on a rational principle inherited from the Stoics, namely, the natural law.

Needless to say, the material rationalization of law under the authority of the princes engendered a variety of conflicts, one of the main ones being the conflict between the material law championed by the sovereign political authority and that of which the orders or the feudal lords constituted themselves champions. It remains, nonetheless, that the material rationalization of that third stage was of decisive importance wherever the basic consideration was not the preservation of any logical norm or abstract legality, but the pursuit of material truth for the sake of objectively and equitably resolving the conflicts between individual interests, as well as between individuals and the collectivity. The fourth stage has seen a return to formalism, the purpose this time being to reconcile legal logic with the material exigencies of extra-juridical origin—that is, individual liberties and collective demands. This process, which originated in the revolutionary movements of the eighteenth century, has not yet been stabilized, because the natural law theory from which it drew its original inspiration has since become outmoded. Various conceptions have been put forward in place of the natural law, such as positivism or historicism, but without success. That being the case, we have in the first place to assess the practical effects of the process, the most substantial of which being the elaboration of civil codes in different countries. The essential characteristic of the new trend is that it abandons both empiricism and casuistry, both a purely didactic approach and the approach of moral counsel.

Nevertheless, the aspiration toward formalism remains ambivalent, like socialism, which seeks to legitimize both the rights of the individual and those of the collectivity. All efforts tend toward the elimination of the exceptional, whether as the result of privileges of birth or of functions or of special jurisdictions, yet at the same time there is a definite trend toward greater docility to authority. The new development is by no means exempt from contradictions. As an example, we might point out that the object of modern penal law is no longer to punish or avenge a crime but to reeducate the convicted. Yet at the same time there is a movement in favor of social legislation, the logic of which is contrary to the spirit of the previous tendency.

In a word, we do not succeed in overcoming the fundamental irrationality of values because we do not succeed in reconciling the antagonisms between them. Formalism therefore remains ambiguous, however much specialization may increase. For life will not let itself be confined within a framework of abstract legal prescriptions. When jurists maintain, for example, that law should be free, and that the judge should create, rather than apply the law, or when they claim to have found an objective standard of value according to which a piece of customs legislation and the authority of the *paterfamilias* could be placed on the same level, then, whatever their intentions, there would seem to be only one conclusion which could satisfy all parties under existing circumstances, namely, that the absolutely logical and systematic coherence of law is a fiction, because no legal theory is absolutely pure and flawless. It is as useless to require of law that it should perfectly apply general axioms as it would be to ask that language should rigorously respect the rules of grammar.

The role of the sociology of law is precisely to interpret this contradiction, as well as the conflicts arising out of the incompatibility between the formal and material aspects of law, in other words, to analyze the development of the legal approach without being influenced by the doctrinal quarrels of the legal professionals. In any case, it is not its business to assess the value of the rationalization, even if present-day law threatens to drive the layman away from legal problems and merely to cultivate his ignorance.

[E]

THE SOCIOLOGY OF ART AND OF TECHNIQUE

1. Purpose of the sociology of art

Weber did not have time to carry out his projected study on this subject. We may glean his intentions, however, from various articles, in particular from his essay on the meaning of ethical neutrality in sociology and economics,[28] or from his lectures, particularly the one on science as a vocation.[29] These scattered fragments give us an idea of what he meant by a sociology of art and of the purpose he assigned to it.

First of all—as in the case of any other sociology—its purpose is not to issue value judgments. While the sociologist should have taste and be alert to the values represented by works of art, he should not concern himself with esthetics. Just as the doctor, in his capacity as a doctor, has no business to ask whether life is worth living, so the sociologist, in his capacity as a sociologist, is not required to answer questions such as, "Is it good that art works exist?" or "Does art have meaning?" or again, "Is art the kingdom of diabolical splendor, hence a kingdom of this world directed to pleasure and turned against God and perhaps, even, against human brotherhood by reason of its aristocratic nature?" The sociologist starts with the fact that art works exist. His task, therefore, is to understand why and how men orient their conduct meaningfully in relation to the existence of such works. In short, he accepts the premise that esthetics are meaningful to man.

He does not even have to give an opinion on the

possible development of art as such, for such an opinion would come under the heading of debatable evaluations. For it is not true that a work executed with new techniques or conceived in a new spirit is for those reasons superior to one in which that technique or that spirit is lacking. The primitives were ignorant of the laws of perspective, yet their works can move us esthetically just as much as those which conform to those laws. Every work of art must be regarded as "finished" in itself; it cannot therefore as such be outmoded, or grow old. Individual views on the value of Inca art, Roman art, the romantic school or modern art will of course differ; but no science—and the sociology of art is an empirical science—can by its procedures assert that one finished work is artistically superior to another. This is borne out by the fact that no theory of esthetics has ever eluded the difficulty simply by contrasting art with non-art. It is possible, of course, to consider a work a failure, yet because its author was motivated by considerations of art, it may be of interest to the sociologist; it was perhaps the first example of a new technique or of the presence of certain conditions which later artists handled more satisfactorily.

It is important, from an empirical point of view, to follow this development. For in this sense it may be appropriate to speak of progress, provided any evaluative comparison is avoided between the earlier work and the others. In other words, the sociologist accepts the general esthetic verdict on these different works and considers only the empirical relationship which may exist between them. The sociologist or historian of art is therefore far from being a connoisseur in the usual sense of that term, even though he often lays claim to that title. He is never more than a theorist or a scientist, just as the expert technologist is not necessarily an engineer. We do not ask the sociologist who specializes in urban problems to be an architect or to construct an ideal city. No one, clearly, can forbid him to have views on the city of tomorrow, provided he bears in mind this elementary fact, that, in assuming the function of a reformer, he ceases to be a scientist; he abandons his role as a sociologist for that of a partisan.

The specific purpose of a sociology of art, considered as an empirical scientific discipline, and governed by the rules flowing from its own premises, is now clear. The sociologist's task consists solely in analyzing the enpirically discernible relationships between the different orientations of the same art or between various arts or styles. This may appear a very modest frame of reference; and so it is. And probably for that reason it is underestimated—mistakenly. For to abandon it while assuming to the title of scientist is to commit an imposture. However narrow the range of scientific inquiry may appear, it is less spurious than the pretentious and anecdotic exploration of the self-styled connoisseur who imagines that he has unveiled the secret of art simply because he has chanced to look into an artist's studio to find out about the external techniques, or the style, of the artist's production. Such inquiries are not to be despised, so long as they remain within the frontiers of sociology and bear on technique and technical development, without involving evaluations. For the development of the processes of artistic creation is one thing, while changes of style are another, and the latter are not conditioned by technique alone. Between esthetic evaluation and the scientific curiosity of the sociologist there is a specific difference.

Another point: while the sociologist of art should endeavor to understand the meaning of a revolution in art forms, he would be guilty of a grave error were he to attribute such a change solely to considerations of class. In the course of a statement on technique and culture, made at the German Congress of Sociologists in 1910, Weber vigorously denounced the confusion between subject and form, between social conditions and cultural means. The fact that an artist is interested, for example, in a category of subjects termed naturalistic, does not necessarily imply that he has discovered a new category of forms. It is absurd, moreover, to imagine that the proletarian understands, and is able to understand only a particular mode or style. Let us take an example from literature. Most workers, Weber points out, acclaim Schiller's plays, and are quite indifferent to naturalism. We may deplore the fact, but it is not the sociologist's place to interfere in the conflict, for in so doing he ceases to function as a scientist. To put it more exactly, to say that a particular social stratum cannot and should not understand a particular artistic form is to show complete ignorance of both art and sociology.

Faithful to his guiding principle, Weber also sought to establish the uniqueness of rationalism in Western civilization in connection with art. Of course, in so doing, he was running the risk of inviting value judgments, and thus derogating from his principle of ethical neutrality. He was nevertheless careful not to assert the intrinsic superiority of our civilization over others, because, as he pointed out, differentiation neither signifies nor necessarily implies progress. The West, thanks to its more advanced rational technique, has succeeded in improving the conditions of artistic production, but this does not mean that it has more satisfactorily resolved the ultimate problems of art.

Similarly, when Weber compared Roman, Gothic and Renaissance art, for instance, he refrained from any esthetic evaluation of those styles. What he sought to understand was the reasons and implications of the technical solution which these styles have provided for certain construction problems. Gothic art, for example, was successful in solving the technical problem of vaulting quadratic spaces, through the construction of abutments for the support of the cross-arched vault, while Renaissance art was oriented rather toward the technical problems of the cupola. The sociology of art must clarify these various solutions, and realize the enthusiasm which each of them must have aroused in the hearts of the builders; it must enable us to understand how sculptors came to give a new plastic "feeling" to the body, and thus to diversify the technique of sculpture. It must also try to explain the possible relationships between these new techniques and the social and religious motivations of artists in those different periods. Once these questions have been elucidated, it has fulfilled its office—assuming that it remains faithful to its premises as an empirical discipline.

The reference to the singularity of Western civilization thus serves only as a value-orientation in the sense defined earlier; its object is to define the matter under discussion and to facilitate the distinction between what is historically essential or secondary. It is not a question of judging the artistic qualities of the works concerned; while a differentiation of this kind may signify an enrichment, it may also be only an impoverishment of forms. The sociology of art would overstep the boundaries of its competence if it tried to evaluate the meaning of the forms peculiar to different styles, or even to different civilizations, with a view to proclaiming the intrinsic superiority of one of them in relation to the others.

2. The example of music

We are able to form a fairly complete notion of the meaning which Weber sought to attach to his sociological analyses of art by taking the example of music. After his death, a text of considerable length was found among the mass of papers which he left, written probably in about 1910, and entitled "The Rational and Social Foundations of Music."[30] It was published in 1921 by Th. Kroyer, the musicologist, and included in the second and third editions of *Wirtschaft und Gesellschaft*. As we have already noted in connection with other works, this one too was only a fragment of a vaster study which Weber never completed. Unfortunately, Weber drafted only the part concerning the rational foundations and stopped at the threshold of the part which was to treat of the social foundations. The text is extremely difficult to read, not only because the author discusses the musical principles of the Byzantine, Islamic, Hindu and Chinese civilizations, but also because he assumes a thorough and precise knowledge of the solfeggio and harmony on the part of the reader. Since we do not possess such knowledge, we shall confine our remarks on the subject to the general principles of Weber's thought by indicating the problems which he raised and which he discussed more cursorily in the pages devoted to music in his essay on ethical neutrality.

The octave is divisible only into two unequal parts, that of the fifth and that of the fourth. This, for Weber, is the starting point of rationalization in music. On this basis, he discusses the problems of modern music (of his time), insisting on the question of tonality and the consequences it entails, namely, consonance and dissonance, and concluding that all rationalization of music based on the principle of the chord expresses a permanent tension in relation to melodic realities, and that it contains in itself a variety of irrationalities by reason of the non-symmetrical position of the seventh. In this connection, Weber examined the possible ways of improving the system of intervals. To illustrate his analysis he turned to the most ancient musical forms of China and Japan, Java and Cambodia, Persia, Arabia, Greece up to Byzantine and Islamic times, and even black Africa and Papua. What interested Weber was the particular ethos accompanying the pentatonic and the latter's preference for the step to measure musical distance and avoid the difficulties of the half-tone. That preference explains why Chinese and Greek music, as well as the music of the earliest Christian churches, had little liking for the chromatic scale, although it was not unknown to them—a point which may be observed in connection with Greek classical music and its divisions into the diatonic, harmonic and chromatic. In passing, Weber discussed a theory put forward by Helmholtz, and argued that it was a mistake to underrate the rationality of ancient music and to regard it as no more than a series of chaotic rhythms, subject to no rules. Similarly, he took issue with the notion that tonality was a modern phenomenon, because, as Stumpf, Gilmann and Filmoore had shown, Indian music and some Oriental music possessed at least a sense for tonality.

Any analysis of the development of music in those periods must take account of the influence of language, rhythm and the dance, both on the articulation and on the formation of tone. In any event, with the rationalization of intervals, "musical memory" began to come into its own. We have to realize, first of all, the importance of practical elements (for example, exorcisms of a medical nature) in the rationalization of music; their role was at least as decisive as that of theoretical research, if not more so. We must also take account of the intervention of mystical tendencies (some instruments were set apart to glorify a particular divinity), so that music to some extent constituted not only a sacred but also a recondite art. These aspects must not be disregarded in a sociological analysis, as though all that mattered was mere technical development. As in every other area, so in the development of music too we observe a constant interaction of human activities.

But music was not truly rationalized until it became an autonomous art, practiced for purely esthetic motives. That came with awareness of tonality; there again, purely technical reasons were often less decisive than practical motives, particularly the necessity to group tones in order to harmonize songs with the musical instruments that accompanied them. The question that arises is the following: what was the significance, in the period of melodic rationalization, of the succession of tones, and how did people express, on the level of musical sentiment, what corresponds to what we mean today by tonality? Weber's reply was of a highly technical nature, based on the studies of Stumpf and his school, as well as on those of von Hornbostel. It would take too long to go into all the details, and we shall examine only one of the consequences of rationalization, namely, polyphonic music. This is a characteristic of musical development in the West.

In actuality, a popular polyphonic music has existed in most parts of the world, but, in contrast to what took place in other geographic regions, where rationalization developed on the basis of an imperfect division of intervals (most often a division of the fourth), Western music took as its basis the harmonic division of the fifth. In his essay on ethical neutrality, Weber also insisted on the importance of the discovery of the properties of the third and of its harmonic significance as an element of the triad, which was to lead the technicians of music to the discovery of harmonic chromatics and the distinction between modern musical rhythm, made up of heavy and light beats, and purely metronomic measuring. The West's innovation was to substitute the harmonic interval for the melodic halftone and quartertone distance.

The real turning point in the rationalization of music thus came with the introduction of what is technically known as polyphony, together with its consequence, the study of counter-point. This is the truly characteristic feature of Western musical culture. Of course, the real development of contra-puntal studies began in the fifteenth century, but their beginnings are to be found in the music of the missionary monks of the early Middle Ages. Thus certain very definite socially and religiously conditioned characteristics of the Western Church gave rise to the musical rationalism of the West. While examining the implications of the controversies stirred up by the idea of counter-point right up to modern times, Weber dwelt at greater length on the immediate consequences of that new technique, principally in its original aspects of canon, fugue and faux-bourdon.

This basic discovery was followed by others, which have been equally conducive to the rationalization of Western music. First, we should mention the invention of modern musical notation, which not only facilitated modern composition, but also made possible its transmission and repeated performance. Attempts at musical transcription have been made elsewhere, but have always left too much room for improvisation and the discretion of the performers. They have thus not been rational.

It might have been expected that, with the introduction of notation, melodic inflections and all forms of irrationality would be eliminated. This has not been the case, however, as composers have deliberately retained irrational elements in order to give themselves greater scope for artistic expression. It would therefore be mistaken to ascribe the presence of irrational elements in present-day music to the survival of certain features of ancient music; they are on the contrary intentional.

The rationalization of Western music is also an effect of the means used by musicians: on the one hand, musical instruments (rationalization by external methods) and, on the other hand, temperament (rationalization by internal methods). The latter means, in Weber's view, was the last word in the evolution of harmonic music by means of chords. In this connection, he disputed the views propounded by A. Schlik and referred back to Bach.

As for instruments, they have everywhere had a preponderant influence on musical development. Weber analyzed several examples of Chinese, Arabic and even Central American music, and concluded that, while in some societies instruments were brought into accord with natural sounds (rationalization by internal development), in others apertures were made in the instruments for external reasons of ornamentation and symmetry and sounds were subjected to this external constraint (rationalization for reasons of esthetic construction).

Weber devoted closest attention to the stringed instruments, and in particular to the keyboard instruments—the organ, the clavichord and the piano. In that connection, he observed that experimentation was just as important for sociology as a completed work. He therefore made a detailed study of the development of the organ from Archimedes' day to the beginning of modern times, and similarly of the clavichord and the piano. Incidentally, musical experimentation in the sixteenth century largely conditioned the development of the experimental movement in the natural sciences.

Alongside his analysis of the technical development, Weber discussed the social implications. From the outset the organ, for example, was a festive instrument, at the court of the Roman emperors as at that of Byzantium; and it has always been used more for religious than for secular music. The clavichord and the piano, on the other hand, have been the favorite instruments of the northern European middle class.

With these considerations, *The Rational and Social Foundations of Music* comes to an end—just at the point where a purely social analysis seems about to take over from the analysis of technical rationalization. From remarks in other works, we know that Weber attached great importance to this social aspect. For instance, the rationalization of the dance measure was in his opinion at the origin of musical forms conditioned by the social life of the Renaissance period; they developed into the sonata. Everything indicates that it was his intention to show that the rational development of art had more influence on the rationalization of modern society than is generally believed.

3. *Some observations on technique*

It has sometimes been remarked with surprise that Weber did not devote a special study to the problem of technique. Yet it would be wrong to consider this omission as a weakness in his thinking. On the contrary, the development and consequences of the phenomenon of technique are referred to and analyzed in nearly all his works, for they constitute one of the decisive factors of the growing rationalization of every area of society, in economics as in religion or art. Weber seems in fact to have been among the sociologists who have placed most emphasis on technique, not only in connection with existing and observable rationalization, but also in connection with the rationalization of the societies of the future. For those societies, he believed, were in danger of being dominated by technique. His analyses of the phenomenon of bureaucracy and its foreseeable development in socialist systems constitute at least indirect evidence to that effect.

Given the persistence with which he employed the concept of technique (we find it at almost every page of his sociological writings), a review should be undertaken of the various meanings which he gave to that term, as well as of its possible applications, before embarking on any interpretation. We should probably find that it was one of his central ideas, as will have been apparent from a perusal of the present study. Only once such a review has been effected will it be possible to indicate clearly the influence exerted in his view by the element of technique in the differentiation of civilizations and the development of the modern world.

Actually, if Weber did not deem it advisable to devote a special study to technique, it was because he found technique everywhere in the course of his investigations. He regarded it as a social phenomenon to be clarified only in terms of the problem or the civilization under consideration; not abstractly, as a self-subsisting entity. Essentially, it is dialectical in nature and not ontological, and it therefore eludes any ideal-typical formulation, in the same way as history. The two concepts, in any case, may be placed on much the same footing.

Weber expressed his views on technique in general in the statement to which we referred earlier, on technique and culture, before the Congress of the German Sociological Society. He began by discussing Marx's application of the concept. That concept, incidentally, was one which Marx himself never defined clearly, whence the many incongruities in his thought, particularly in connection with the theory that the hand-mill produced feudalism and the steam-mill, capitalism. Such an assertion does not explain economic activity; it is merely a construct of history in terms of technology. And even on that definition it is not accurate. For the period of hand-mills, which extended up to the threshold of the modern world, cannot really be understood save in the light of other factors quite unrelated to technique. The method of combining two phenomena —that of technique on the one hand and that of politics or economics on the other—in order to establish a definite causal relationship, can be justified neither scientifically nor historically. The Marxist technological explanation therefore remains debatable, notwithstanding the dialectical suppleness of the relationships between infrastructure and superstructure.

It is not true that the same technique always produces or conditions the same type of economy. Capitalism, for instance, is not a modern phenomenon corresponding to a historical stage in the development of a civilization, in the sense of being the necessary consequence of a previous stage. For this type of economy is to be found in antiquity too, as well as in other civilizations whose economic and cultural development has differed greatly from our own. Furthermore, if our historical data are correct, we know that the capitalism of antiquity reached its summit at the very point where technical development came to a halt.

Similar observations may be made in connection with the argument of the non-Marxist technologists that capitalistic and technological development are so closely related that the element of technique must be considered as the virtually exclusive factor of cultural development. Such an assertion will remain gratuitous so long as it has not been tested by precise sociological investigation. Only once this research has been completed will it be possible to say whether this correlation really does or does not exist, and whether the development of contemporary culture differs wholly from that of other periods. In the meanwhile, we are dealing only with a problem, and not with a certitude.

It would in any case be surprising that technique should serve as an exclusive causal factor, or even as the ultimately decisive factor, when analogous theories attributing the same function to religion or economics have collapsed upon a rigorous analysis of the facts. It was thought, at one time, that the discovery of new processes or techniques would be capable of altering completely the fundamental meaning of art and of rendering intuition and creative originality superfluous. Yet changes of style in the domain of art have never been determined solely by technical factors; moreover, whatever techniques an artist needs for his work, he selects for himself, without submitting to the dictates of the latest technical developments; he remains master of the choice of his methods as of his colors or words. We may say, indeed, that whatever the type of civilization—and a purely technological civilization will probably be no exception to this rule—extremely divergent elements combine to give art its meaning; and not only are many of these elements far removed from technique, but they are also frequently irrational in character.

Causality is a very complex thing made up of the most unlikely concatenations of factors: sometimes politics will determine economic activity, and sometimes the reverse will be the case; sometimes economic or political considerations will prevail over religion, and sometimes it will be the other way round, etc. It would therefore appear vain to hope that a criterion will one day be established which would completely satisfy our intellectual curiosity.

A final question arises: what, basically, is meant by technique? Can it be defined specifically? For example, does it consist solely in a particular way of using material things? The word is used in such widely differing senses that it eventually becomes unintelligible, being applied to anything whatsoever, from a simple action to the work of an unskilled laborer or the operation of a machine. Just as the distinction between art and non-art is insufficient to explain the essence of the esthetic phenomenon, so the suggestion of some technologists that everything that is not technical should be called non-technique cannot serve as a guideline for consistent reflection on the matter. One of the tasks of sociology is precisely to clarify the term in as univocal a manner as possible, always in the context of the specific investigation, in order to obviate the confusions and over-simplifications popularized, for instance, in Ostwald's philosophy; Ostwald, a chemist, attempted to reduce all human values, including intellectual and ideal values, to pure technique and the laws of energy.

Thus, in Weber's view, technique is no more able to escape the tensions and antagonisms of values peculiar to every civilization than is any other human activity. While it is one of the essential factors, and perhaps even the most important one, in the growing trend toward rationalization which we observe today, it will not triumph over the inertia of the irrational. In a sense, Weber's position on technique is identical with his position on methodology, namely, that technique could lead to an extremism which, on the basis of a wholesale determinism, underrates the importance of the multiplicity of angles of vision from which man can know and act. In short, precisely because the process of rationalization cannot foresee its own term, it is inappropriate and meaningless to speak of absolute perfection from a technical standpoint. Human genius must necessarily transcend its own works. Indeed, man achieves the possible only by constantly aiming at the impossible, so that his task can never be exactly delimited.

Conclusion

Throughout this presentation of Weber's sociology, we have perforce either summarized lengthy passages very perfunctorily or neglected subtle distinctions in the author's reasoning, in order to bring out the general pattern of his work. We might, for instance, have devoted a section to the sociology of morals, although Weber treated the subject concurrently with the sociology of religion and the sociology of economics. Again, we confine ourselves to merely mentioning a sociology of education, since the author made only passing references to this subject. We should also note that he attempted, but without logical elaboration, to outline a sociology of knowledge under the heading of a "sociology of science." The idea was taken up some three or four years later by one of his students, Karl Mannheim, and by Max Scheler. Weber's interests and the directions of his investigations were so varied that they constantly open up new fields of research.

One point emerging from this presentation should be particularly stressed. For Weber, sociology was not the science of the social phenomenon as such. Indeed, the latter concept is so vague, and its meaning so diffuse, that it cannot be used independently to define the specific nature of an investigation. Weber explained this in his study " 'Objectivity' in Social Science and Social Policy":

> The belief that it is the task of scientific work to cure the "one-sidedness" of the economic approach by broadening it into a general social science suffers primarily from the weakness that the "social" criterion (i.e., the relationship among persons) acquires the specificity necessary for the delimitation of scientific problems only when it is accompanied by some substantive predicate. Otherwise, as the subject matter of a science, it would naturally comprehend philology, for example, as well as church history and particularly all those disciplines which concern themselves with the state, which is the most important form of the normative regulation of cultural life.[1]

In a sense, every human science deals in one way or another with the social phenomenon. The questions with which sociology deals constitute merely one aspect of the possible forms of social analysis, alongside those raised by political science, economics, legal science or ethnology. More precisely, as a discipline using both the causal and the interpretative methods, it attempts to explain certain social relationships and to understand the meaningful approach adopted by men in the face of the historical and empirical development of various sequences and given correlations of factors.

Space does not permit us to deal adequately with the criticisms made of Weber's work. Some are wholly justified, as for instance those concerning his definition of law, or his description of certain ties between capitalism and Protestantism, etc. Others are less so, particularly when they seek to discredit his work on the grounds that it contains certain inaccuracies. He was the first to recognize such faults, since he did not always possess all the necessary information on a matter under discussion. In any case, it would be absurd to reject a method merely because of certain informational lacunae. As for the attempts to disparage his work in the light of recent discoveries which he obviously could not have known, there is no better reply than the one which Weber himself made:

In science, each of us knows that what he has accomplished will be antiquated in ten, twenty, fifty years. . . . Every scientific "fulfilment" raises new "questions"; it *asks* to be "surpassed" and outdated. Whoever wishes to serve science has to resign himself to this fact.[2]

Neither will his censors escape this common lot of all specialists of the human and social sciences.

An author's influence is largely dependent upon translation. The first of any of Weber's writings to be translated was into Russian, in 1904. This was his essay on the social causes of the decay of ancient civilization.[3] His *Wirtschaftsgeschichte* and *Herrschaftssoziologie* were also first translated into Russian, in 1923, under Soviet rule. The English translations, although later in date, are the most numerous. It is thus natural that Weber's influence should be very strong in America, although many interpretations remain doubtful, probably by reason of the particular turn of mind of the German immigrants who introduced him. The other countries where his work is most widely known are Italy, Spain and Japan. In France, his influence was initially very unsubstantial. Thanks to R. Aron's studies, on the eve of the last war, Weber's philosophy and sociology have impressed themselves on the French specialists of the human sciences. It is to be hoped that the few translations which have recently been published in France, and the others which are in progress, will contribute to a more thorough knowledge of his ideas.

But Weber's fate has been most curious of all in his own country, Germany. Many German university teachers vaunt the illustrious title of being a former student of Max Weber. The claim is a surprising one, since Weber stopped teaching in 1903 and did not return to it until 1920, a few months before his death. Be that as it may, the fact remains that Weber's name is venerated and respected in Germany—at a distance. His work is treated as a monument to be admired from afar, as though the author's ideas might prove embarrassing on closer inspection. His theory of knowledge, indeed, is viewed with favor. But as soon as some writer assumes to analyze Weber's political or sociological thinking more thoroughly, as did Mommsen, for example, he arouses very complex reactions. One gets the impression that modern German sociology, repudiating Weber's ethical neutrality, has adopted a defensive position in his regard, precisely in order to avoid raising the political problem which haunted Weber throughout his life. With the exception of a few authors, German sociologists are trying to construct an "inoffensive" sociology which will wound no one and stir up no new ideas, and they take refuge in graphs and statistics. Thus the great tradition of German sociology, as represented not only by Weber but also by Toennies and Simmel, is virtually thrown overboard. One might be tempted to write a sociological study on present-day German sociology, taking as a basis the motivations which Weber treated so masterfully in his *Protestant Ethic and the Spirit of Capitalism*. But what purpose would that serve? Weber's reputation, now, is universal.

Notes

Notes

CHAPTER I

[1] E. Durkheim, *The Rules of Sociological Method*, Glencoe, Illinois, The Free Press, 1950.

[2] H.H. Gerth and C. Wright Mills, *From Max Weber: Essays in Sociology*, New York, Oxford University Press, 1946, p. 135.

[3] Included by H.H. Gerth and C. Wright Mills in *From Max Weber: Essays in Sociology*.

[4] See E. A. Shils and H.A. Finch, *Max Weber on the Methodology of the Social Sciences*, Glencoe, Illinois, The Free Press, 1949, p. 1.

[5] See Weber's statement on technology and culture, made to the First Congress of the German Sociological Society in 1910, in *Gesammelte Aufsätze zur Soziologie und Sozialpolitik*, pp. 449–56.

[6] H.H. Gerth and C. Wright Mills, *op. cit.*, p. 139.

[7] Edited by Don Martindale and Johannes Riedel and published by the Southern Illinois Press, Carbondale, 1958.

[8] E.A. Shils and H.A. Finch, *op. cit.*, pp. 124–5.

CHAPTER 2

[1] E.A. Shils and H.A. Finch, *op. cit.*, p. 187.

[2] *Ibid.*, p. 84.

[3] Max Weber, *Basic Concepts in Sociology*, New York, The Citadel Press, 1964, p. 30.

[4] E.A. Shils and H.A. Finch, *op. cit.*, p. 90.

[5] *Ibid.*, p. 104.

[6] *Ibid.*, p. 107.

[7] *Ibid.*, p. 164.

[8] *Ibid.*, pp. 185–6.

[9] R. Aron, *German Sociology*, New York, The Free Press, 1964, p. 80.

[10] E.A. Shils and H.A. Finch, *op. cit.*, pp. 58–9.

CHAPTER 3

[1] Cf. J. Freund, *Max Weber, Essais sur la théorie de la science*, Paris, Plon, 1965, pp. 395–6.

[2] Max Weber, *Basic Concepts in Sociology*, p. 29.

[3] *Ibid.*, p. 30.

[4] *Ibid.*, p. 36.

[5] *Ibid.*, p. 29.

[6] H.H. Gerth and C. Wright Mills, *From Max Weber: Essays in Sociology*, New York, Oxford University Press, 1946, p. 122.

[7] Max Weber, *The Theory of Social and Economic Organization*, New York, The Free Press, 1966, p. 101.

[8] Part I of *Wirtschaft und Gesellschaft* appears in English translation as *The Theory of Social and Economic Organization*, ed. Talcott Parsons, New York, The Free Press, 1966.

[9] Published by the Beacon Press, Boston, 1963.

[10] Published by Collier Books, New York, 1966.

CHAPTER 4

[1] R. Aron, *op. cit.*, p. 67.

[2] From " 'Objectivity' in Social Science," included by E.A. Shils and H.A. Finch in *Max Weber on the Methodology of the Social Sciences*, p. 81.

[3] E. Durkheim, *The Rules of Sociological Method*, Glencoe, Illinois, The Free Press, 1950.

[4] See Max Weber, *The Protestant Ethic and the Spirit of Capitalism*, New York, Scribner, 1958, pp. 13–31.

[5] *Ibid.*, pp. 30–31.

[6] See Max Weber, *The Theory of Social and Economic Organization*, pp. 158–323.

[7] *Ibid.*, p. 164.

[8] Max Weber, *General Economic History*, New York, Collier Books, 1966, p. 207.

[9] *Ibid.*, p. 267.

[10] *Ibid.*, p. 268.

[11] Included by H.H. Gerth and C. Wright Mills in *From Max Weber: Essays in Sociology*.

[12] Max Weber, *The Sociology of Religion*, Boston, Beacon Press, 1963, p. 138.

[13] Max Weber, *The Protestant Ethic and the Spirit of Capitalism*, p. 68.

[14] R. Aron, *German Sociology*, p. 95.

[15] Max Weber, *The Protestant Ethic and the Spirit of Capitalism*, p. 96.

[16] *Ibid.*, p. 183.

[17] The collection of Max Weber's political writings was published in Tübingen in 1958. W. Mommsen's work was also published in Tübingen, in 1959.

[18] Max Weber, *The Theory of Social and Economic Organization*, New York, Free Press, 1966, p. 154.

[19] *Ibid.*, p. 152.

[20] Max Weber, *The Theory of Social and Economic Organization*, p. 407.

[21] *Ibid.*, pp. 337-8.

[22] *Ibid.*, p. 352.

[23] *Ibid.*, p. 127.

[24] *Ibid.*, p. 121.

[25] M. Rheinstein, *Max Weber on Law in Economy and Society*, Cambridge, Mass., Harvard University Press, 1966, p. 41.

[26] *Ibid.*, p. 42.

[27] *Ibid.*, pp. 303-4.

[28] Included by E.A. Shils and H.A. Finch in *Max Weber on the Methodology of the Social Sciences*.

[29] Included by H.H. Gerth and C. Wright Mills in *From Max Weber: Essays in Sociology*.

[30] See Max Weber, *The Rational and Social Foundations of Music*, Carbondale, Southern Illinois Press, 1958.

CONCLUSION

[1] From " 'Objectivity' in Social Science and Social Policy," included by E.A. Shils and H.A. Finch in *Max Weber on the Methodology of the Social Sciences*, p. 67.

[2] From "Science as a Vocation," included by H.H. Gerth and C. Wright Mills in *From Max Weber: Essays in Sociology*, p. 138.

[3] Included in *Journal of General Education*, University of Chicago Press, 1950, Vol. V, pp. 75–88.

Bibliography

Bibliography

I. GENERAL STUDIES

Aron, R., *La philosophie critique de l'histoire*, Paris, J. Vrin, 1950.

Baumgarten, E., *Max Weber, Werk und der Person*, Tübingen, 1964.

Bendix, R., *Max Weber, An Intellectual Portrait*, New York, Doubleday Anchor Books, 1962.

Fleischmann, E., *De Weber à Nietzsche, Archives européennes de sociologie*, Vol. V, 1964.

Jaspers, K., *Max Weber, Politiker, Forscher und Philosoph*, Munich, 1958.

Special issue of the *Kölner Zeitschrift für Soziologie und Sozialpsychologie*, 1963, entitled *"Max Weber zum Gedächtnis."*

Mettler, A., *Max Weber und die philosophische Problematik in unserer Zeit*, Leipzig, 1934.

Parsons, T., *The Structure of Social Action*, New York, McGraw Hill, 1937.

Strauss, L., *Natural Right and History*, University of Chicago Press, 1953.

Troeltsch, E., *Gesammelte Schriften*, Vol. III, *Der Historismus und seine Probleme*, Tübingen, 1922.

Weber, M., *Max Weber*, Heidelberg, Lambert Schneider, 1950.

Weinreich, M., *Max Weber, l'homme et le savant*, Paris, J. Vrin, 1938.

II.   SPECIAL STUDIES

Antoni, C., "La logica del tipo ideal di Max Weber," *Studi germanici*, III, 3, 1939.

Becker, H., "Culture case study and idealtypical method, with special reference to Max Weber, *Social Forces*, XII, 3, Baltimore, Johns Hopkins, 1934.

Bennion, L., *Max Weber's Methodology*, 1934.

Bienfait, W., *Max Webers Lehre vom geschichtlichen Erkennen*, 1930.

Fechner, E., "*Der Begriff des kapitalistischen Geistes bei Sombart und Weber,*" *Weltwirtschaftliches Archiv*, 1929.

Mommsen, W., *Max Weber und die deutsche Politik*, Tübingen, 1959.

Oppenheimer, H., *Die Logik der soziologischen Begriffsbildung*, 1925.

Pfister, B., *Die Entwicklung zum Idealtypus*, 1928.

Schaaf, J., *Geschichte und Begriff*, Tübingen, 1946.

Schelting, A. von, *Max Webers Wissenschaftslehre*, Tübingen, 1934.

III. STUDIES ON THE SOCIOLOGIST

Aron, R., *German Sociology*, New York, The Free Press, 1964.

Flug, O., *Die soziologische Typenbildung bei Max Weber*, Göttingen, and *Jahrbuch der philosophischen Fakultät Göttingen*, 1923.

Grab, H., *Der Begriff des Rationalen in der Soziologie Max Webers*, 1927.

Heymann, F., *Die Polarität in der verstehenden Soziologie Max Webers*, thesis, Frankfurt, 1924.

Honigsheim, P., "Max Weber als Soziologe," *Kölner Vierteljahrshefte für Soziologie*, 1921.

Mises, L., "Soziologie und Geschichte," *Archiv fur Sozialwissenschaft und Sozialpolitik*, T. LXVII, 1932.

Oppenheimer, F. "Max Webers soziologische und sozialpolitische Bedeutung," *Arbeit und Wissenschaft*, Vienna, T. III.

Ronai, Z., "Max Webers soziologische und sozialpolitische Bedeutung," *Arbeit und Wissenschaft*, Vienna, T. III.

Rothacker, E., "Webers Arbeiten zur Soziologie," *Vierteljahrshefte für Soziologie*, T. XVI, 1922.

Singer, K., "Krisis der Soziologie," *Weltwirtschaftliches Archiv*, 1920.

Spann, O., "Bemerkungen zu Webers Soziologie," in *Tote und Lebendige Wissenschaft*, 1928.

Walter, A., "Max Weber als Soziologe," *Jahrbuch für Soziologie*, 1926.

Willbrandt, R., "Kritisches zur Webers Soziologie," *Kölner Vierteljahrshefte für Soziologie*, T.V, 1926.

———, "Weber als Erkenntniskritiker der Soziologie," *Zeitschrift für Statistik*, 1925.

Winkelmann, J., "Die Herrschaftskategorien der politischen Soziologie und die Legitimität der Demokratie," *Archiv für Rects- und Sozialphilosophie*, 1956.

Index

Index